D0247462

Fairest Isle

BBC Radio 3
Book of British Music

BBC

Edited by David Fraser

BBC RADIO 3
90-93 FM

CONTRIBUTORS

Margaret Bent
is a Fellow of All Souls College, Oxford, has co-edited the Old Hall manuscript and written extensively about late medieval music, including the book *Dunstaple*

David Byers
is a composer, musicologist (with a particular interest in 18th and 19th century music) and Senior Producer, Music and Arts, BBC Northern Ireland

Lewis Foreman,
biographer of Sir Arnold Bax, has published many books on British music, most recently *Music in England 1885–1920*

Alain Frogley
lectures in music at the University of Connecticut and is an authority on the music of Vaughan Williams; he is currently editing a book of essays about the composer. A shorter version of his Vaughan Williams article originally appeared in BBC Music Magazine

David Gallagher
is a music producer for Radio 3 and co-ordinator of *Fairest Isle*, BBC Radio 3's Year of British Music and Culture 1995

Peter Holman
is director of The Parley of Instruments, musical director of Opera Restor'd and author of *Four and Twenty Fiddlers* and a new study of Purcell

Stephen Johnson
writes on music in The Independent, reviews for Gramophone and broadcasts regularly on BBC Radio 3

Michael Kennedy,
opera critic of the Sunday Telegraph, has written many books on composers, including Britten, Elgar, Vaughan Williams and Walton, biographies of Barbirolli and Boult, and *The Oxford Dictionary of Music*

Diana McVeagh
is a freelance writer. She is the author of *Edward Elgar: His Life and Music* and the Elgar article in *The New Grove Dictionary of Music and Musicians*

Robert Maycock
is a writer on music, contributing regularly to The Independent and BBC Music Magazine. He is a former chair of the Society for the Promotion of New Music

John Milsom
has written extensively on the music of Tallis and Byrd. He is Lecturer in Music at Christ Church, Oxford, and contributes regularly to BBC Music Magazine, Radio 3 and the World Service

Nick Sandon,
Professor of Music at Exeter University, has published numerous articles on, and editions of, early English church music and is especially interested in the role of music within a liturgical context

Roderick Swanston
broadcasts regularly on BBC Radio 3 (including a monthly series on British music during 1995), and is Head of Undergraduate Academic Studies at the Royal College of Music

Bruce Wood
is Senior Lecturer in Music at the University of Wales, Bangor. His publications include editions of royal and Cecilian odes in the Purcell Society Edition and John Blow's symphony anthems for *Musica Britannica*

Piers Burton-Page
is a producer and presenter for BBC Radio 3, and author of the recent biography of Sir Malcolm Arnold, *Philharmonic Concerto*

Chris de Souza,
a BBC Radio 3 producer and presenter, has made a concert version of Britten's music for *The Rescue*

Andrew Green
presents *In Tune* on BBC Radio 3 and is a freelance music journalist

Paul Hindmarsh,
a BBC music producer in Manchester, is the author of *Frank Bridge: a thematic catalogue* and editor of previously unpublished music by Bridge and Britten

Andrew Huth
is a writer on music who works for Decca, and wrote the booklet *The Proms: A Living Tradition*

Martin Neary
is Organist and Master of the Choristers at Westminster Abbey

Anthony Payne
is a composer and music critic of The Independent

Robert Philip
works as a BBC arts producer for the Open University and broadcasts regularly on Radio 3

Nicholas Williams
is a music publisher and writes for The Independent

COVER ILLUSTRATIONS
Front cover (clockwise from top right):
Musicians frieze from Gilling Castle,
Henry Purcell, Peter Grimes costume design,
bar of *Britannia* by James MacMillan,
William Walton, late 17th-century English
violin bearing arms of the Stuart kings,
title page of *Parthenia*
Back cover (clockwise from top right):
Spy and Ape caricatures of Gilbert and Sullivan,
Henry VIII playing the lute, Sir Edward Elgar,
ticket for 1793 Hanover Square concert,
angel lutenist on 13th–14th-century cope
Inside front cover:
Awake Sweet Love by John Dowland
Inside back cover:
Britannia by James MacMillan

Published by BBC Radio 3 in association with BBC Books,
a division of BBC Enterprises Ltd, 80 Wood Lane, London W12 0TT

First published in 1995
© 1995 BBC

ISBN 0-563-37162-5
All rights reserved

Designed by Andrew Barron and Collis Clements Associates
Picture research by Jenny de Gex and Elisabeth Agate

Printed and bound in Great Britain by BPC Paulton Books Ltd

CONTENTS

FOREWORD
The Adventurous Conservatism of British Music
Nicholas Kenyon 4

THE ADVENTUROUS CONSERVATISM OF BRITISH MUSIC

The famous (though doubtless apocryphal) 19th-century newspaper headline 'FOG IN CHANNEL: THE CONTINENT ISOLATED' is a nice example of an attitude to British music and culture which has been hard to shake: that of an island race, complacent in its remoteness from the European mainstream, pursuing its own cultural agenda regardless of the world around it.

Part of this attitude stems not from arrogant over-confidence but from chronic lack of confidence. 'None of the other nations of Europe', wrote Nikolaus Pevsner, 'has so abject an inferiority complex about its own aesthetic capabilities as England.' In music, Britain has hardly ever led the world. We have probably not showed the way forward to the Continent since John Dunstable in the 15th century was among those who, as a contemporary poet put it, 'a newer way have found/in music loud and soft/Of making lively concordance'. Our best young composers today are having the same effect: we live in a golden age of richly varied new music.

But the British, musically and culturally, also have other skills: one of them, as the composer Hugh Wood identified some years ago, is that of doing things outstandingly well rather late in the day. The viol fantasias of Purcell, the English madrigalists, the symphonies of Elgar – all are superb examples of their genre which came very late in the life of the form. This characteristic has given British music a special quality which goes some way to pinning down that elusive 'Britishness' which many have sensed but rarely identified in our music.

BBC Radio 3's Year of British Music and Culture, inspired by the tercentenary of Henry Purcell, the 90th birthday of Sir Michael Tippett, and many other anniversaries, is an attempt to look at the most striking, the most adventurous, and the liveliest areas of our national culture. This book is designed as a companion to the year. It does not slavishly follow the contents of our broadcasts, though there will be a chronological thread to follow through the year in, for instance, Roderick Swanston's Sunday features and in *Composer of the Week*. The book is intended to add a general perspective to the hundreds of individual broadcasts: with it at your side, listening to the Radio 3 year will be enhanced, and it will provide a lastingly useful reference work.

My thanks to the expert contributors, the editor, David Fraser, and the designer, Andrew Barron, for assembling this splendid publication against the unforgiving speed of broadcasting deadlines. Enjoy it, and enjoy the year.

Nicholas Kenyon
Controller, BBC Radio 3

Sounds and Sweet Airs,
That Give Delight

An Unabashed Celebration of
The Perennial Abundance of
British Music

Roderick Swanston

The most commonly quoted remark about music and Britain is that it is a 'Land without Music'. It is not true, nor ever has been, even though foreigners and natives have sometimes believed it. Britain has been an island that has teemed with music since records begun. When the Dutch humanist Erasmus visited England in the early 16th century, he complained: ' ... music, nothing but music ... they have so much of it in England that the monks attend to nothing else'. True, Erasmus was writing about church music, but contemporary sources show his remark could as easily have been made about contemporary secular music. Moreover, if he were to visit Britain again today wouldn't his observation still be apt? Indeed when would it not have been?

From their inception public concerts abounded in Britain. So avid, for instance, were concert-goers to hear the Italian virtuoso Paganini that his concerts in 1831 managed to sell out a 3,000-seat opera-house 27 times, and the Crystal Palace, after its move to Sydenham, had to be adapted to

Chapter opener shows, *top right:* **John Tavener** *top left:* **Manuscript of *If Ye Love Me* by Tallis** *bottom:* ***The Opera Rehearsal* by Marco Ricci, c1709, said to be of Nicola Haym's *Pyrrhus and Demetrius*, held in a practice room at Haymarket.**

below: **The Sharp Family by Johann Zoffany, 1779-81. The musical sons and daughters of Thomas Sharp, Archdeacon of Northumberland, gave regular fortnightly concerts on Sundays from the 1750s. This portrait shows them aboard their barge at Fulham.**

accommodate both the Saturday concerts, and the Handel extravaganzas which at their peak in the 1880s numbered a chorus of 4,000, an orchestra of 500 and an audience on one occasion of 87,769. Outside London similar situations were found. New town-halls boasted new concerts with large audiences of different (though not all) social classes, and the uniting of the three cathedral choirs of Gloucester, Worcester and Hereford (since c 1715) can still boast of being the oldest music festival in the world. Nor have things changed in our own age. In the years since 1945 London has been more than once described as the musical capital of the world, because of the sheer quantity and diversity of music performed.

It is true the development of British music has been different from that of other countries, for which in part its religious, political and social developments have been responsible. Popular, vernacular religious music is part of its core, from the 14th-century Lollards, who helped form and spread the 'educational' English carol, through such minor masterpieces as Sheryngham's *Ah gentle Jesu* from the 15th century to the privately devotional *Never weather-beaten sail* (1613) by Thomas Campion. The development of a popular vein of vernacular religious music is not only older in Britain than its most obvious rival, the German chorale, but equally politically rooted and embedded in the collective memory, as the spirited defence of Tate and Brady's psalter [1696] in Thomas Hardy's *Under the Greenwood Tree* (1872) shows, or Vaughan Williams' declaration in his *A Musical Autobiography* that, while editing the music for the English Hymnal, close encounter with the best (and some-times the worst) tunes was 'a better musical education than any amount of sonatas and fugues'.

Of course, it will be argued that what was meant by the Land without Music was neither the absence of public or domestic music-making, nor the lack of a plethora of popular hymns, folk-songs, popular dances and instrumental tutors (as published by

Thing, *an* Englishman.'

DANIEL DEFOE, THE TRUE-BORN ENGLISHMAN

Playford in the 1650s), nor the 19th-century musical educational movements of John Hullah and the External Departments of Universities. What was meant was that there was no indigenous art music, nor great composers; no Bach nor Brahms, nor any in-between. The British, it might have been said, performed only foreign music because they had no art-music of their own.

It is true, Britain has been a good host to foreign musicians who have either settled here, such as Handel and Geminiani in the 18th century, and Berthold Goldschmidt and Roberto Gerhard in the 20th; or who have just visited, as Haydn, Mendelssohn, Dvořák and many others. Yet visitors and settlers have not just influenced British music; their own styles have been affected by indigenous British music and taste. Who, for instance, can escape the compliment Handel paid his future homeland in *Rinaldo* when he infused his 'most celebrated' air, 'Cara sposa', with so Purcellian an accompaniment? Or who can miss the changes Haydn wrought in his Viennese style to accommodate British taste: the Broadwood piano-inspired use of the middle range of the fortepiano, for instance, in his final keyboard sonatas, or the obvious new blend of experiment and seriousness that characterizes the 'London'

symphonies, so clearly written for London ears?

Even so, the die-hard critics will say, British music, except in rare moments, has neither blazed new trails nor avoided European imitation, as a result only a handful of its composers can stand comparison with their Continental contemporaries; so unlike the case of British plays and poetry. Yet, apart from the fact that language is compelled to emphasise its national origins, whereas music by its very nature, need not, it should be remembered that both poetry and playwriting have thrived on foreign influence. What, for instance, is so un-British about the French-inspired Chaucer, the Italian-saturated Shakespeare or the century of Augustans championing Graeco-Roman nation-state ideals, translating their epics and paraphrasing their authors? We do not think of Schütz or Bach as any less German for their Italian and French imitations, nor Berlioz less French for his love of Beethoven. Foreign interaction has proved a constant source of enrichment, as the pages following will show.

However British music has not just been based on foreign models, it has also forged an audible identity of its own as a closer examination of the facts and an increasing familiarity with the music from the editions of E H Fellowes and the volumes of *Musica Britannica* to the plethora of modern recordings demonstrates.

The following chapters will make clearer what I

left: Medieval entertainment illustrated in the Luttrell Psalter from East Anglia, c1340
above right: Ralph Vaughan Williams
right: A firework display on the Thames, 15 May 1749, promoted by the Duke of Richmond to emulate the Royal Fireworks which celebrated the Treaty of Aix-la-Chapelle

mean by an audible identity, but I offer here two suggestions. One of the earliest English features noticed by the 15th-century theorist Tinctoris was the 'contenance angloise'. The 'contenance' consisted of rich polyphony organised to produce a resonantly euphonious effect unspoilt by excessive rhythmic fussiness. Such features can still be heard differentiating the music of the Eton Choirbook from its contemporaries at the end of the 15th century. But isn't it also the same effect Roger North identified in Purcell's trio sonatas, which he described as 'clog'd with somewhat of an English vein' despite their being (as Purcell claimed) 'just imitations of the fam'd Italian masters'? Isn't it also the same love of richer textured euphony part of what distinguishes early Tippett from Stravinsky, Delius from Debussy or even Elgar from Strauss or Mahler?

British folk music is plentiful and varied, so it would be hard to identify features that unite Irish, Scottish, Welsh and English varieties; yet a characteristic British melodiousness has crept into a wide range of native music from the jauntily catchy *Sumer is icumen in* through the madrigals of Wilbye and Gibbons (when compared with de Wert or Marenzio) to those limpid, often slightly folky melodies that Handel's English contemporaries favoured, such as Arne's *Blow, blow thou winter wind* or *Where the bee sucks*, which he wrote

right: **Delius in Frankfurt in 1923 with his wife Jelka and, standing, Percy Grainger**
below: **A view of Elgar's beloved Malvern Hills with, inset, a photograph of the composer**

for Garrick's Shakespearean revivals. Arne's albeit stylised rhythms capture not only the lilt of the original words, but their balladic quality marks out a particular kind of British melodic demoticism that Handel had to learn while living here. Somehow the strains of four-square tunes like *While Shepherds watched*, folk-tunes such as *Bushes and Briars* or traditional melodies such as *Greensleeves* have crept into the British musical persona and emerged in works as varied as *The Beggar's Opera*, Stanford's *Irish Symphony*, Holst's *St Paul's Suite* and Maxwell Davies's *Farewell to Stromness*. True, each of these works may be considered overtly 'nationalistic', but their melodic turns of phrase can be found echoed in countless works, forming a kind of under-the-table conspiracy of British inflections of sources drawn from all over the place. Maybe, at some deep level these demotic tunes, and the love of them, reflect the various forms of liberty (real or imagined) that visitors and settlers in this country have come to value so much.

Of course much music besides marks out the British Isles: the Scottish and Irish pipes and their repertoire, English folk-singing and dancing, the brass-band and choral traditions, the long line of non-Conformist and revolutionary hymns and songs, the Welsh harpists, the West-Gallery minstrels, the organ and cathedral traditions, and so on. It is true also that British music has often followed in the wake, making its identity in adaptation rather than inauguration; but, as the following chapters will show, on the crest of this great wave of music-making there have been more than a handful of great, gifted and original composers in all periods, quite the equal of other countries. Far from being a 'land without music,' 'the isle is full of noises, Sounds and sweet airs, that give delight' (Shakespeare, *The Tempest*).

2

LA CONTENANCE ANGLOISE

FROM THE BEGINNINGS TO 1485

MARGARET BENT

Isidore of Seville observed in the seventh century that sounds perish because they cannot be written down. Music of the past could only be recovered for modern performance when it became, after Isidore's time, notated more specifically than as a mere reminder of sounds already familiar. The notes and rhythms of British music before the Norman Conquest are almost entirely opaque to us.

In any case, blueprints for performance can never convey what music actually sounds like; they assume knowledge and skills which may have been lost with the passage of time. Each generation remakes music for its own time; only some external aspects (like the reconstruction of instruments, the notes on the page) can aspire to be 'authentic'. We now have the benefit of many remarkable modern readings of early music by groups such as Gothic Voices, the Orlando Consort and the Hilliard Ensemble, which reflect the developments in performance over the last 20 years since the pioneering work of British performers such as Michael Morrow and David Munrow. They bring us closer to the music through their understanding and skill, but we know that we will never be able to hear it as they did.

The history of medieval English music has to be told in terms of surviving handwritten copies, which means that we are largely confined to liter-

Chapter opener shows,
top right: **13th – 14th century cope – English embroidery showing lutenist – from Steeple Aston Church, Oxfordshire**
middle left: **Angel playing harp, one of the 14th – century gilded roof-bosses from Gloucester Cathedral**
bottom right: **Warwick Castle gittern, carved with hunting scenes and grotesques, late 13th or early 14th century**

left: **Panel showing Christ in glory and elders with musical instruments, from wall painting in Westminster Abbey chapter house c1390**

ate music. Contemporaries leave us tantalising hints of rich but vanished Celtic traditions; the little notated music from Scotland, Ireland and Wales largely reflects imported repertory.

There is plenty of literary and pictorial evidence *about* musical activity in pre-Conquest and Celtic Britain, which shared with its Germanic and Scandinavian settlers a tradition of long narrative epic poems (*Beowulf* is the oldest) that may have been partly sung or declaimed. They provide descriptive contexts for aristocratic and minstrel performance of secular song – probably in a narrative genre – to the accompaniment of lyre or harp. Minstrels could be hired for festivities, while noble men and women cultivated the more elegant instrumental skills at leisure. Music was used in daily life for entertainment, dance, work songs, traders' cries, battle rallying and drinking songs as well as for edification and polemics and for embellishment of the liturgy and civic events.

Music was not then available at the press of a button. It always required skilled, live players or singers performing for their own pleasure or for payment; music needed regularity, routine or planning. Although their art was often functional and ephemeral, musicians took delight in exercising the highest craft, just as carvers and glaziers did in statuary or stained glass that would rarely be seen.

Some early manuscripts, including some epic poetry and the so-called 'Cambridge songs' in secular Latin verse, have sketchy musical notation, for which a few tunes can be recovered when they happen to match later melodies. The 12th-century Durham hermit St Godric has left us three modest songs which are the earliest with English words and transcribable melodies.

European Christendom celebrated its liturgy with chant derived from a common tradition allegedly going back to Pope Gregory in the sixth century. British dialects of Christian chant must have taken root in these islands along missionary routes. By the time liturgical manuscripts had musical notation, Britain had come to follow Roman practice more closely than the older Celtic Christian traditions. The major monument of pre-Conquest music in Britain, and indeed the earliest recorded repertory of part-music in Europe, is the Winchester Troper, or rather Tropers, from about 1000 AD, two complementary manuscripts that provide 'reminder' musical notation for a large two-part collection, some of which can be deciphered with reference to later versions in staff notation.

Some medieval service-books contain drama-tised enactments of the events of the main Church festivals, Easter and Christmas. These 'liturgical dramas' emphasised the ritual liturgical functions that they embellish, much as polyphonic (multi-voice) music embellished the performance of monophonic (single-line) chant. They also led to vernacular plays and later independent drama. There are very early English dialogue enactments of the Visitation to the Sepulchre. (The famous *Play of Daniel* is now preserved in a manuscript in the British Library but is not itself of British origin.)

The new French-speaking ruling classes brought massive change following the Norman Conquest, confining English vernacular art to a lower social status. But many institutions (especially the monasteries) kept their pre-Conquest character, and others were revitalised rather than suppressed. When the Norman royal line died out in 1135, the throne passed to the – still French-speaking – Plantagenet dynasty. Henry II, Count of Anjou (r 1154-89), had married the heiress Eleanor of Aquitaine. The King of England now held these fiefdoms in addition to Normandy, and thus ruled more of France than the French king. To talk about 'France' and 'Britain' at this time is misleading in terms of modern geography. The court of Henry II and Eleanor provided a two-way exchange route for French and English musical culture.

Something of the culture of the southern French troubadours, and later the northern French trouvères was transmitted to England, though it did not transplant well without its own courtly surroundings; nor did the low status of the English language furnish the conditions for a courtly vernacular song tradition. But the few Anglo-Norman songs that survive from the 13th century suggest more activity than has been documented. A few dozen little-known English songs remain. Only about 20 have English words; the others are in Anglo-French or Anglo-Latin. Most are monophonic, belong to no common tradition, and were never anthologised. Wholly unwritten traditions are even harder to document: Henry's chaplain Gerald of Wales (Giraldus Cambrensis) is

above: **King David and musicians, from the so-called Hunterian Psalter written and illuminated in the North of England c 1170**
below: **John I of Portugal entertains John of Gaunt to a feast accompanied by musicians; a miniature by Jean de Wavrin from Froissart's *Chroniques d'Angleterre***

well known for hinting at a long pedigree for the tradition of unwritten part-singing in Wales and of instrumental accomplishment in Ireland.

In addition, the precocious English cultivation of composed polyphony may have enriched French developments. Continental successors to the Winchester Troper are the 12th-century collections from the great pilgrim resort of St James of Compostela (Spain) and from St Martial in Limoges (Aquitaine). The St Martial music broke away from two-part 'chords' and began a new elaborated style where the parts had more independence. It also was not confined to liturgical texts. English rule embraced Aquitaine and included major pilgrim routes to Compostela; it is from those two places that the earliest readable polyphony survives. While it would be going too far to treat this repertory as English music, the primacy and influence of English musical innovations has been underestimated, and the notion of French cultural dominance fostered by German and American musicology is ripe for its current revision.

The next large collection of music in these islands probably originated in St Andrews, in Scotland. The manuscript known as W1 includes the earliest version of the liturgical polyphonic repertory from 12th-century Paris, associated with Master Leonin (his *Magnus liber organi*). But it also includes a considerable and strikingly new repertory that may be of Scottish origin. Even to

describe it as 'insular' perpetuates the self-deprecation of 'British' music by implying surprise at its high technical accomplishment.

Before and around 1300 there was two-way contact between English and French musical dialects. After 1300, French developments in the notation of rhythm were rapid, and had far-reaching implications for French musical style. Between about 1315 and 1350, the initial stages of the hostilities of the 100 Years' War (starting in 1337 when Edward III claimed the title of King of France), no foreign compositions enter native manuscripts, no native compositions reflect foreign influence. The French and English go their separate ways, evolving independent techniques, styles and notations from the starting point of their brief confluence c 1300. Then from about 1350 there is evidence of French music in England, perhaps following the captivity here of the French King John V and his retinue.

By the 14th century it was not only the church that provided music for the liturgy. Extensive patronage by wealthy laymen and noble households supported choral and memorial services in the larger parish churches, and began to support household musicians for private devotions as well as for entertainment. Freelance minstrels travelled in search of weddings, feasts and other opportunities to exercise their talents and earn their keep. The music that must have been played on the instruments we know from (often idealised) angel pictures was largely unwritten and therefore lost. Composers of – primarily vocal – 'art music' earned their living as singers and choirmasters. They worked within or, later, outside monastic communities. They might be members of religious colleges established within a cathedral or church, or employees of a noble household. Winchester had a famous organ before the Conquest, and it is from England in the 14th century that the earliest document of what may be organ music survives (the so-called Robertsbridge manuscript).

English 14th-century music has been neglected at the expense of the better-known repertories of France and Italy. We cannot usually attach composers' names or historical events. Much of it has only recently been published, in the l'Oiseau-Lyre 14th-century series. There is nothing comparable to the rich source material we have for the French contemporary Guillaume de Machaut, who supervised the compilation of handsome volumes of his collected works for his patrons and posterity.

English music had a distinctive national voice at least from the late 13th century. From the period around 1300 there is a very substantial collection of fragments from Worcester, thereafter only bits and pieces ranging from one to eight pages each. The English fragments, nearly all devotional music to Latin texts, nevertheless point to a rich and

right: Angel musicians, stained glass window by John Prudde, c1447, from the Beauchamp Chapel, St Mary's, Warwick

varied repertory, many lost manuscripts, and quite distinctive styles. A fondness for more modest rounds and canons follows the unique Sumer canon, as does the cultivation of 'rondellus' compositions whose successive sections are repeated with exchanged voice-parts. An example is the well-known *Alle psallite cum luya*, which also shows the troping or 'stuffing' of a word, here *Alle — luya*, with other text. The general effect of this music is tuneful and sonorous, projecting the words with care.

If the Sumer canon [*Sumer is icumen in*, pictured far left] of around 1300 was an isolated national landmark, so in a different way is the famous late 14th-century motet *Sub Arturo plebs/ Fons citharizancium/In omnem terram*, whose three textual strands symptomise its imported French techniques. The top-part text sings the praises of English musicians, lining them up against the middle-part text, which gives a potted history of music listing the ancient authorities Tubalcain, Pythagoras, Boethius, Gregory, Guido and Franco – to which the composer, J Alanus, modestly appends his own name. Multi-textual motets of cleverly proportioned construction were taken up by the English; a famous example from the early 15th century is Dunstable's *Veni sancte spiritus/Veni creator*. English composers in the period around 1400 seem to have worked on mastering and even surpassing French techniques of notation and rhythmic vocabulary, and many English mannerisms disappear. Then, for the first 25 years of the 15th century, English composers showed a vigorous burst of creativity in fusing their existing sound ideals with French techniques and rhythms. The combination was a powerful one and led to the forging of a distinctive new style.

The later Plantagenets take us to the 15th-century Lancastrian Kings Henry IV, V, VI (deposed 1461). This period saw the closing stages of the 100 Years' War (1337-1453), and the beginning of the civil Wars of the Roses preceding the establishment of the Tudor dynasty in 1485. Henry IV was the first anglophone king since the Conquest. In the generation after Chaucer, English gained a new status, not only in the composition of French courtly forms to English texts but to the indigenous English carol which often mixed English and Latin, and was certainly not confined to Christmas [see the Agincourt carol, pictured

below]. The major monument of late-medieval English music is the so-called Old Hall manuscript [pictured over page] from the reign of Henry V. Remnants of an associated younger manuscript compiled for the infant King Henry VI show slightly more modern but overlapping repertory, giving more prominence to Dunstable.

The main composers of the 15th century are the first English composers known to us by name and biography: Lionel (or Leonel) Power and John Dunstable (or Dunstaple). They have left us mainly Mass music and motets, though Dunstable may have written one of the most famous 15th-century songs, *O rosa bella*. He was associated first with the dowager Queen Joan, perhaps with John Duke of Bedford, then with Humfrey Duke of Gloucester, a close associate of John of Wheathampstead, Abbot of St Albans, who wrote

THE AGINCOURT CAROL
The Trinity Carol Roll, *right,* **is a scroll of parchment containing on one side workaday copies of carols for various occasions. The Agincourt Carol alternates Latin refrains thanking God for the victory with English narrative verses about the Normandy campaign of 1415–16; the Old Hall manuscript contains more learned motets celebrating the same events.**
   Deo gracias Anglia, redde pro victoria,
   Our king went forth to Normandy, etc.

at least one of Dunstable's surviving epitaphs. Power served the Duke of Clarence who, as the next brother of Henry V, was heir to the throne until his own prior death. Both composers were thus closely associated with the Queen Mother and her four sons. This fairly new biographical knowledge confirms that English composers must have travelled on the continent in order to account for the spread of their music and its influence. Knowledge of their music comes predominantly from foreign manuscripts, where English music was much sought after and highly praised – in the words of the poet Martin le Franc that head this chapter – as the *contenance angloise*.

After Agincourt, this newly fused product was 're-exported' especially between 1420 and 1435, a distinctive English voice stiffened with French techniques, coinciding with the English occupation of France; it exerted a strong influence on Burgundian-patronised composers of the slightly younger generation of Dufay. Indeed, not until the Beatles has English music been so popular outside this country. English music of the generation of Dunstable and Power was very important for the stylistic and technical development of their younger contemporaries on the continent, as poetry, treatises and above all the music itself attest. Much of it can be recognised as English, or was so labelled in the manuscripts, even where we lack composers' names, as is usually the case. In particular, a major achievement of the English was to establish the techniques of a musically unified Mass Ordinary (the Kyrie, Gloria, Credo, Sanctus and Agnus Dei), creating works of symphonic proportions in which European composers for the next 200 years invested their most elaborate musical thinking.

The continental demand for English music receded after France recovered all territory except Calais, and England became immersed in civil war. English composers including Walter Frye, John Plummer, John Benet and John Bedingham continue to appear in foreign manuscripts, even with English-language songs, but thereafter there is little discernible influence until the early 16th century. Instead, there was a surge of native architecture and music of wondrous decorative quality, culminating in the Eton Choirbook (see the next chapter) which gives us a wealth of beautiful music by another collection of named composers.

THE OLD HALL MANUSCRIPT

The first important collection of English church music (147 pieces), with 25 named composers of whom Lionel Power is the best represented, is the so-called Old Hall manuscript. Dating from the second decade of the 15th century, it was probably prepared for Henry V's brother Thomas, Duke of Clarence, in whose chapel he was employed. Music from this manuscript has been recorded by the Hilliard Ensemble and Gothic Voices. Two compositions are ascribed to a 'Roy' (or King) Henry, probably Henry V. One is this Sanctus, whose three parts are notated in aligned score with the words under the lowest part. The capital letters 'S' seen here are 19th-century replacements for the originals that were cut out. The blobs at the beginning of each staff are middle-C clefs.

Sanctus, sanctus, sanctus, dominus deus sabaoth. Pleni sunt celi et terra gloria tua. Osanna in excelsis.

Benedictus qui venit in nomine domini. Osanna in excelsis.

3

CONNYNG SYNGYNG MEN

THE EARLY TUDOR PERIOD 1485–1558

NICK SANDON

uring the reigns of Henry VII (1485–1509) and Henry VIII (1509–47) the musical culture of Britain reached unsurpassed levels of vitality and achievement. Music was prized, not merely as a means of recreation but also as a powerful spiritual and moral agent, and in consequence it played a prominent role in public and private life. Enthusiastic and discerning patronage greatly stimulated the musical profession and rewarded outstanding talent. The average level of skill among composers and performers seems to have been remarkably high, and the prevailing musical idiom was extremely distinctive, yet able to accommodate stylistic experiment and innovation.

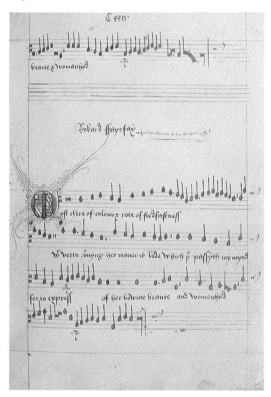

This chapter concentrates on polyphonic music; the term refers to its characteristic texture, which consists of interweaving melodic lines. Composed and performed for a discriminating elite by highly trained professionals, and carefully notated in expertly copied manuscripts, this is the art music of its time. Plainchant and folk music are not discussed. Although plainchant continued to form the major musical constituent of church services until the advent of Protestantism, the chant repertory was an inheritance, complete as it stood; early Tudor composers might incorporate

Chapter opener shows,
top left: **A decorative initial incorporating a portrait of John Taverner from the manuscript of his mass** *Gloria tibi trinitas*
middle right: **King Henry VIII playing the harp, an illustration from the king's psalter c1540**
bottom left: **Musical instruments, including a fiddle, recovered from Henry VIII's flagship, the** *Mary Rose* **which sank in 1545**

left: **A song by Robert Fayrfax from** *The Fayrfax MS,* **a collection from c1500 including songs by Cornysh, Davy, Sheryngham, Browne and others**

plainchant into their own works, but they did not compose it. Folk music depends on memory, improvisation and oral transmission; except for the few instances in which popular material found its way into composed music (for instance in John Taverner's *Western Wind* Mass), it cannot now be retrieved. If the following account pays more attention to composers than to performers, it is because more evidence survives of their activity, and because they tended to hold the most prestigious and best documented musical positions, particularly those of choirmaster and organist.

In many respects the musical culture of early Tudor England was deeply traditional, continuing and developing usages, techniques and styles traceable back several centuries. Had John Dunstable and Lionel Power been able to time-travel forwards a century to the musical world of John Taverner, they would probably have felt quite at home. In the 1520s as in the 1420s, most musicians worked in various kinds of religious environment, and they made a closely defined contribution to the performance of the Opus Dei. Although separated by a century, the music of Dunstable and Taverner relies on similar principles of design and techniques of composition, and its sound reflects the same delight in concord and full sonority.

This is not to deny that changes took place. Employers were considerably more numerous in Henry VIII's England than they had been in Henry V's, a larger proportion of them were laymen, and some operated on an exceptionally lavish scale. Musically, the changes were less radical than those in contemporary continental music. To take four works: Power's Mass *Alma redemptoris mater* (c 1425) and Taverner's Mass *Corona spinea* (c 1525) are far more alike than are Guillaume Dufay's Mass *Sine nomine* (c 1420) and Josquin des Prez's Mass *Pange lingua* (c 1515). This conservative tendency was recognised at the time; in the 1470s the Flemish music theorist Tinctoris criticised English composers for their failure to keep pace with mainstream musical fashion. The recurrent critical complaint about the conservatism of English music is itself five centuries old!

Church music was cultivated in a surprisingly wide variety of institutions, prominent among which were some of the secular cathedrals. At Lincoln, for example, the list of choirmasters includes an impressive number of outstanding composers, from William Horwood in the 1470s, through Thomas Ashwell and Thomas Appleby, to William Byrd in the 1560s. Rather different circumstances prevailed in those cathedrals, such as Canterbury and Durham, which were also Benedictine priories. Ever since the mid-14th century it had proved difficult for monasteries to keep pace with musical developments. The fact that only the brethren were allowed to participate in the main services of the community made it impossible simply to draft professional lay singers into the choir, an expedient readily available to secular churches and chapels. On the other hand, many of the larger houses already maintained small choirs of boys and/or laymen to sing services in the Lady Chapel, where no such prohibition existed, and towards 1500 some monasteries began to augment these choirs and to provide them with a master skilled in polyphony, so that they could perform the current polyphonic repertory. Several major composers held such positions at some stage of their careers: for example, Ashwell had moved from Lincoln Cathedral to Durham Cathedral by 1513, while Robert Fayrfax seems to have been connected with the Lady Chapel choir at St Alban's Abbey in the 1490s. Not all the foundations concerned were Benedictine; in the late 1530s Thomas Tallis was briefly employed at Waltham Abbey, an Augustinian house.

Collegiate foundations, so-called because they supported a college or resident community of clergy, often made ample provision for music. They were mainly the product of private patron-

below: **The Field of the Cloth of Gold, the French setting for a meeting in 1520 between the French king, Francis I and Henry VIII to secure an alliance (which failed) between the two countries. Robert Fayrfax (and other composers) accompanied the English monarch to France and organised the music**

age, either recent or past, and they varied greatly in scale, from enormous new projects such as Cardinal College, Oxford, founded by Cardinal Wolsey, to modest enlargements of existing institutions. Some, such as Tattershall in Lincolnshire, where John Taverner sang before he became choirmaster at Cardinal College, were parish churches raised to collegiate status by a wealthy patron. Tattershall was typical of many collegiate establishments in having a charitable dimension, being provided with a small almshouse; St Mary Newarke, Leicester, where Taverner's contemporary Hugh Aston was choirmaster, had a much larger one. Other collegiate institutions, such as Eton College and the colleges of Oxford and Cambridge, were associated with education; some of these, notably Eton, King's College, Cambridge, and Magdalen College, Oxford, were extremely active musically. The Eton Choirbook, still owned by the college, is by far the largest and most important surviving source of early Tudor church music. Whatever their ancillary functions might be, the central purpose of these collegiate foundations was to sustain a perpetual round of prayer for the souls of the founder and his nominees. In that it was believed to reinforce and intensify the effect of prayer, music was an invaluable resource.

The most influential manifestations of lay patronage were the household chapels maintained by royalty and the lay and spiritual magnates; in this context 'chapel' means a group of clergy. It had long been customary for great men to employ clerics whose duties included the performance of

divine service for the household. By the mid-14th century ambitious patrons were adding specialist musicians to their chapel staff, so that the worship conducted on their behalf could incorporate polyphonic music in fashionable styles. This probably began in the royal household, but it was quickly and extensively copied, until by 1471 a commentator on the organisation of Edward IV's household could consider it normal for dukes, marquises and earls to maintain private chapels. The practice was, in fact, even more widespread: Ralph, baron Cromwell, the founder of Tattershall College, also kept a household chapel, as did some mere knights.

The royal household chapel, often called the Chapel Royal, was usually considered pre-eminent, although with typical arrogance Wolsey allowed his own chapel, headed by the composer Richard Pygott, to outnumber and even out-perform that of his master Henry VIII. Many leading composers were members of the Chapel Royal: Fayrfax and William Cornysh under Henry VII and VIII, Richard Pygott under Henry VIII and Edward VI, John Sheppard under Mary, and Byrd under Elizabeth. Tallis was a member for more than 40 years under four monarchs, managing to accommodate himself to successive changes of religion. Windsor Castle and the Palace of Westminster had their own chapel choirs; composers associated with

above: **Thomas More and his family, a 1590s copy by Rowland Lockey of a lost Holbein painting from 1528. A lute and a viol are placed beside books and coats of arms forming part of the background, as does a view of More's Chelsea garden, reflecting tastes of the period**

them include Walter Lambe and John Merbecke at Windsor and Nicholas Ludford at Westminster.

Lay patronage of church music created that fertile blend of religion and worldliness, piety and pride, which was such a strong stimulant of later medieval and renaissance culture. Such patronage was not entirely limited to the great. A striking musical development in early Tudor England was the spread of polyphony into some parish churches. This was mainly financed by the parishioners themselves, and by gilds or charitable associations connected with the church. Some churches were apparently able to finance a permanent choir; many of these were in London, for example St-Mary-at-Hill, Billingsgate, where Tallis sang for a few months before moving to Waltham Abbey. Taverner, after leaving Cardinal College, seems to have taken charge of the music in the parish church of his home town of Boston, Lincolnshire. More often, however, singers might be hired for a particular service on an important day in the church's calendar. Churchwardens' accounts quite often include such entries as the following, from St Stephen's, Walbrooke, in 1526: 'To the alehouse over the syngers on Seynt Stephyn Evyn vid.'

The prime duty of church musicians was to make divine service more acceptable to God and more impressive to man. Polyphony was mainly intended for performance either during Mass or Vespers – the two services most frequented by the laity – or as part of an extra-liturgical act of devotion towards the end of the day. For Mass the unchanging texts known as the Ordinary – the Gloria, Credo, Sanctus and Agnus Dei – were set, often quoting the same musical material in each movement in order to create what is known as a cycle. The material quoted was usually a plainchant melody selected to make the composition relevant to a particular day or purpose, as in Taverner's Mass *Gloria tibi trinitas*, which takes its title from the Trinity Sunday plainchant on which it is based. This Mass may well have been written for Cardinal College: an antiphon to the Trinity was sung there daily, a representation of the Trinity appears on the College seal; and the Mass is the first item in a set of partbooks which belonged to the College.

Some Masses, in contrast, are based on a secular tune, as in the three *Western Wind* Masses by Taverner, Christopher Tye and Sheppard, or even on an elementary musical tag, as in Ashwell's Mass *God Save King Harry*. Other Masses utilised music from existing polyphonic compositions; Tallis's Mass *Salve intemerata*, for example, is a polished reworking of material from his eponymous votive antiphon, and Sheppard's Mass *Cantate* appears to be based on a lost polyphonic original. The chief polyphonic constituent of Vespers was the Magnificat, of which numerous settings survive. Fayrfax's Magnificat entitled *Regale* is typical in its alternation of plainchant and polyphonic verses and in basing the latter on a special kind of cantus firmus called a faburden.

Musically the evening devotion was a very productive expression of late medieval piety. Originally a monastic observance, it had spread to secular churches by the 14th century, and in the 15th it grew ever more popular with benefactors, because it offered a ready means whereby an institution or an individual could seek the intercession of a favourite saint. Performed following Vespers or Compline before the image of the saint to whom it was directed, it took the form of a miniature service: a votive antiphon sung by the choir, a versicle and response exchanged between officiant and choir, and a prayer addressed by the officiant to the saint. During the 15th century the votive antiphon was sung increasingly often in polyphony rather than in plainchant, and by the end of the century it had become the predominant polyphonic genre.

For most of the century votive antiphon texts remained relatively few in number, and these few were repeatedly set in polyphony. Towards 1500, however, numerous new texts began to appear, a high proportion of which survive in a single musical composition, as if they were written to be set by a particular composer in order to adorn a specific occasion. The 67 votive antiphons in the Eton Choirbook exemplify the old and new fashions: 26 of them are settings of either *Salve regina* or *Gaude flore virginali*, whereas another 24 texts are set only once. Some of these unique texts seem to have stimulated composers to unusual efforts. For example, Richard Davy's *In honore summae matris* is an astonishingly imaginative and well-sustained setting of a long and intricate poem addressing the Virgin and her Son; Davy bases his composition on a plainchant cantus firmus from All Saints' Day, and it is probably no accident that the poem alludes to a passage from the ninth lesson at Matins on that day.

As reformist ideas gained a hold during the 1520s and 30s the votive antiphon attracted criticism because of its non-scriptural texts and implicit reliance on the intercession of saints. It did not immediately disappear – Taverner's *Mater Christi* must date from the late 1520s and Ludford's *Ave cujus conceptio* probably belongs to the mid-1530s – but some composers seem to have sought less controversial types of text. Prayer-motets – settings of liturgical prayers or texts modelled on them, such as Ludford's *Domine Jesu Christe* – were already being written in the mid-1530s. The polyphonic responsory, a setting of a plainchant item from the service of Matins, seems to have been born in the

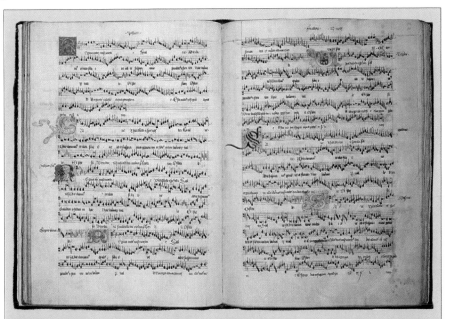

THE ETON CHOIRBOOK
Apparently copied for Eton College at the very beginning of the 16th century, the Eton Choirbook is by far the largest and most important surviving source of early Tudor church music. When complete it contained 93 compositions including 24 Magnificats and 67 votive antiphons. This opening shows the first half of *Salve Regina* by John Sutton, a Fellow of the College in 1477–8. The seven voices are written separately on the page and all but the highest are labelled: Tenor, Inferior (Lower) Contratenor, Superior (Higher) Contratenor, Triplex (Treble), Medius (Mean or Alto), Bassus. The capital at the beginning of the Triplex incorporates the College's arms. The statutes required that *Salve Regina* be sung in polyphony every evening and that each member say daily the antiphon *Libera nos*. Sutton incorporates the *Libera nos* plainchant into his setting as a tenor cantus firmus; the stepwise movement, narrow range and longer note values of this voice reveal its special function. The text is written in black ink in the fully-scored sections and in red in the reduced-voice sections, perhaps indicating that the latter should be sung by soloists.

same decade – Taverner's *Dum transisset sabbatum* was apparently one of the first – but most of the surviving examples, such as Sheppard's *Reges Tharsis* and Tallis's *Videte miraculum*, were probably written in the reign of Mary. The earliest surviving settings of complete psalms, such as Tye's *In quo corrigit*, date either from Edward VI's reign or from late in that of his father. It is worth remarking that Josquin and his contemporaries had been setting such texts at least a generation earlier.

Among the most significant musical developments during the 15th century were the increase in size and the change in makeup of polyphonic choirs. In Dunstable's day polyphony was sung not by the whole ecclesiastical choir but by a small group of adult professional singers called clerks. There would normally be no more than three or four of these, allowing one voice to a part in the standard polyphonic textures. During the 15th century the number of clerks tended to increase, and other members of the choir such as the vicars-choral and the boys began to take part in performing polyphony, so that by the early 16th century the polyphonic ensemble could be considerably larger. In the 1470s Edward IV modernised the choir of St George's Chapel, Windsor, by adding nine clerks to the existing four and seven choris-

below: The Ambassadors by Hans Holbein, 1533. Two renaissance noblemen stand beside a lute, an open hymnbook with music to Luther's Veni Creator Spiritus and scientific instruments

ters to the existing six, producing 13 of each. In the 1480s Magdalen College had 16 choristers and eight clerks, plus four chaplains who might have been capable of taking part in polyphony. Under Henry VIII the Chapel Royal included 12 choristers and about 20 clerks, usually called gentlemen. Obviously not every early Tudor choir could boast such numbers; there must have been ensembles hard pressed to find even one singer for each line. It is difficult to suggest an average size, but 12 to 18 would probably not be wide of the mark. Although many churches possessed an organ, the instrument apparently played a relatively minor role, supporting the singing of plainchant and playing solos based upon chant rather than participating in polyphonic music. There is no evidence that any other instrument habitually made a contribution to church services.

Early-15th-century polyphony was performed by adult male singers; the two-octave range between its highest and lowest notes allows it to be sung by two adjacent types of voice, either alto and tenor or perhaps tenor and bass. By 1500, however, the picture had changed: most of the polyphony in the Eton Choirbook has an overall range of three octaves, and it requires the four kinds of voice recognised today: treble, alto, tenor and bass. Precisely how this change came about is very obscure. Two distinct processes are involved – the addition of a true bass part below the customary alto-tenor-tenor trio, and the addition of a part for boy trebles above it. Both of these probably began in the 1450s; but it is not clear which came first, if indeed either consistently preceded the other. Here, as with many other aspects of style, we are hampered by the very meagre survival of music dating from the third quarter of the century.

At any rate, by 1500 the preferred number of parts had increased from three to five – treble, alto or mean, two tenors and bass – and this was to remain standard until the Reformation. The treble was certainly sung by boys and the three lowest parts by men; the alto may have been sung by boys in some choirs and men in others. Composers also wrote for other vocal combinations, mostly for all-male ensembles. Sometimes they composed in a larger number of parts: John Browne's *O Maria salvatoris* is in eight, Robert Wylkynson's *Salve regina* is in nine, the Scottish

composer Robert Carver's Mass *Dum sacrum mysterium* is in ten and his *O bone Jesu* is in the unprecedented number of 19. On the other hand, composers would still write in fewer voices if the occasion demanded it, either because the choir itself was small or because not all the singers would be present at a particular service; Ludford's Lady-Masses, for example, are for three voices.

These innovations affected the size of musical manuscripts. The early-15th-century Old Hall manuscript, which has an unusually large format for its period, measures about 42 centimetres by 28; the early-16th-century Eton Choirbook measures some 60 by 43, and is by no means the largest choirbook of its time. During the 1520s and 30s choirbooks, in which every part is on the same page, were supplanted by partbooks, in which each part is in a separate book; this was more practical for large ensembles. There were also important developments in musical style. Early Tudor composers enthusiastically exploited the greatly enlarged range of contrasts at their disposal: contrasts of texture, from duets to full scoring; contrasts of vocal type, from high treble to low bass; contrasts between intricate soloistic effects and broader gestures for the whole choir. Exuberant and tender by turns, William Cornysh's *Salve regina* exploits musical contrast more fully than most works of its time, and also emphasises the vocal virtuosity for which English singers were famous.

In many other respects style remained extremely traditional, evincing many features – emphasis upon concord and fullness of sound, harmonic solidity, melodic directness, and smoothly flowing rhythm – that had characterised English music for generations. On the other hand, there is also evidence of stylistic innovation more typical of continental music. For example, several turn-of-the-century composers, particularly Browne and Fayrfax, were already experimenting with imitative writing, and a generation later Taverner, Ludford and Aston were to take these experiments much further. If most English music of the period is old-fashioned in treating words as abstract objects, Fayrfax's gravely eloquent *Maria plena virtute* marries music to text in a way that Josquin himself could scarcely have bettered.

Music in Scotland experienced a remarkable flowering under the Stewart kings James IV

'... the King's chapel, which truly is more divine than human; they do not sing but exult, particularly the basses, whose equals I do not believe exist in the whole world.'

NICCOLO SAGUDINO, A MEMBER OF THE VENETIAN EMBASSY OF 1515, AFTER HEARING MASS SUNG BY THE CHAPEL ROYAL

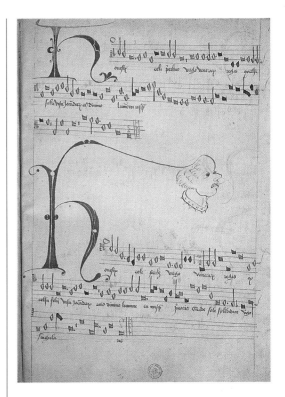

above right: A page of the Carver Choirbook

(1488–1513) and James V (1513–42). Both monarchs were anxious that their kingdom should figure upon the international stage and enter the cultural mainstream. One took an English bride, Henry VII's daughter Margaret, the other a French one, Mary of Guise. English and continental influence can be seen strongly at work in Scottish music of this period, the former in the works of Robert Carver and the latter in those of Robert Johnson, for instance in his setting of the psalm *Deus misereatur*. Spectacular though this efflorescence was, it was almost entirely dependent upon the royal court, and in the mid-century political crisis it withered overnight.

In concentrating upon church music this chapter simply reflects reality. Secular music was much less highly developed than church music, having hardly begun to find markets or evolve characteristic forms and idioms. There was, for instance, no equivalent of the Italian frottola or the Parisian chanson through which English music publishing could establish itself. The only music published in England during the first half of the 16th century, the *XX Songes* of 1530, was apparently a commercial failure. The cultivation of secular music was largely confined to the great households, where players of various instruments – lute, harpsichord, recorders, viols and so on – were employed and where the talents of chapel singers could be put to alternative use in hall and chamber. The musicians of the Chapel Royal often provided entertainment while the king dined, and during the reign of Edward VI the boys of the chapel performed plays before the young monarch. Two large collections of early Tudor song have come down to us: the Fayrfax manuscript of the early 1500s, and King Henry VIII's book of about 1520. The differences between them are instructive. The Fayrfax manuscript contains songs by composers active around the turn of the century, many of whom, such as Cornysh, Browne and Davy, were primarily employed as chapel musicians. Some of the songs are religious, calling mankind to repentance, as in Davy's *Ah, mine heart*, or musing on the Passion, as in Cornysh's *Woefully arrayed*. Most of the amorous songs, for instance Fayrfax's *Benedicite! What dreamed I?*, set high-flown, ponderous courtly lyrics of a kind that continental composers had abandoned a generation earlier. Stylistically these works strongly resemble the same composers' church music.

King Henry VIII's book breathes a new spirit. Most of the songs in it are more concise; their poetry is succinct and direct; and their music is simpler (see for example Cornysh's *You and I and Amyas*). The book also contains instrumental consorts of varying lengths and degrees of difficulty. There is a strong impression of catering for amateurs as well as professionals; the king and his intimates would have been capable of performing much of this repertory, and Henry himself is credited with the authorship of several compositions. These developments do not seem to have been sustained; we have virtually no secular songs from the 1530s and 40s, and when they reappear around the middle of the century, for example in Tallis's *Like as the doleful dove*, they have taken on a plodding character and sententious tone strongly evident also in Thomas Whythorne's collection *Songes for Three, Fower and Five Voyces* (1571). The development of instrumental music is even harder to trace because so little survives; this is particular-

above: **The Chapel Royal at Hampton Court, rebuilt by Henry VIII in the 1530s, the only Chapel Royal still in use today**

ly frustrating because one would like to assess the extent to which the numerous Netherlandish and Italian instrumentalists at the royal court helped to create an awareness of continental style. The 1550s probably saw the birth of the long-lived genre known as the In Nomine, a piece for instrumental consort built around a presentation of the *Gloria tibi trinitas* plainchant in a similar rhythmic guise to that which Taverner had given it at the words 'in nomine Domini' in the Sanctus of his Mass of the same name.

During the reign of Edward VI (1547–53) church music suffered immensely, mainly because the English rite gave less opportunity for music and the reformers' obsession with clarity of declamation obliged composers to write in a style that was so elementary and self-effacing as to be virtually devoid of interest; Tallis's Dorian Service shows how such constraints could effectively cramp even a composer of genius. Even more disastrous was the forced closure of many important choral foundations, which severely damaged the country's musical infrastructure. Mary's reign (1553–8) brought a brief resumption of the old ways. Musically Queen Mary sought to return to the England of her childhood in the 1520s, as if to reject even the changes which had occurred in the following decade. One of the masterpieces of her reign, Tallis's Mass *Puer natus*, is a traditional cantus firmus Mass; another, his votive antiphon *Gaude gloriosa*, is unequivocally addressed to the Virgin. But ironically these two compositions and many contemporary works by Sheppard and Tye show clear signs of having been touched by continental musical style, perhaps through the chapel musicians whom Philip of Spain brought with him when he came to England for his marriage with the queen. These continental traits, rather than those of the insular tradition, were to form the basis of English musical style under Elizabeth and James I.

The title quotation 'connyng syngyng men' comes from a description of Cardinal Wolsey's household chapel by George Cavendish, Wolsey's first biographer.

4

THE TRIUMPHES OF ORIANA

ELIZABETHAN MUSIC 1558–1603

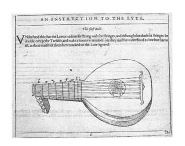

JOHN MILSOM

We begin in 1588, the 30th year of Queen Elizabeth's reign. The Spanish Armada has been scattered, and England is freed from the threat of invasion. In a spirit of national rejoicing, crowds line the streets of London, hoping to catch sight of the queen as she processes in state to St Paul's Cathedral, where she will give thanks for the victory. Our reporter, John Stow, Freeman of the Company of Merchant Tailors and author of *The Annals of England*, was there in the crowd:

'The four and twentieth of November, being Sunday, her Majesty – having attendant upon her the Privy Council and nobility, and other honourable persons as well spiritual as temporal in great number, the French Ambassador, the judges of the realm, the heralds, trumpeters, and all on horseback – did come in a chariot-throne ... from Somerset House to the Cathedral Church of St Paul. ... Over the gate of the Temple Bar were placed the waits of the city. And at the same Bar, the Lord Mayor and

Tomaso Inglese   *Tallis Compositore*

Guglielmo Inglese   *Bird Compositore*

Chapter opener shows,
***top right:* Four musicians playing lutes and viols, from a painted frieze in the Great Chamber of Gilling Castle, North Yorkshire, c1585**
***middle left:* Drawing of a lute from William Barley's *A New Booke of Tabliture*, 1596, containing seven lute solos by Dowland**
***bottom right:* Virginals by Stephen Keene, 1668**

***left:* Engravings thought to be of Thomas Tallis (top) and William Byrd (below)**

his brethren the Aldermen in scarlet received and welcomed her majesty to her city ... She proceeded along to [St] Paul's Church, where at the great west door she ... was received by the Bishop of London, the Dean of Paul's, and other of the clergy to the number of more than fifty, all in rich copes; where her highness, on her knees, made her hearty prayers unto God. Which prayers being finished, she was under a rich canopy brought through the long west aisle to the choir, the clergy singing the Litany; which, being ended, ... she heard a sermon ... and then returned through the church to the Bishop's palace, where she dined, and returned in like order as afore (but with great light of torches) to Somerset House.'

It is a summary account, but we can flesh out some of the details. The queen's trumpeters, for example, announced her presence with blazons of sound similar to those still heard today on occasions of state. At Temple Bar (the gateway leading from the Strand into Fleet Street, marking the westward limit of the City of London), Elizabeth was greeted by waits (civic minstrels) playing loud music on shawms, sackbuts and drums, outdoor instruments capable of making more noise than even the liveliest of crowds. From there she was carried along Fleet Street, with pageants and songs to entertain her. The best part of an hour later, she completed the half-mile journey to St Paul's – not Sir Christopher Wren's great temple, but rather the gothic cathedral destroyed by the Fire of London. There she heard choirs singing the Litany and Te Deum, the playing of the organs, and air thick with the pealing of bells.

At some point in all this, a party of boys from Christ's Hospital stepped forward to present a specially composed victory song. It was a unique creation. William Byrd, organist of the queen's Chapel Royal, wrote the music. Queen Elizabeth herself devised the words, 'in manner of a thanksgiving to God for her and our deliverance from the invincible navy of the Spaniard'. They began as follows:

'Look and bow down thine ear, O Lord;
From thy bright sphere behold and see
Thy handmaid and thy handywork
Among thy priests, offering to thee

Zeal for incense, reaching the skies;
Myself and sceptre sacrifice.'

In a day of otherwise public ostentation it must have seemed an almost intimate moment, for Elizabeth's verse is decidedly personal. She speaks of 'myself', 'my days' and 'mine enemies'; she thanks the Lord who 'hath preserved in tender love / The spirit of his turtle dove'. Byrd's music appears to have been solemn – it survives today only as a fragment – and uses a grave minor key. Neither words nor music show any sign of braying, and it is hard to imagine them being bawled out. In short, 'Look and bow down' is a work of refinement and artistry. In that respect it differs from everything else in the day's musical fare. Those Londoners in the crowd who got close enough to hear it must have enjoyed a rare treat: a glimpse into the otherwise inaccessible world of chamber music, normally the exclusive preserve of the privileged.

This is an important point, easily overlooked from our 20th-century vantage point. The Elizabethan era is often described as the 'golden age' of English music, an age characterized by the superb artistry of Tallis's *Lamentations*, Byrd's *Lullaby*, Dowland's *Lachrimae* and Morley's *Fire, fire*. But it was a golden age only for those people who had access to its riches: the high-born, the powerful, the wealthy and the educated. To the men and women in the streets it was an age like

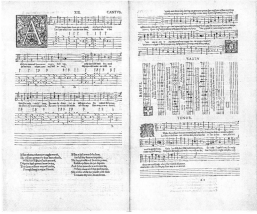

above: John Dowland's song *Awake Sweet Love* from the 1597 edition of *The Firste Book of Songes or Ayres*, showing the layout of the parts so that a single book can be read by performers round a table. The left hand page also contains the lute part in tablature
below: Gentlemen and Children of the Chapel Royal in the funeral procession for Queen Elizabeth I in 1603

any other, an age of folksong, balladry, hymn-tunes and morris dancing. To understand what 'Elizabethan music' meant to them, we should turn to Shakespeare. His plays are full of references to music, but almost without exception those references are to the music of the streets – to ballads and popular songs such as *Greensleeves* that were on everyone's lips, to fanfares and the sounds of public ceremony, not to the motets of Thomas Tallis, the songs of William Byrd, the ayres of John Dowland or the madrigals of Thomas Morley. If Shakespeare knew such highbrow music, he rarely alludes to it. It was not the music of common experience.

Returning, then, to John Stow, we should take note of the point at which his vivid description of the festivities on 24 November 1588 runs out of steam. As Elizabeth stepped from public gaze into the privacy of the Bishop's palace, Stow falls silent. Presumably he was not counted among the honoured guests. The next thing we hear about is the queen's departure. If we are to fill in the gap, we will have to do some imagining:

Over her sumptuous dinner, Queen Elizabeth was entertained by the plucking of lutes, by consorts of viols, and by that most dazzling of ensembles, the mixed (or 'broken') consort – an odd array of plucked, bowed and blown instruments, which you will see illustrated in the

The Serjeant of the Vestrie

Children of the Chappell.

Gentlemen of the Chappell.

Deputie clarke of the Markett
Clarks
Clarks extraordinary
Offecer
Dyett

picture of Sir Henry Unton's wedding feast. As the queen took her dessert, five singers stepped forward to greet her with music in that new fashion called the madrigal. The pieces they sang were taken from a recently published book called *Musica Transalpina* – 'Music from beyond the Alps' – in which Mr Nicholas Yonge, a London singer, has gathered together some madrigals by the best Italian composers alive today, and substituted new English words for the Italian originals. From that same book they sang a new piece in similar style by our own William Byrd, called *The fair young virgin*, and also some madrigals by Alfonso Ferrabosco, the Italian musician-cum-spy who frequents the royal court and vies with Byrd for musical excellence. Dinner being finished, there was some dancing, again to choice music, which was played by the royal violin band; after which

right: **Title page of the madrigal collection, *The Triumphes of Oriana***
below: **Detail from a memorial panel, 1596, with scenes from the life of soldier and diplomat, Sir Henry Unton, showing his wedding feast with masquers and two consorts of musicians. Dowland composed the pavan *Lachrimae or Seaven Teares* as a memorial to Unton in 1604**

the queen returned in like order as afore (but with great light of torches) to Somerset House.

Although this is pure surmise, none of its details lie beyond the bounds of possibility. Like her father, Henry VIII, Elizabeth was a connoisseur of fine music. Not only was she used to having it around her, sung and played by professionals. She was an able musician herself. In one of Nicholas Hilliard's most exquisite miniatures she is shown playing the lute. A spinet now in the Victoria and Albert Museum evidently belonged to her, and we know for a fact that she was an expert player of keyboard instruments. Her dancing was famed; in one picture, painted around 1580, we can see her in full flight, supported physically by the hands of Robert Dudley, Earl of Leicester, and musically by the

royal violin band. She maintained the choir of the Chapel Royal to high standards throughout her reign – and this at a time when church music, distrusted by many of the Protestant reformers, was generally at a low ebb. ('If it were not the queen's majesty that did favour that excellent science', wrote John Boswell in 1572, 'singing-men and choristers might go a-begging, together with their master the player of the organs.') Heading her choir for some 30 years was William Byrd, England's foremost composer, who provided it with magnificent pieces such as *The Great Service* and *Sing joyfully*. Other well-known names linked with the Chapel Royal include Thomas Tallis, Richard Farrant, Robert Parsons, John Bull and Thomas Morley. The last of these mustered the services of 23 composers to write a grand set of madrigals in honour of Elizabeth, published in 1601 under the title *The Triumphes of Oriana*.

The musical finery of Queen Elizabeth's court inevitably set the standard for her subjects. We need look no further than inventories of belongings or account-books of expenses to see how seriously music was taken by the Elizabethan aristocracy and nobility. The Earl of Leicester, for

instance, had a store of musical instruments at each of his principal residences: in 1583, Kenilworth could boast six viols, twelve flutes, three lutes, three bandoras and two keyboard instruments, while in the great chamber of Leicester House in London there were violins, viols, an organ and a virginals. At Nonsuch Palace in Surrey the 12th Earl of Arundel, Henry Fitzalan, built up an unrivalled library of music, printed and manuscript, together with performing resources that could do justice to it. One report praises '... his solemn choir / By voice and instruments so sweet to hear.'

Musical education for the heirs of the nobility became the norm rather than the exception. In the accounts of the Cavendishes of Chatsworth we read of payments in 1599 'For a set of singing books', 'For a treble viol for Master William', 'To Mr Newcom's man for lute strings', 'To Thomas

above: **Queen Elizabeth dancing with her favourite Robert Dudley, Earl of Leicester, by the Flemish artist Marcus Gheeraerts**

Banes for teaching Master William and Mistress Frances to sing'. Throughout England there were prestigious connections to be forged with high-ranking individuals and their families. Byrd, for example, secured either employment as a teacher or patronage as a composer from the Earls of Worcester and Northumberland, and the Lords Lumley, Paget and Petre. John Wilbye spent most of his life in the service of Sir Thomas and Lady Kytson of Hengrave Hall in Suffolk, and dedicated his *First Set of English Madrigals* (1598) to their son-in-law, Sir Charles Cavendish (whom Wilbye praises for his 'excellent skill in ... [and] great love and favour of music'). On rare occasions we can even see how the hands of the powerful and wealthy actually shaped some aspect of English music – most spectacularly in the case of Tallis's famous 40-part motet, *Spem in alium*.

'In Queen Elizabeth's time [around the year 1571] there was a song sent [from Italy] into England of 30 parts ... which, being sung, made a heavenly harmony. The Duke of [Norfolk], bearing a great love of music, asked whether none of our Englishmen could set as good a song, and Tallis (being very skilful) was felt to try whether he could undertake the matter – which he did, and made one of 40 parts, which was sung in the long gallery at Arundel House; which so far surpassed the other that the Duke, hearing of it sung, took his chain of gold from his neck and put it around Tallis's neck and gave it to him.'

Just as the nobility followed the example of the court, so the professional classes took their lead from the nobility, and explored the pleasures of music as a mode of recreation. Grammar schools began to teach its rudiments as part of the curriculum. At the Universities of Cambridge and Oxford it could be both studied at a theoretical level and pursued for leisure. Writing in 1599, Edward Herbert, Lord Cherbury, recalls his under-graduate days at Oxford:

'During this time of living in the University ... I attained also to sing my part at first sight in music, and to play on the lute with very little or almost no teaching ... and my learning of music was for this end, that I might entertain myself at home, and together refresh my mind

above: **Title page of Morley's *A Plaine and Easie Introduction to Practicall Musicke*** *left:* **Miniature of Queen Elizabeth, painted c1580 by Nicholas Hilliard, celebrating the Tudor monarch's musical virtuosity**

As did he live, so also did he die/In mild and quiet sort/(O! happy man)

EPITAPH FOR THOMAS TALLIS, ST ALFEGE CHURCHYARD, GREENWICH

after my studies, to which I was exceedingly inclined, and that I might not need the company of young men in whom I observed in those times much ill example and debauchery.'

For those gentlemen and women who were unable to secure or afford tuition, help was at hand in the form of printed books. The first English manual on lute-playing, translated from the French, appeared in 1568. Sixteen years later, the Oxford-trained teacher William Bathe published his *Introduction to the True Art of Music*, containing 'exact and easy rules, with arguments and their solutions, for such as seek to know'. Most famous and comprehensive of all, however, was Thomas Morley's *A Plain and Easy Introduction to Practical Music*, first published in 1597. Expressed in the form of an imaginary dialogue, it opens with the embarrassed confession of Philomathes, an aspiring but untrained musician:

'... supper being ended and music books (according to the custom) being brought to the table, the mistress of the house presented me with a part, earnestly requesting me to sing. But when after many excuses I protested unfeignedly that I could not, everyone began to wonder – yea, some whispered to others, demanding how I was brought up; so that upon shame of mine ignorance I go now to seek out mine old friend Master Gnorimus, to make myself his scholar.'

Even from these few references, we can begin to sense the nature of the world that nurtured Elizabethan music. When Nicholas Yonge published his *Musica Transalpina* in 1588, he must have envisaged copies falling into the hands of everyone from Queen Elizabeth herself, and all her noble earls and lords, right down to the 'great number of gentlemen and merchants of good account' with whom he kept company in London. Typically he would have printed about 1,000 copies, all of which must have been intended for sale in Great Britain, since English was barely spoken abroad. Evidently the book sold well, for a second edition appeared around 1594. It is important to realize how different this is from the standards of Henry VIII's reign, when music-making was largely the province of professionals rather than amateurs.

Demand and supply on such a scale represents an astonishing cultural change. Had keyboard and lute notations not posed technical problems to the printers, they too would have been mass-produced in similar numbers. Instead the needs of players were satisfied by manuscript copies, which proliferated as never before.

In short, secular music came of age in the Elizabethan era. Curiously, it did so at the very time when church music was falling into its sharpest decline for centuries. According to Thomas Whythorne – a musician of somewhat dubious ability whose fame today rests largely on his autobiography of c 1576 – music had become 'so slenderly maintained in the cathedral churches

below: **A Fête at Bermondsey by Joris Hoefnagel, c1570**

and colleges and parish churches that, when the old store of the musicians be worn out ... (which is like to be in short time), ye shall have few or none remaining except it be a few singing men and players on musical instruments'. A later (anonymous) writer laid the blame for the decline squarely on the shoulders of the Protestants. 'Few or none of the people', he says, 'would vouchsafe to come into the choir during the singing service, but would stand without, dancing and sporting themselves, until the sermons and lectures did begin.' For those of a Puritan leaning, the spoken word was preferable to any 'unnecessary piping and minstrelsy' of choristers and singing-men. Put crudely, the Elizabethan church no longer had

much to offer the ambitious composer.

Here we face an apparent contradiction. If the standards of Elizabethan choirs had fallen so very low, how are we to account for masterpieces such as Tallis's *Lamentations* and Byrd's Mass for Four Voices, works that many listeners would place at the very pinnacle of the Tudor church music tradition? How can these possibly be cited as evidence of church music in decline?

There is a simple answer. These pieces are not church music at all, at least not in the strict meaning of the term. Although by constitution Elizabethan England was a Protestant nation, in practice many of its citizens remained loyal to the Roman Catholic faith. Since there was no possibility of worshipping in the new Anglican churches, the Elizabethan Catholics turned instead to private devotion. They sang motets, pieces with texts from the Bible or the liturgy that expressed their aspirations and beliefs. More defiantly still, they heard Mass in the privacy of their own

below: Portrait of John Bull c1589

homes, using whatever singers they could muster. For music they turned to sympathetic composers, and above all to a seemingly unlikely collaborator: none other than Queen Elizabeth's organist and chapelmaster, William Byrd.

Byrd's adherence to the Catholic cause is undisputed. When not on duty with the Chapel Royal, he moved in an almost exclusively Catholic circle of patrons and friends. It was in the houses of prominent Catholics such as the Earl of Worcester and Sir John Petre that many of Byrd's best known works were given their first performances, works such as *Haec dies*, *Ne irascaris*, *Laudibus in sanctis*, *Ave verum corpus* and the Masses for three, four and five voices. Some of them are jubilant; some are pious; and an unusually large number of them speak of oppression and liberation, themes that were of special relevance to the English recusant community. It does not take much imagination to grasp the allegory in *Domine, tu iurasti*, a motet which (in the words of an apparently reliable source) Byrd himself reckoned to be 'the best [piece] he ever composed':

> 'Lord, you swore to our fathers that you would give to their offspring a land flowing with milk and honey. Now, Lord, remember the covenant you made with our fathers, and deliver us from the hand of Pharaoh, the king of Egypt, and from bondage under the Egyptians.'

Here as in so much of the Elizabethan repertoire, music has become meshed with broader issues of politics and power. *Domine, tu iurasti* speaks no less seriously to its audience of attentive Catholics than Byrd's Armada song, *Look and bow down*, voices the relief of a queen and country spared from the threat of foreign invasion. In these works and many others like them we can, if we look hard enough, see with quite vivid clarity the world as it was for our Elizabethan ancestors, and find it to be in many ways surprisingly similar to our own – a world in which religious strife, political conflict and social aspiration were as real and important as they are today. No one will dispute the fact that, as art alone, the music of Tallis, Byrd, Morley, Dowland and Bull can still give us exquisite pleasure. How much more intense that pleasure, however, when its original context too is known to us.

5

COURT AND COUNTRY

THE EARLY SEVENTEENTH CENTURY

1603–1660

PETER HOLMAN

When James VI of Scotland rode down to London in the spring of 1603 to become James I of England he took possession of one of the most centralised countries in Europe. London, with a population of over 200,000, was more than ten times the size of her nearest rivals, Norwich, Bristol and York. An extraordinarily large proportion of the nation's commercial, intellectual and artistic life was conducted in her noisy and crowded streets. Nearby, at Whitehall, was the seat of England's centralised form of government, organised around the court and the person of the monarch. The court was by far the most important musical centre in the country. Nearly all of England's important composers were associated with it in one way or another, and by 1625, when Charles I came to the throne, it employed around 140 musicians; they were divided into a number of separate groups, each with its own personnel, repertory, and role in court life.

The oldest and largest of these groups was the Chapel Royal, which had its origins at least as far back as the 12th century. Its main function was to provide the king with daily choral services in the small chapel at Whitehall, though its members also took part in court plays and masques, and probably contributed a good deal to its secular musical life. The Chapel Royal was not large – 12 boys were supported by 20 men, who attended in a rota – but it employed England's leading church

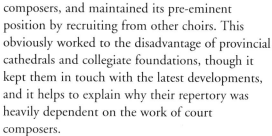

Chapter opener shows, *top left:* **Figure with a lute, an early 17th-century painting on the Nine Muses ceiling of Crathes Castle, Scotland** *middle right:* **The title page of** *Parthenia* **(1613), one of the first English music books printed from engraved plates, containing keyboard music by Byrd, Bull and Gibbons** *bottom:* **Painting of the Thames at Hampton Court by an unknown artist c1640**

below: **A stylised engraving of a ceremony between James I and the Spanish ambassador in the Whitehall Chapel in 1623 at which they ratified the projected marriage of Prince Charles to the Spanish Infanta. Note the musicians' gallery housing the organ, instrumentalists and singers**

composers, and maintained its pre-eminent position by recruiting from other choirs. This obviously worked to the disadvantage of provincial cathedrals and collegiate foundations, though it kept them in touch with the latest developments, and it helps to explain why their repertory was heavily dependent on the work of court composers.

The Anglican liturgy, then as now, required settings of services (the unchanging texts prescribed for Morning Prayer, Evening Prayer and Holy Communion) and anthems (texts proper to each day). In addition, a distinction was made between full and verse settings. The former, an offshoot of the central European contrapuntal tradition, was purely choral, while the latter was an Elizabethan invention in which sections for solo voices alternate with those for full choir. Verse anthems also divide into those with organ accompaniment, and 'consort anthems' with parts for a group of instruments, though some exist in both forms. It is not entirely clear how and why the two types developed. Consorts of viols were probably used in early Chapel Royal anthems, but were usually replaced by organ when they were performed in cathedrals. Wind consorts were used in Whitehall chapel and in some cathedrals and were sometimes an alternative, but most later consort anthems come from secular manuscripts, and were presumably mostly performed with viols as devotional chamber music.

Full anthems continued to be written throughout the reigns of James I and Charles I, though verse anthems increasingly dominated the reper-tory. This is certainly true of the output of the three greatest Jacobean anthem composers, Orlando Gibbons, Thomas Tomkins and Thomas Weelkes. Indeed, the verse anthem achieved its classic form with Gibbons, a member of the Chapel Royal from 1603. In his simpler and presumably earlier ones, like the famous 'This is the record of John', there is only one soloist, and the choir takes up the words and the music of the solos, as in Elizabethan verse anthems. But in a work such as 'See, see the word is incarnate', one of the masterpieces of the genre, he developed a much more complex relationship between the verse and full sections. The striking text (by Godfrey Goodman, Dean of Rochester) is a compressed, allusive narrative of Christ's life from

Christmas to Ascension, and Gibbons matches it with vivid, dramatic music, passing rapidly from voice to voice in the solos, creating complex ensembles, and casting the choir now as angels at the Nativity, now as the Jews welcoming Christ into Jerusalem.

By and large, however, Gibbons exemplifies the Jacobean virtues of restraint, decorum and proportion, with the potentially conflicting demands of traditional linear counterpoint and forward-looking harmonic patterns kept in fruitful balance. The same is true of Thomas Tomkins. Tomkins was organist of Worcester Cathedral from 1596 to the Civil War, and has therefore been thought of as a provincial composer, but he was also a member of the Chapel Royal from at least 1603, and much of his large and fine output of anthems must have been written for Whitehall chapel; most of them were published by his son Nathaniel in *Musica Deo sacra* (1668). Thomas Weelkes, organist of Chichester Cathedral from 1601–2, was the one outstanding provincial church composer who never received a Chapel Royal post, though this probably had more to do with his sad reputation as 'a comon drunkard and notorious swearer & blasphemer' than with his abilities as a musician. We think of him mainly as a madrigalist, but that is because less than half of his known church music survives complete. Furthermore, some of his best-known 'anthems', such as the six-part 'When David heard' and 'Gloria in excelsis Deo', survive only in secular sources, and may in reality be devotional madrigals. The Chichester choir, like a number of others, was at a low ebb in Weelkes's time, and would have been hard put to do justice to his characteristically powerful and brilliant choral style. During Charles I's reign, provincial composers such as John Amner (at Ely) and Michael East (at Lichfield) largely continued to work in the Jacobean idiom, and the leaders of the next generation were more interested in secular music.

At court, the secular musicians were traditionally divided into the few, who provided the royal family with chamber music and tuition in private, and the many, who manned instrumental consorts in the public areas of the palace. The vogue for consorts – usually three or four sizes of one instrument – developed in England in Henry VIII's reign. The English court maintained separate

'It is proportion that beautifies everything, this whole universe consists of it, and music is measured by it...'

ORLANDO GIBBONS

above: Orlando Gibbons
right: A viol player
illustrated in
Christopher Simpson's
***The Division-violist* (1659)**

shawm and sackbut, flute, recorder and violin consorts well into Charles I's reign, though by then the fashion abroad was for groups that mixed several types of melody instrument with lutes or keyboards. In this respect, court instrumentalists lagged behind their less eminent colleagues. A distinctive and sophisticated six-man mixed consort consisting of violin or treble viol, flute or recorder, bass viol, lute, cittern and bandora emerged in the 1570s and spread rapidly from aristocratic households to waits and theatre musicians; some of its repertory, largely settings of popular tunes and dances, was published by Thomas Morley in 1599 and Philip Rosseter in 1609. In a modified form (with a second violin instead of the flute/recorder and theorbos replacing the plucked instruments) it remained the favoured urban dance band throughout our period, with a sizeable repertory by William Lawes, Charles Coleman, Simon Ives and others. When mixed consorts finally appeared at James I's court it was in the households of his

sons Henry and Charles rather than in the main royal music.

At the same time, a repertory for viols was belatedly developing in England. Until about 1600 aristocratic English children were usually taught music through a solo instrument; the more advanced skills needed to play in ensembles were found only in the most musical households. The lute was most favoured, since it was cheap and portable and its tablature notation was easy for beginners to learn. Virtually all the Tudors were lutenists, but Prince Henry and Prince Charles were taught the viol, and around 1620 it began to supplant the lute, acquiring a solo repertory

below: **Traditionally known as *The Cabal* by J B Medina, this painting is now thought to be a portrait of members of the King's Private Music c1661–3, with the German violin virtuoso Thomas Baltzar and the composer John Banister seated left and right at the front**

played 'lyra-way' in chords from tablature in addition to its consort repertory. Harpsichords and rectangular virginals were relatively expensive and rare, and were used mainly for solo music; until Purcell's time chamber organs were the only keyboard instruments used to any extent in ensemble music.

Instrumental music, whether for ensembles or solo instruments, was based either on dance forms or contrapuntal idioms derived from vocal music. Around 1600 the main dances were the grave pavan and galliard, and the livelier almain and corant, both duple/triple-time pairs; the fast triple-time saraband was introduced around 1625. They

all consist of two or three repeated sections, and their repeats encouraged running ornamentation or 'divisions', usually improvised in consort music but written out for the benefit of amateurs in the solo repertory. In the 16th century dances and popular songs were often settings of Italian chord sequences; after 1600 this was formalised into a repertory of divisions on newly-devised ground basses, mostly for one or two bass viols; the art of improvising or composing divisions was fully dealt with by Christopher Simpson in his treatise *The Division-violist* (1659).

Dance music and settings of popular tunes in dance patterns make up the bulk of the music for lute and 'virginal' (a term that includes in this context harpsichord and even chamber organ). This does not mean that the repertories are trivial: settings of pavans and galliards by the best composers – John Dowland, Daniel Bacheler, Francis Cutting, John Bull, William Byrd, Orlando Gibbons and Thomas Tomkins – are frequently extended, complex and highly expressive. Most lute and keyboard music circulated in manuscript, and is often met with today in editions of collections such as The Fitzwilliam Virginal Book (supposedly compiled by the Catholic Francis Tregian while imprisoned in the Tower 1609–19), though there are printed collections such as the *Varietie of Lute-Lessons* (1610) and *Parthenia* (1613), the latter containing keyboard music by Byrd, Bull and Gibbons. The complex, division-laden style of English lute and keyboard music declined in the 1620s, and was replaced by a simpler and more delicate idiom, using the arpeggiated *style brisé* developed by French lutenists – several of whom worked at the English court.

The consort repertory consists largely of fantasias in three, four, five and six parts, though there are also some collections of dance music – such as Dowland's *Lachrimae* (1605) for five viols or violins with lute, which opens with a matchless variation sequence based on his pavan of the same title. The fantasy is essentially a wordless motet or

right: **Corranto by William Byrd from the** *Fitzwilliam Virginal Book,* **the most remarkable collection of English 17th-century instrumental music** *below left:* **Mary Sidney, Lady Wroth holding a theorbo, c1620**

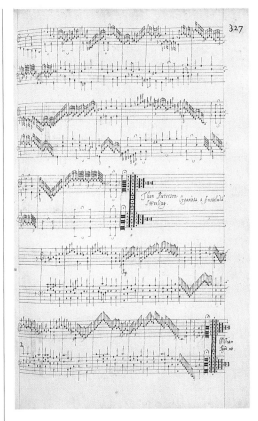

madrigal, typically consisting of a succession of contrasted and unrelated contrapuntal ideas, though sometimes works were based on a given theme, taken from plainsong or folksong. The 'In nomine' plainsong, for instance, taken from a passage in John Taverner's mass *Gloria tibi trinitas* (c 1520), was used as the basis for more than 150 works written over more than a century. There are a fair number of Elizabethan fantasias, but the heyday of the genre was in James I's reign, when Alfonso Ferrabosco, John Ward, Thomas Lupo, John Coprario, Orlando Gibbons, Richard Dering, Thomas Tomkins and others created a repertory of unparalleled richness, still only partially explored by modern viol consorts.

Lupo, Gibbons and Coprario, working in Prince Charles's household around 1620, also invented new types of contrapuntal music using varied combinations of violins, viols and chamber organ. Hitherto, the violin had been largely a dance instrument in England, so the new repertory had strong dance elements. Coprario's quirky and unpredictable sets of fantasia-suites, a fixed grouping of fantasy-alman-galliard, are scored specifically for one or two violins, bass viol and organ, and provided models for William Lawes,

John Jenkins and others. Lawes and Jenkins, the greatest Caroline consort composers, greatly expanded the repertory, devising new scorings. They are a fascinating study in opposites, the one a dashing courtier killed in the Civil War, the other a genial, long-lived household musician in remote East Anglian country houses; the one a restless, mercurial and daring musical personality, the other more serene and traditional, though with an inexhaustible harmonic and textural imagination.

There were three main types of secular vocal music at the beginning of this period. The oldest, the consort song, originated in laments performed in early Elizabethan choirboy plays. They were usually sung by boys, accompanied by four busy viol parts, and were often strophic, with the

below: **A self-portrait painted c1640 by the composer Nicholas Lanier**

MASTER OF THE KING'S MUSIC

Monarchs and music have historically been willing partners, but it seems to have been Charles I's particular enthusiasm for a good tune that gave rise to the appointment of the first-recorded 'master of the music'. The composer and performer Nicholas Lanier is seen in charge of Charles's sizeable 'Band' of players and singers in 1626. Even so, it was only from 1700, with the appointment of John Eccles, that the post formally carried with it the added responsibility for composition. Until then Purcell, Blow, Cooke and Humfrey had provided works for the royal court under the title 'composers in the private music'. For over a century successive Masters such as Greene, Boyce and Stanley provided birthday and new year odes (and more besides) for their respective sovereigns. This practice

of odes-to-order ended around 1820, but in one form or another royalty continued to make use of private bands (under the control of the Master) until the reign of George V. Walter Parratt, in office at that time, was thus the last Master to have official duties. Subsequent holders of the post (Elgar, Walford Davies, Bax, Bliss and now Australian-born Malcolm Williamson) have essen-

tially been appointed in recognition of their musical achievements. The job does not have to be a sinecure, however – Walford Davies and Bax were heavily involved with planning coronation music, for example. Malcolm Williamson has written a series of works with royalty in mind, including the *Mass of Christ the King*, dedicated to the Queen.

Andrew Green

musical interest created by sharp dissonance rather than word-painting. Word-painting was the novel feature of the madrigal, the Italian pastoral genre for unaccompanied voices that largely supplanted the consort song in the 1590s. Like their Italian counterparts, English madrigals were disseminated in printed editions, while consort songs mostly circulated in manuscript (though they sometimes appear in disguise in madrigal books, with words added to the viol parts). The greatest madrigal collections, such as the anthology *The Triumphes of Oriana* and the sets by Thomas Weelkes and John Wilbye, appeared in the years around 1600, and the genre declined soon after. At the same time, there was a revival of interest in the consort song, which began to be used as a vehicle for humorous evocations of urban and rural life, notably by Thomas Ravenscroft and in the Cries of London by Weelkes, Gibbons and Dering; the latter are effectively extended viol fantasias larded with snatches of street cries.

Lute songs also circulated mostly in print, but in a distinctive form, with parts placed around an opening of a large book, so that it could be read by performers crowded around a single copy placed on a small table. This unusual format, apparently invented by Dowland for his *First Booke* (1597), dictated the genre's subsequent development. The same music could be performed by a single voice with lute, as a part-song, or with voices replaced by viols, but it had to be simple enough to work in the various alternative scorings, and short enough to fit on a single page. Thus lute songs are typically short, strophic settings of light verse, using dance forms and rhythms, and frequently achieve a high degree of correlation between poetic and musical accent, line endings and phrase ending, rhyme schemes and matching cadences.

The lute song had a brief life: its heyday was effectively the period spanned by Dowland's four books, from 1597 to 1612 when *A Pilgrimes Solace* appeared. By then the theorbo had been introduced into England from Italy, and with it the technique of reading from a figured or unfigured bass, which made it unnecessary to write out tablature lute parts. At the same time, a new generation of composers – notably Robert Johnson, Alfonso Ferrabosco and Nicholas Lanier – began to write declamatory songs. They are partially influenced by Italian monody, so their vocal lines mirror the inflections of speech, and many of them survive with florid ornamentation. The best, such as those by Robert Johnson for plays given by Shakespeare's company (including *The Tempest* and *The Winter's Tale*), have considerable originality and dramatic force, though they survive mostly in poor manuscript sources. Music publishing was governed by a monopoly that more or less went into abeyance around 1620, and few editions appeared from then until John Playford began publishing during the Commonwealth. As a result, there was much catching up to do, and Playford's early song books are effectively retrospectives from the three previous decades. They give pride of place to Henry Lawes (William's elder brother), the most prolific and distinguished song composer of the Caroline generation.

The most ambitious dramatic music of the period was written for masques, the lavish occasional entertainments that combined courtly dancing and elaborate vocal music with spectacular stagecraft and the elements of spoken drama. Masques used the full resources of the royal music: the wind musicians played incidental music and covered the sound of stage machinery in scene changes; the violins played specially-composed dance music; and vocal music was provided by groups of singers cast as minor characters, often accompanied by multiple lutes. Unfortunately, we have no complete score for any court masque, but

Masque drawings by Inigo Jones – *far right:* A Daughter of Niger from *The Masque of Blackness* (1605) and *right:* Torch bearer: a Fiery Spirit from Thomas Campion's *The Lord's Masque* (1613) *below: An Idyll* by Sir Peter Lely, c late 1640s. The theme is probably the familiar allegory of Music – the voice, flute and bass viol – in the service of Love and Beauty

a number of Jacobean masque songs survive, mostly by Thomas Campion, Alfonso Ferrabosco and John Coprario, and we have a large number of Jacobean masque dances, most of which cannot be assigned to a particular production. The situation is much worse for Caroline masques, though we have portions of William Lawes' vocal music for *The Triumph of Peace* (1634), *The Triumphs of the Prince d'Amour* (1636) and *Britannia Triumphans* (1638). They consist of stately instrumental passages, solo sections and choruses in intricate, anthem-like sequences.

The court masque was killed off by the Civil War, but a diminutive private variant continued to be produced in country houses and schools. Freed of the requirement to produce court propaganda,

authors expanded the role of the spoken drama, creating a hybrid, half masque, half play. An early example is Milton's *Comus* (1634), produced for the Earl of Bridgewater at Ludlow; Henry Lawes provided the music and played the part of the Attendant Spirit. A number of works in the private masque tradition were put on in Commonwealth London as part of attempts to circumvent Parliament's ban on spoken plays. Thus, William Davenant had his play *The Siege of Rhodes* (1656) set to recitative by a consortium of composers, and Matthew Locke greatly expanded the role of music in James Shirley's *Cupid and Death* (1653) for a semi-public revival in 1659, probably for the same reason. *Cupid and Death*, an amusing comedy in which chaos ensues when the arrows of the protagonists are exchanged, is the only masque to survive with substantially complete music.

What of music in the Interregnum? The court broke up in confusion at the start of the Civil War in 1642, and the royal musicians were left to fend for themselves. Some went abroad, some joined the Royalist army, but most were forced to eke out a living as best as they could; they were joined soon after by the members of church choirs, disbanded by Act of Parliament. It used to be thought that the Civil War produced conditions universally detrimental to music, but Percy Scholes pointed out in the 1930s that the Puritans were not against music as such, only

right: Garton Orme at the Spinet, painted by Jonathan Richardson
below left: The impressario and actor Thomas Betterton (1635–1710) as Solyman in *The Siege of Rhodes*
below: The first shutter showing the prospect of Rhodes, designed by John Webb (a pupil of Inigo Jones) for *The Siege of Rhodes* (1656)

against its use in the theatre and in elaborate church music. Cromwell employed a group of musicians at Whitehall, and even ordered performances of Dering's Latin motets, originally written for the Catholic chapel of Henrietta Maria, Charles I's queen.

Furthermore, consort music flourished during the troubles. As the writer Roger North put it, 'when most other good arts languished Musick held up her head, not at Court nor (in the cant of those times) profane Theatres, but in private society, for many chose to fidle at home, than to goe out, and be knockt on the head abroad.' Oxford, in particular, became a musical centre: first, between 1642 and 1646, when the court was there; later, during the Commonwealth, when William Ellis put on weekly music meetings in his house; and later still, from 1657, when the university Music School was reopened by the professor, John Wilson. These Oxford music meetings were largely devoted to consort music, and were the precursors of the public concerts that developed in London during the Restoration period. At the Restoration the court reassembled, and the royal music was revived in its pre-war glory. But things were never quite the same, and before long the centre of London's musical life shifted for good from the court to its burgeoning public concerts and commercial theatres.

6

GENIUS OF ENGLAND

PURCELL AND HIS AGE 1660–1715

BRUCE WOOD

The restoration of King Charles II to the throne of his fathers marked an end to nearly 20 years' disruption of cultural life. The dismantling of choral foundations during the Commonwealth, and the burning of many of their music libraries; the abolition of the royal musical establishment, and the scattering of its members; the banning of play-acting, as a precaution against seditious satire: all these acts of destruction had now to be reversed, presenting the restored monarch with a formidable task. Much in the outcome was new, though some pre-War practices reasserted themselves, and persisted long afterwards – a feature of the Restoration scene which it is easy to overlook – while some of the most conspicuous innovations had roots, ironically, in the Puritan years.

Charles gave prompt attention to the rebuilding of the royal musical establishment. Musicians who had served his father were reinstated wherever possible, but after the long interregnum many new appointments were necessary. Only one change was more radical. The royal violin band dated back to the reign of Elizabeth, its humble function being to provide music for dancing. Now it was enlarged to 24 players, in emulation of Louis XIV's celebrated court orchestra, which Charles had heard during his exile, and drilled to formidable excellence.

The resumption of choral services in the Anglican church presented a greater challenge, for the continuity of chorister training had been broken. Henry Cooke, choirmaster at the Chapel

Chapter opener shows,
top left: **Detail of lime-wood carving by Grinling Gibbons in the carved room at Petworth House, 1692**
middle right: **Portrait of Henry Purcell in his final year, 1695, attributed to John Closterman**
bottom: **Musicians – trumpeters and kettle-drummer – in the Coronation procession for King James II, 1685**

above: **John Blow, an engraving from *Amphion Anglicus*, the collection of his songs published in 1700**
left: **The Coronation of Charles II in Westminster Abbey on 22 April 1660**

Royal, resorted to conscripting the ablest boys from cathedral and parish choirs – a long disused prerogative – and by this means assembled perhaps the most talented group ever to sing together anywhere. It included all the leading English musicians of the next generation: Pelham Humfrey, John Blow, William Turner and Thomas Tudway.

At first, for want of any recent compositions, the choral repertory was broadly the same as it had been before the Civil War – astonishingly conservative by Continental standards, for its prevailing musical language was still that of the late Renaissance. But Cooke soon introduced striking novelties. At Charles II's coronation in Westminster Abbey the music, much of it composed for the occasion by Cooke, featured spatial separation in the Venetian fashion, with separate galleries accommodating the choir, a group of solo voices, and the Twenty-Four Violins. Within the year the same principle was being applied, on Sundays and feast days, to anthems in the Chapel Royal. In this much more intimate performing space the violins were reduced to a small consort. Placed in a gallery above the choir-stalls, they played in the lively French manner favoured by the King (but deplored by an outraged John Evelyn as music for the ale-house, not for the church). Their preludes and ritornellos complemented vocal passages that included solos in the declamatory style – long familiar in Italy, but in England only much more recently infiltrated into solo song and still virtually unknown in church music.

Though important as a pioneer, Cooke was not a composer of any distinction; but the 'symphony anthem' was soon consolidated by others into the most glamorous genre in Restoration church music. As such, its value was political as well as artistic: it could serve as a suitably impressive vehicle for texts which – judiciously selected from the Scriptures, and sometimes even compiled from unrelated verses – sought to cast a spurious light of divine approval upon the actions of the king. (This artless technique for manipulating public opinion was presumably effective, for the practice persisted at the Chapel Royal to the end of the century and beyond.)

Matthew Locke, a senior figure among the royal musicians, was a composer of fiery individuality. A Roman Catholic, and organist to Charles's

Catholic queen, he nevertheless composed most of his sacred music for the Anglican rite. Among his anthems is one audacious example, *Be thou exalted, Lord*, laid out for no fewer than five groups of performers: three choirs, a violin band, and a mixed or 'broken' consort of violins, viols and theorbos. He also scored several of his anthems for the cornetts and sackbuts of the royal wind music – the same ensemble which, again playing music he had composed for them, had greeted the king on his triumphal entry into London at the Restoration.

That anciently-established group, however, was soon eclipsed by the newly fashionable violins, and younger composers never wrote for it. The most precocious of the Chapel choristers, Humfrey, was sent to study abroad after his voice broke – returning in 1667 so Frenchified, bumptious and scheming that it was, as a disgusted Samuel Pepys put it, enough to make a man piss. Over the next seven years Humfrey doubled the repertory of symphony anthems. His musical language, more urbane than that of Locke, was also more expressive, especially in penitential mood. In 1672, on Cooke's death, Humfrey assumed the post of royal choirmaster, with the young Henry Purcell among his first charges. But within two years his own tenure was cut short by death.

Blow, who succeeded him, was to hold the post for nearly 35 years and wield enormous influence. A busy pluralist as a performer, he was a composer of vigorous creativity, and far more versatile than Humfrey. Among his large and varied output he himself gave pride of place to his church music, which includes over 100 anthems. Nearly a third of these are scored for strings, and a few for other instruments too: at first oboes and baroque recorders, imported from France in the mid-1670s along with their players, and in the 1690s another newcomer to English sacred music, the trumpet.

Blow's symphony anthems, and his equally numerous verse anthems without instruments, range from modestly-scored examples written for the Chapel Royal to grandiose pieces for state occasions. During a creative life spanning 40 years his musical language changed considerably – the stubborn autonomy of part-writing which Dr Burney was to deplore as 'bestiality' a century later, and the reckless harmonic clashes that resulted from it, gradually yielding to a

right: **Henry Purcell by an unknown artist, showing the composer at an earlier age than other existing portraits** *below:* **Thomas Britton (1644–1714), the English patron of music who in 1678 established a series of weekly concerts in a room above his small-coal business in Clerkenwell. The subscription concerts were to last for 36 years**

smoother, more euphonious manner that anticipates Handel. But to the end of his days he continued composing in the old polyphonic manner: anthems mostly for full choir, though sometimes with inset ensemble verses – virtually the last examples, though by no means the least, of a genre that stretched back to the Reformation. In the same conservative style he also composed over a dozen settings of the service: more than were produced by all his leading contemporaries put together.

Within a year or two of Blow's appointment at the Chapel Royal, the most brilliant of his pupils had already become a colleague in the royal music. Purcell's earliest works almost certainly date from his chorister days; he was soon composing music of astonishing assurance, and rivalling his teacher in both technical and expressive versatility. The enchantingly vernal symphony anthem *My beloved spake*, for instance, and the massively polyphonic *Blow up the trumpet in Zion*, striking in its penitential rhetoric, both date from before his 18th birthday.

Purcell's life of a busy practical musician, as organist both of Westminster Abbey, where Blow resigned in his favour, and of the Chapel Royal, did not stunt his creative development. His musical language, at once fastidious and virile, owes much to Blow and something to Locke and Humfrey, but is yet so individual that it is adequately described only by his name: Purcellian. His one setting of the complete service is the finest of the period, full of ingenious canons concealed by the sheer variety of scoring and invention. But most of his energy as a church composer went into his anthems, of which he poured out nearly 70 between about 1675 and 1688. The best of them are polar opposites in style: symphony anthems featuring exuberant display passages for solo singers (most memorably for the great bass John Gostling, in *They that go down to the sea in ships*), and pieces in the old-fashioned polyphonic style, sometimes abounding in contrapuntal devices – inversion, augmentation and the like – deployed with a casual ease worthy of the greatest of his Renaissance predecessors. On rare occasions he brought the two styles together in a potent synthesis, as in the spacious 1685 coronation anthem *My heart is inditing* – a carefully planned companion-piece for Blow's identically scored and equally splendid *God spake sometime in visions*.

Purcell could, however, be uneven – something for which pressure of work was probably to blame. Many of his verse anthems, with and without instruments, are perfunctory in their treatment of the full choir, which is sometimes given only the single word 'Allelujah' set to a few bars of block chords. On the other hand, he was undeterred by indifference to his Chapel Royal music after 1685 on the part of the Catholic James II, during whose reign he (unlike Blow) continued to compose not only workaday music but also some impressive symphony anthems. The last of these, *O sing unto the Lord*, is a masterpiece by any standards. Also to James's reign belong most of Purcell's declamatory sacred songs – a remarkable series of powerful settings, designed for private devotional use, of texts by an intriguingly recondite selection of poets and divines.

After the 1688 Revolution the glory days of the Chapel Royal ended abruptly. William III, who

right: **A model of Dorset Garden Theatre, made by a present-day Dutch designer Frans Muller, showing the masque for Act V of Purcell's semi-opera The *Prophetess, or the History of Dioclesian*. *Dioclesian* was first staged at the theatre, London's biggest and best equipped at the time, in 1690**
below: Still Life with Musical Instruments **by Edwaert Collier (fl 1673–1700). In the centre is an open copy of a posthumous anthology of music by Purcell, *A Collection of Ayres, composed for the theatre and upon other occasions*, 1697.**

opposite top: **Westminster Abbey in Canaletto's famous painting of 1749**
opposite bottom: **Ticket for the Coronation of George III, Westminster Abbey, 22 September 1761**

disapproved of elaborate church music, forbade the use of instruments other than the organ; and financial retrenchments affected the entire musical establishment at court (in the process giving a powerful fillip to public concert-giving, still in its infancy in London). Purcell cut his losses, left Blow to shoulder almost unaided the burden of writing for the Chapel, and turned his own energies elsewhere. His subsequent sacred works are few and mostly unremarkable, but one of them is of unforgettable nobility. The tiny anthem *Thou knowest, Lord, the secrets of our hearts* was composed for the funeral of Queen Mary, in 1695; deliberately archaic in style, it replaced a lost movement in a dignified Tudor setting of the Burial Sentences – that by Thomas Morley, whose performance was a time-honoured feature of state funerals.

The symphony anthem produced one vigorous offshoot which long outlived it. During the 1660s it became customary for the king to be offered a loyal birthday tribute, written by one of the court poets and set to music by Cooke, Locke or Humfrey, and it was not long before odes were being composed for other occasions in the court calendar. Like the symphony anthem, the ode remained the preserve of the small circle of court composers. From 1675 onwards Blow, with occasional assistance from Turner, set an ode for New Year and another for the king's birthday, while from 1680 to 1688 Purcell contributed a welcome song on the king's return to London after his summer absence, and after the Revolution a birthday ode for the queen. A parallel series outside the court, initiated in 1683 by Purcell and contributed to by all the established composers of the day, celebrated the festival of St Cecilia. Individual odes were commissioned for other occasions too, as were some of their smaller and fewer-voiced

cousins, symphony songs.

During the 1680s the court ode gradually outgrew its parent genre, and began to assume a more popular style. But it was only after the Revolution, with the symphony anthem all but extinct, that the ode reached the peak of its development. The two most ambitious examples by Purcell, *The Yorkshire Feast Song* (1690) and *Hail, bright Cecilia* (1692), were richly scored for full baroque orchestra, of whose use he was the chief pioneer; so too were most of the magnificent series of birthday odes which he composed for Queen Mary – a final burst of splendour for a royal musical establishment which was soon to fall into decay. Many of these works displayed the talents of singers from the theatre as well as from the Chapel Royal, and the Private Music in solos whose open-hearted tuneful style echoes that of the show-stopping numbers in Purcell's biggest and greatest works of the 1690s – his dramatic operas.

Opera in England had curious origins. It began during the Commonwealth, when the former theatrical impresario Sir William Davenant circumvented the ban on play-acting by presenting a 'Story sung in Recitative Musick' – a possibility the legislators had not envisaged. *The Siege of Rhodes*, staged at Davenant's London residence, was successful enough to lead to two further all-sung entertainments. But when the theatres reopened after the Restoration, London's two acting companies, the King's Men and the Duke's Men, were naturally more concerned to rebuild a repertory of spoken drama than to explore operatic possibilities. The increasing popularity of music within plays, however, prompted Davenant, who headed the Duke's Company, to make bolder plans. He commissioned from Christopher Wren a new theatre, at Dorset Garden on Thames-side, fully equipped for lavish productions.

Davenant did not live to see the building completed, but his successor, the energetic Thomas Betterton, shared his ambitions for the company. A visit to France in the summer of 1671, just before Dorset Garden opened for business, enabled him to see the hit of the Paris season, the Corneille/Quinault/Molière *comédie-ballet Psyché*. Such works, with their separate casts of actors, singers and dancers, offered a more suitable model than all-sung opera for a London theatre company dominated by actors. An English *Psyche* was duly

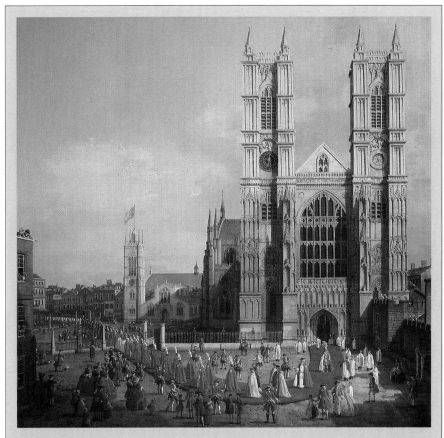

PURCELL AND HIS PREDECESSORS AT WESTMINSTER ABBEY
It was as an organ tuner that Henry Purcell's name first appeared in the records at Westminster Abbey in 1675. Four years later, at the age of 20, he was appointed Organist, though whether he became Master of the Choristers as well is not known.

Since 1388 various professional musicians had been employed at the Abbey, initially to sing the daily mass in the Lady Chapel. We know that boys were taught descant to decorate the plainchant, and a few compositions by Masters of the Choir such as John Tyes (1399–1402) are still sung by the Abbey Choir today.

The foundation to which Purcell was appointed dated from 1540, when Henry VIII granted the first charter and the Master of the Lady Chapel Choir, William Green, became the Master of the New Choir. It is only from this era that the names of Organists as such appear in the Chapter minutes.

Of the Abbey Organists between 1560 and 1640 two names stand out – Robert Whyte (d 1574) and Orlando Gibbons (d 1625). Whyte's glorious polyphony, often woven around a *cantus firmus*, provides a link with the musical inheritance from before the English Reformation, while the verse anthems of Gibbons anticipate some of Purcell's finest settings.

Probably the greatest influence on Purcell, however, was his predecessor and successor, John Blow (d 1708).

Purcell clearly profited from this rich musical heritage. But what set him apart was the naturalness of his word-setting and his exquisite use of dissonance and harmony as an expressive force, as acknowledged on his memorial in Westminster Abbey, which declares him: '... gone to that Blessed Place where only his Harmony can be exceeded'.

Martin Neary

commissioned. The libretto was by Thomas Shadwell, the setting by Locke; the dances were composed by the expatriate Italian Giovanni Battista Draghi, and choreographed by Josias Priest; the elaborate scenery and stage machines – as important to Restoration audiences as the music – were designed by John Webb, who had worked with Inigo Jones on pre-War court masques.

Interweaving these various strands took time. The rival company, sensing delay, announced a short season of authentic French opera, importing the performers as well as the works. As a stop-gap response Betterton devised an 'operatic' version of Shakespeare's *The Tempest* (a play already re-worked for the company by Davenant and Dryden), and transferred to it the entire creative team from *Psyche*. Assisted by several other composers, they added songs, dances and other orchestral numbers, and two self-contained masques inserted into the main plot. The resulting

above: **Matthew Locke portrait 1662, attributed to Isaac Fuller**
left: ***Dido and Aeneas,* a design for a staircase by Sir James Thornhill (1675–1734), the fore-most English artist of the time**

hotch-potch, staged in 1674, was a smash hit, earning the company far more money than *Psyche* did when finally produced. The efforts lavished on integrating *Psyche* had been largely wasted on the public – a lesson that Betterton took to heart. And the music had been laid out not for strings alone (as in *The Tempest*) but for full orchestra, including oboes, trumpets and kettledrums, though Locke published it only in short score. Needlessly extravagant or not, it was to offer an inspiring model for Purcell 15 years later.

In the early 1680s there was a flurry of interest in all-sung opera, instigated by the king himself. Blow's *Venus and Adonis*, a miniature but power-fully affecting three-act masque performed at court probably in 1683, may have been a first response to royal enthusiasm. And there is a strong possibility that Purcell's *Dido and Aeneas* – another small-scale masterpiece, and clearly modelled on *Venus and Adonis* – belongs to this same period and con-text. (The subsequent revival of both pieces, by pupils at a school run by the choreographer Josias Priest, forms a further link between them.) The two works may have been conceived as a pre-emptive strike against plans to import all-sung opera from France; for Betterton – now London's only theatre manager, after a merger of the King's company with the Duke's – was dispatched to Paris to arrange for the entire opera company there to visit London and play before the king, just as French and Italian comedians regularly did.

In this he failed. Instead, he brought back a composer prepared to write an opera. Louis Grabu, a French-trained Catalan, had been Master of the King's Musick to Charles II in the early years of the Restoration, and had planned at that time to establish an opera company in London, but was forced out on the grounds of his Catholicism. His return now was ill-fated. It re-ignited old resentments among English musicians; and the fact that the projected opera was to be all-sung caused ill-feeling among the actors, whom its production would deprive of work. Nevertheless Dryden, the Poet Laureate, duly penned a libretto for the opera – entitled *Albion and Albanius*, and allegorising Charles II as its hero – and Grabu duly composed the setting. But Charles died while the opera was in rehearsal, necessitating hasty modifications so that it could compliment his suc-cessor James II as well. The final misfortune was that its eventual production, in May 1685, coincided with Monmouth's rebellion, which made the opera politically hazardous and emptied the theatre, saddling the company with heavy losses. Grabu's enemies gleefully blamed him for this fiasco – a judgment which history has uncritically repeated, though his score, admittedly marred by awkward setting of the English words, is otherwise decidedly impressive. Nevertheless, it was five years before the company plucked up courage to mount another opera.

This time they shunned the pitfalls of all-sung opera, but made no attempt at any complex synthesis of music and spoken drama on the model of *Psyche*. Instead, mindful of the success of *The Tempest*, they contented themselves with adapting an old play – Fletcher and Massinger's *The Prophetess, or the History of Dioclesian* – inserting a substantial amount of music only tenuously connected with the main action, and providing spectacular staging and special effects. The score was commissioned from Purcell: an historic choice. Sumptuously laid out for full orchestra (still a novelty in England), the music was a crucial factor in the resounding success of the production. Even Dryden, previously a staunch defender of Grabu, now acclaimed Purcell. The triumph of *Dioclesian* guaranteed the young composer any future operatic commissions, and the lion's share of theatrical work in general.

During the next five years he composed scores for over 30 plays. Further dramatic operas also followed. *King Arthur* (1691) enjoyed even greater success than *Dioclesian*, though it was more complex in conception: in Dryden's libretto – written seven years earlier as a sequel to *Albion and Albanius*, with Grabu the intended composer (an irony Purcell doubtless relished) – the music was woven more closely into the main drama, somewhat after the fashion of *Psyche*. *The Fairy Queen* (1692) reverted to the earlier formula, taking as its basis Shakespeare's *A Midsummer Night's Dream* and inserting extravagant self-contained masques, replete with exotica – from magic swans, dancing monkeys and amorous Chinamen and women to figures of Night, Secrecy, Mystery, Sleep and the Four Seasons – and set to the richest of all Purcell's scores. *The Fairy Queen* was the biggest hit of all; but as with the two previous operas its initial run failed, even at the usual double ticket

above: Venus and Adonis by Peter Paul Rubens, c1635

prices, to recoup the huge expense of mounting it.

When the management sought to meet the shortfall by reducing the actors' salaries, unrest naturally followed. The eventual upshot, early in 1695, was a split in the company. Purcell's last opera, *The Indian Queen*, was in preparation at the time. Probably planned on a fairly modest scale for economy's sake, it emerged with only half as much music as its predecessors, and lacking a final-act masque altogether. The one subsequently added was composed by Purcell's brother Daniel, for only weeks after the premiere came Henry's sudden death. It was a loss that English music could not afford. Blow was widely esteemed as Purcell's equal (a view sharply at odds with that of the 20th century – and uncomfortably so, given that Restoration England identified its great men with unerring accuracy); but his creative energies were soon to diminish. Among younger musicians, Jeremiah Clarke was also to die young, while Daniel Purcell and William Croft were worthy but minor figures. Worst affected by Purcell's death was dramatic opera: already hamstrung with the accountants' knives, it now joined the royal musical establishment in terminal decline, despite the popularity of a few pieces – most notably Clarke's and Daniel Purcell's *The Island Princess* (1699). The scene was set for the arrival of Handel and the triumph of Italian opera.

Music in Restoration Britain, or even England, was not synonymous with music in London. Much of the present chapter has necessarily been concerned with a handful of leading composers, working in one royal household and one theatre. But pockets of expertise also exist elsewhere, in the provincial cathedral and collegiate choirs: eager performers, some of them, of the latest music from London, though their own standards were mostly far below those of the Chapel Royal. Some cathedral organists – Henry Hall at Hereford, for instance – were themselves composers of modest distinction. There were other contexts, too, for professional music-making: regular Cecilian concerts in Oxford and Salisbury, and occasional revivals of Purcell operas in several cities. And the rapid growth of music publishing testifies to a vigorous market among musical amateurs.

During the 1680s and 1690s song-books poured from the presses, their titles – *Comes Amoris: or the Companion of Love*, *The Banquet of Musick*, *Apollo's Banquet*, *Deliciae Musicae* – devised to appeal to a burgeoning and well-educated middle class. The chief beneficiary was Purcell, for whom success bred success. His name on a title-page guaranteed sales, whilst unprecedented availability, coupled with the sterling quality of his single songs as well as of the hit numbers from the operas, earned him a reputation greater and more durable than any previous English composer had enjoyed. His early death increased rather than diminished his stand-

'Genius of England, from thy pleasant bower / of bliss arise and spread thy sacred wings'

FROM D'URFEY'S *DON QUIXOTE* FOR WHICH PURCELL WROTE THE MUSIC

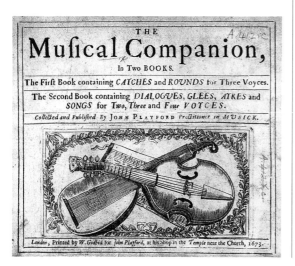

left: The Musical Companion, published by John Playford in 1673. Purcell, William Lawes and Locke were among the composers represented in this edition

ing – as witness the very title chosen by Henry Playford for his great memorial collection of Purcell's songs: *Orpheus Britannicus*. Even in after years, with musical fashion reformed *all'Italiana*, Purcell was not neglected. His music doubtless sounded old-fashioned alongside the latest Italian arias, but he remained unrivalled for his skill at setting English words, whether in the declamatory style or to one of his characteristic melodies, somehow inevitable yet never predictable. *Orpheus Britannicus* itself proved astonishingly durable and was re-published at intervals throughout the 18th century. In contrast *Amphion Anglicus*, Pearson's volume of songs by Blow, was issued only once, in 1700.

Instrumental chamber music was a different matter. There was no shortage of new works: Locke, for instance, wrote copiously, mostly for strings, and published several collections. Public taste was generally conservative, with the viols still sufficiently popular to sustain two editions of a major publication, Christopher Simpson's *The Division-violist*, in seven years (1659–1665). And as late as 1680 Purcell composed, in the space of a few weeks, a collection of fantasias for viols (or possibly for a broken consort of viols and violins) which are breathtaking in their combination of contrapuntal complexity and disturbing expressiveness. But these were the last of their line. The Italian tide was already running.

In 1683 Purcell published a dozen trio sonatas for violins and continuo. He claimed them to be 'a just imitation of the most fam'd Italian masters', but besides their Italianate verve and clarity they have strong indigenous features: polyphonic richness and dissonant, often intensely chromatic harmony. This 'English vein' disadvantaged them, in a market that preferred logic and superficial brilliance to waywardness and profundity. The edition had still not sold out when the composer's widow published a second set in 1697; and after her death in 1706 both volumes of these musical jewels – worthy to stand alongside the chamber music of Haydn or Bartók – were remaindered. Though Britain's Orpheus was revered for his voice, his lyre went largely unheard. Poetic justice swiftly followed: his indifferent compatriots were to have no unquestionably great composer of their own, instrumental or vocal, for the next two centuries.

7

PRIDE OR PREJUDICE?

MUSIC IN THE 18TH CENTURY

1715–1800

PETER HOLMAN

Eighteenth-century British music has long had a bad press. Historians have traditionally seen Purcell's death in 1695 and Handel's arrival in London in 1710 as events that ushered in a century and a half of decline and foreign domination. It is true that the establishment of Italian opera in London in 1705 caused the downfall of the Purcellian type of semi-opera, and effectively ended the theatre careers of a talented generation of Englishmen: John Weldon, William Croft and Daniel Purcell fell back largely on church music; John Eccles, it is said, retired to Kingston-upon-Thames to fish, and Jeremiah Clarke shot himself – though in a fit of despairing love rather than professional jealousy. Nevertheless, within a few years English operas were once more in production, and English composers continued to flourish in the theatre throughout the century.

It is also true that England attracted hundreds of immigrant musicians during the century, but this is because she was the leading mercantile nation in the world at the time, and had a correspondingly rich musical life, in the provinces as well as in London. The myth that Handel's presence in England caused its native music to decline gained ground in the 19th century, when the English oratorio – the genre he effectively invented – dominated musical life. Englishmen certainly held their own in other genres – theatre music, odes, songs and cantatas, *concerti grossi*, trio sonatas – though we often know them for their

Chapter opener shows, *top:* **The Coronation procession in 1727 for King George II, for whom Handel composed the Coronation Anthems, including** *Zadok the Priest* *middle left:* **Ticket for Hanover Square concert in 1793** *bottom right:* *The Beggar's Opera,* **William Hogarth's first painting of the John Gay/J C Pepusch ballad opera**

left: **George Frideric Handel, painted by Philip Mercier in 1735-36, the earliest authenticated portrait of the composer** *right:* **Johann Christian Bach, painted by Gainsborough in 1776**

lesser works. William Boyce's charming and cheerful symphonies have often been recorded, but he would hardly have wanted to be remembered for them; most were written, probably in extreme haste, as the overtures to operas or court odes. His finest music is to be found in his major vocal works, still hardly known.

Any account of music in 18th-century England has to begin with that exotic and irrational import, Italian opera, if only because it was the genre that most consistently engaged the attention of fashionable society. All-sung opera came later to England than to other European countries; the few works before the 18th century, such as *Dido and Aeneas*, were experiments within a native tradition of small-scale country house and school masques. But once established, it was sung in Italian, and was composed and performed largely

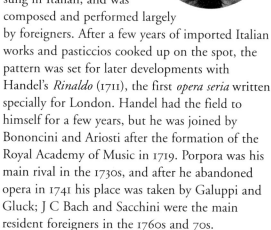

by foreigners. After a few years of imported Italian works and pasticcios cooked up on the spot, the pattern was set for later developments with Handel's *Rinaldo* (1711), the first *opera seria* written specially for London. Handel had the field to himself for a few years, but he was joined by Bononcini and Ariosti after the formation of the Royal Academy of Music in 1719. Porpora was his main rival in the 1730s, and after he abandoned opera in 1741 his place was taken by Galuppi and Gluck; J C Bach and Sacchini were the main resident foreigners in the 1760s and 70s.

Opera seria was essentially a vehicle for great singing. Many of Handel's operas require only a handful of singers, with castrati and female voices taking the leading roles. The action is carried swiftly forward by the recitative, and character is depicted by a series of contrasted arias, usually *da capo* in structure to allow the singer to decorate the repeat of the first section. The mood of each aria is often determined by the orchestral scoring – trumpets for heroism and battle, oboes for bacchic jollity, recorders for rustic peace and love, and so on – or by the use of appropriate dance patterns – from the amorous sarabande and minuet to the joyful gavotte and gigue. The plots, mostly taken from classical history or mediaeval romance, were concerned with the conflicting demands of love and duty among the aristocracy. The lower orders hardly feature: many Italian operas have no choruses and conclude merely with an ensemble of soloists. *Opera seria* has been routinely ridiculed by modern critics accustomed to Wagnerian music-drama, but the genre can be powerfully expressive in the hands of a great dramatic composer such as Handel – and in a production that respects the conventions of the 18th-century theatre.

Throughout the century there were attempts to develop an English alternative to Italian opera. Oddly, some were made by Germans: J C Pepusch and J E Galliard wrote some charming miniature English operas as afterpieces to spoken plays between 1715 and 1718 (they were the model for Handel's *Acis and Galatea*, 1718), while J F Lampe and J C Smith were involved with Henry Carey

below: The Music Party, Philip Mercier's well-known portrait showing Frederick, Prince of Wales and his sisters in harmonious mood, 1733

and the young Thomas Arne in the short-lived English opera company of 1732-3. By then it was clear that humour was the best way to beat the Italians; indeed, the English musical theatre was mostly confined to comedy after then. Pantomime, a favourite type of afterpiece that combined all-sung mythological scenes with *commedia dell'arte* horseplay, became popular in the 1720s, largely because of the antics of John Rich, the greatest Harlequin of the century. But the most effective weapon was John Gay's *The Beggar's Opera*, produced in 1728 with music arranged by Pepusch. It transferred the heroics of *opera seria* to the London underworld, replacing the recitative with spoken dialogue and the arias with simple folk tunes. It was a sensation: it ran for 62 nights, was frequently revived throughout the century, and inspired more than 100 ballad operas over the next decade.

Thomas Arne was by far the most wide-ranging and important English theatre composer in the middle of the century. He made his name with *Comus* (1738), a reworking of Milton's 1634 masque. This modified revival of Purcellian semi-opera, which profited from a temporary collapse of Italian opera, started a fashion for old texts, and its pre-Romantic rural atmosphere attracted many imitations, including Handel's Milton oratorio *L'Allegro* (1740). Arne did not have a success to equal it for 20 years, though he wrote an immense amount of theatre music of all types during that period, much of it lost. But he never ceased to experiment, and in the early 1760s he produced three smash hits in a row, each an original master-piece. In *Thomas and Sally* (1760) he combined all-sung *opera buffa* (as in Pergolesi's *La serva padrona*) with English ballad opera for the first time. In *Artaxerxes* (1761), his grand setting of Metastasio in translation, he produced a true English *opera seria*, a work that held the stage until the 1830s. In *Love in a Village* (1762), a reworking of *The Village Opera* (1729), he created a new form of ballad opera, with borrowed Italian arias and specially-composed numbers as well as folk tunes, all orchestrated in a modern way. It began a vogue for pastiche operas that lasted to the end of the century and beyond.

Arne was a variable composer in several senses. He was frequently hasty and careless, but at his best he is much more memorable than those who display consistently good craftsmanship – such as William Boyce. He was also the first English com-poser to use stylistic variety as part of his composi-tional technique, in one number using the charm-ing folk-like idiom he had pioneered in the 1730s, in the next cultivating a grand Handelian style, in

a third adopting an advanced *galant* idiom. It aided characterisation, and made large-scale works agreeably varied, but modern critics, influenced by 19th-century ideas of progress and unity in art, tend to see it as a weakness.

English theatre music after Arne is still a dark void, and attempts to illuminate it are hampered by a lack of surviving material. The London theatres and their music libraries were repeatedly destroyed by fire, and operas were usually printed in vocal score, without choruses, dances or recita-tives. Thus we have only one opera in orchestral score by Charles Dibdin, William Shield and Stephen Storace (though two of his Viennese operas survive complete), and none by Samuel Arnold and James Hook. Dibdin and Storace were the most talented of this group, but neither lived up to the promise of their early works: Storace, a friend and follower of Mozart, succumbed to illness and overwork at 33, while Dibdin spread his talents too thinly, and was continually hampered by his quarrelsome disposition and his chaotic private life.

William Boyce, Arne's main rival, also wrote a good deal of theatre music, though most of it does not live up to the promise of *Peleus and Thetis* (c 1740) and *The Secular Masque* (c 1745), both all-sung set-tings of old masque texts using an assured blend of Purcellian and Handelian idioms. In fact, *The Secular Masque*, a setting of Dryden's 1700 celebra-tion of the new century, has virtually no plot and is closer to an ode than an opera, and Boyce was at his best in this middle ground between genres. His masterpiece, the serenata *Solomon* (1742), a setting of a text derived from the Song of Songs, is a lyrical dialogue in which two characters, 'He' and 'She', express their love in ecstatic terms, though it has a strong feeling of time and place – there are sensuous evocations of the passing sea-sons – and several moments of overt drama. It is a pity Boyce did not write more works of this sort, but his later life was taken up largely with the pro-duction of court odes and church music. There is, however, a rich repertory of extended occasional works by English composers, still hardly explored

in modern times; notable examples are the St Cecilia odes by Boyce and Maurice Greene, the Shakespeare odes by Boyce, Arne and Thomas Linley junior, and the orchestral anthems written for festivals or special events by Thomas Roseingrave, William Croft, Boyce, Greene, Linley and others.

English oratorio effectively came into being when Handel revised *Esther* for London performances in 1732. Initially, it was given in semi-staged form, as it probably had been in the original 1718 performance for the Duke of Chandos. But the Bishop of London evidently objected, and it was subsequently given in concert form in a theatre, setting the pattern for later oratorios. Handel's oratorios divide into two main types: most are Biblical dramas, in which the solo singers represent particular characters and the chorus takes the role of the people, Jewish or heathen, but there are also some works on more abstract themes, such as *Israel in Egypt* (1739) and *Messiah* (1741). In this type there are no particular characters, and the chorus has a more prominent role; at first they were less popular than the Biblical dramas, but they came into their own towards the end of the century, when the fledgling amateur choral movement took them up. Handel's first oratorios inspired a few imitations in the 1730s, such as Greene's *Song of Deborah and Barak* (1732) and Boyce's *David's Lamentation over Saul and Jonathan* (1736), but most composers preferred not to challenge him on his own ground; the most important later examples are Arne's *Judith* (1761) and Thomas Linley junior's *Song of Moses* (1777).

Cathedral music was at a low ebb. Most cathedrals and collegiate foundations had already reduced their spending on music to a minimum, and inflation gradually made things worse. This deterred active and capable musicians from becoming provincial cathedral organists, and most preferred to become organists of urban parish churches; many distinguished 18th-century musicians, including Greene, Pepusch, Boyce, Roseingrave and John Stanley, found it convenient to com-

below: A Musical Party (The Mathias Family, c 1731) by William Hogarth, showing a typical trio-sonata ensemble of the time

bine such a post with other activities. Anthems and services of the time generally use an idiom derived from Restoration composers. Full anthems and services alternate contrapuntal sections with verse passages in block chords, the whole underpinned with organ continuo. Verse anthems largely consist of music for solo voices, divided into Purcellian declamatory passages and florid Italianate airs, framed with written-out organ ritornellos; choruses are often short and perfunctory. The best and most influential collections were published in the first half of the century, by Croft (1724) and Greene (1743), though there are also two fine posthumous publications of Boyce's anthems (1780 and 1790).

In general, however, there was a crisis of confidence among anthem composers late in the century, perhaps because the study and publication of Tudor and Stuart cathedral music was gathering pace. Greene began collecting material for a comprehensive collection, which he passed on to Boyce, who eventually published it as *Cathedral Music* (1760, 1768, 1773); Samuel Arnold produced a revised and enlarged edition in 1790. More of the repertory appeared in collections edited by William Thomson (c 1780) and John Page (1800),

while a volume of Purcell anthems appeared in the 1790s as part of an abortive complete edition. Such ventures had their counterpart in the activities of the Ancient Concerts, the Madrigal Society, and the great histories of Burney and Hawkins. In part, they reflected the traditional conservatism of English musicians, but they should also be seen as expressions of the same fashionable nostalgia for the past that produced Strawberry Hill gothic and the fake mediaeval poems of Thomas Chatterton.

In many ways, the music written for parish churches and dissenting chapels is considerably more interesting than the cathedral repertory, though it was often the work of self-taught composers, and remains virtually unknown today. Efforts were made to improve parish church music around 1700 through the establishment of choirs and the purchase of organs, though most country parishes were still without an instrument at the end of the century, and many employed bands of wind and stringed instruments to support the singing. This 'west gallery' repertory was founded on the metrical psalms of Sternhold and Hopkins,

above: **Handel directing an oratorio rehearsal in a private house, possibly belonging to the Prince of Wales**
below: **The Thames on Lord Mayor's Day by Canaletto, c1747**

but it was gradually supplemented by the New Version of Tate and Brady and other newly-composed hymns, anthems, and elaborate psalm settings with solo passages and contrapuntal sections. The latter, the 'fuguing tune', was once thought to be an American invention; we now know it was exported from England to its American colonies.

Much of the gallery repertory is extremely crude by the standards of 'art' music – consecutives and forbidden dissonances abound – but it often has a vigour and stark grandeur lacking in more 'accomplished' music.

The public concert was an English invention, though until the end of the 18th century concerts were given by amateurs as often as professionals, and in the absence of purpose-built concert halls were held in taverns, theatres, pleasure gardens, assembly rooms or private houses. Concerts were normally given by orchestras, and nearly always included vocal music and instrumental solos; the concert devoted to a single combination – be it keyboard, choir, orchestra or chamber ensemble – belongs to a later period. Many concert series were

essentially private and relied on word of mouth rather than advertising, and those that were ostensibly public often restricted admission by keeping subscriptions artificially high.

However, ordinary people could hear a good deal of orchestral music in the theatres. The repertory of concertos for fifth and sixth flute (small recorders in C and D) by William Babell, Robert Woodcock and John Baston, as well as the concertos and sonatas of John Humphries, seem to have been written for Lincoln's Inn Fields in the second and third decades of the century; Handel's concertos fulfilled the same function in his operas and oratorios. In the summer, ordinary people could also hear good music in the pleasure gardens. Vauxhall existed in Restoration times, but only began to put on regular concerts in 1732; its major rivals were Marylebone and Ranelagh, opened in 1738 and 1742. In the early days, the repertory of the pleasure gardens was probably similar to that in public concerts, though a large number of collections of 'Vauxhall songs' were published by Arne and others from the 1740s, which suggests that the main fare there was songs and cantatas with orchestral accompaniment. Organ concertos – easily audible in the open air – became popular later in the century; James Hook is said to have played one every night during his 45 summers at Vauxhall.

Around 1700 the orchestral repertory consisted mainly of suites originally written as incidental music for plays, but Corelli's Op 6, published in Amsterdam in 1714 and in London the following year, created a fashion for *concerti grossi*. The first English 'grand concertos' were probably by Corelli's pupil Francesco Geminiani, who arrived in London from Lucca in 1714. His influential Opp 2 and 3 appeared in 1732, but he had already published concerto elaborations of Corelli's Op 5 violin sonatas in 1726 and 1729. Geminiani's grand concertos, like Handel's Opp 3 and 6 (1734 and 1740) and other early sets, were originally written for London's professional orchestras, but before long the genre was taken up by the amateur orchestral societies that were springing up in every sizeable town in the middle of the century.

The grand concerto was ideal for these groups, for the difficult *concertino* parts for two violins and cello could be played by hired hands, while the easy orchestral *ripieno* parts could be taken by

their employers, the gentlemen amateurs. Such was the rage for grand concertos that demand soon exceeded supply, and composers and publishers began to cash in with arrangements. Handel's concertos are partly reworkings of orchestral music from vocal works, while Charles Avison published a remarkable set of arrangements of Domenico Scarlatti's harpsichord sonatas in 1744, and around the same time Benjamin Cooke even cobbled together a spurious set of concertos by Alessandro Scarlatti from disparate sources. After 1750 most grand concertos were written by provincial composers, and some of them, such as those by Avison (Newcastle), John Alcock (Lichfield) and Capel Bond (Coventry) are attractive and accomplished – a testimony to the vitality of provincial musical life. Handel's Op 6 concertos are unquestionably the masterpieces of the genre, but Geminiani's

below: **A Sunday concert at the home of Dr Charles Burney, 1782, which shows Burney gossiping (bottom right)**

DR CHARLES BURNEY
Dr Charles Burney (1726–1814), an admired member of Dr Johnson's prestigious intellectual circle, was one of the most intelligent men of his day. He knew personally many musicians, including Haydn, Gluck, C P E Bach, the antiquarian Padre Martini and the famous librettist Metastasio, often leaving vivid accounts of their conversations. After starting as an organist, Burney decided in the 1760s to write a *History of Music* (four volumes published 1776–89) for which he travelled extensively in Europe in pursuit of manuscripts, treatises and personal encounters (*The Present State of Music in France and Italy* [1771], *The Present State of Music in Germany, the Netherlands and United Provinces* [1773]). His pioneering and indefatigable search for these gave him a unique, though sometimes idiosyncratic, insight into 'ancient' music; but his profound knowledge of contemporary music and musicians make his ever elegant accounts of them perennially interesting and good reading.
Roderick Swanston

COMFORTS of BATH.
Pl 2

were more popular at the time, and the way they mix conservative counterpoint and formal patterns with forward-looking ornamental violin writing was widely imitated. English composers were still writing in the Corelli-Geminiani style in the 1780s, long after the arrival of the German *galant* symphony.

The English type of keyboard concerto began as an offshoot of the grand concerto, with the organ replacing the *concertino*. Handel made a few experiments before he came to England, but only began to play organ concertos regularly in his oratorios in the 1730s. Six were published as his Op 4 in 1738; a·second set appeared posthumously as Op 7 in 1761. Handel used the light and sparkling type of chamber organ common in English homes and concert halls, and wrote for it in an attractively varied fashion, sometimes using it in alternation

above: **Gertrud Elisabeth Mara singing at a concert in the Assembly Rooms, Bath, c1795, a watercolour by Thomas Rowlandson**

with the orchestra, like the *concertino* in a grand concerto, sometimes giving it florid right-hand solos, like a wind instrument. Within two years the first imitations appeared, by Avison and Henry Burgess, and by the 1750s there was a large repertory available, though some of it consisted of simple arrangements of string concertos: several of Handel's Op 6 were pressed into service, as were John Stanley's Op 2 of 1742. At first, English organ concertos tended to be solidly Handelian in style, though some composers began to look abroad for models during the 1740s and 50s – the Revd William Felton of Hereford to Vivaldi, for instance, and Thomas Chilcot of Bath to Domenico Scarlatti. The range of idioms available increased in the 1760s and 70s when J C Bach popularised the *galant* keyboard concerto, though only the best composers, such as Stanley (Op 10,

1775) and Arne (a set published posthumously in 1793), had the imagination and technique to take advantage of what was on offer. By then, too, the harpsichord and the piano had become common alternatives to the organ.

The other main orchestral genre was the overture or symphony. The French overture, with a solemn dotted introduction followed by a fugue and one or more dances, was the standard early in the century; it was gradually replaced by the Italianate three- or four-movement symphony (which, confusingly, was often called 'overture'). At first, both types were normally part of large-scale vocal works, though they were frequently detached from them and published together in sets. The overtures to Handel's operas and oratorios entered the orchestral repertory in this way, as did Boyce's two sets of symphonies (1760 and 1770) and Arne's *Eight Overtures* (1751). The link with vocal music was broken around 1760, when German concert symphonies in the *galant* style were introduced. The Scottish aristocrat Thomas Erskine, Earl of Kelly, a former pupil of Johann Stamitz in Mannheim, published his Op 1 symphonies in Edinburgh in 1761, and was probably behind the series of 'periodical overtures' started by his compatriot Robert Bremner in London in 1763, which initially consisted largely of Mannheim works. J C Bach, who started his famous subscription concerts with C F Abel in 1765, wrote symphonies of considerable charm and refinement (they sound Mozartian to us), though they only had a limited influence. English composers were mostly too rooted in the past to be able to learn much from J C Bach, just as they had difficulties with Haydn in the 1790s, and with Beethoven in the next century. Samuel Wesley (see Chapter 8) was about the only Englishman to write convincing classical symphonies.

We think of the Tudor and Stuart period as the golden age of amateur music-making, but there must have been a great deal of activity in Georgian homes, to judge from the vast quantities of music of all sorts published in editions clearly intended for domestic use. Women continued to learn music mainly by way of key-

above: Tickets for performances in 1752 of Handel's oratorios, *Samson* and *Hercules*
below: Concert at Vauxhall Gardens, a 1784 watercolour by Thomas Rowlandson. Mrs Weischel sings from the 'Moorish-Gothick' orchestra while the audience promenades below and Dr Johnson, Boswell and possibly Mrs Thrale and Oliver Goldsmith eat in a supper box

board instruments, though there was a vogue for the cittern-like English guitar in the middle of the century, and for the new pedal harp in the 1790s. The socially-acceptable instruments for men were the flute and the violin; for them to learn the keyboard was to risk becoming tainted with professionalism, or worse, to be thought effeminate. The main domestic keyboard instrument was the simple wing-shaped spinet, with a single row of strings, though it was gradually supplanted by the square piano in the 1770s and 80s. Harpsichords were the preserve of professionals and the wealthy, and were mainly made by the two rival firms of the Swiss Burkat Shudi and the Alsatian Jacob Kirckman. Their large and powerful instruments combined elements of the Italian, French and Flemish national schools, and matched the eclectic taste of the English public, which devoured imported keyboard music of all sorts, and encouraged local composers to work in a variety of styles. English grand pianos were initially built like English harpsichords, and thus had a powerful tone; Haydn and Beethoven, among others, preferred them to the more delicate Viennese instruments.

There was little distinction between domestic music and music written for public performance. A great deal of domestic ensemble music was derived from the public forms already discussed:

vocal music from the theatres, concert rooms and pleasure gardens was usually published in condensed score, so that it could easily be played at home, just as orchestral music often appeared in key-board arrangements. Conversely, many of the forms of 'chamber music' – the solo sonata with continuo, the trio sonata, the string quartet – were used in concerts as well as in the home. Some trio sonatas even have solo and tutti indications, and Boyce's famous set of 1747 was the staple diet of theatre orchestras and orchestral societies for many years. Even genres so apparently domesticated as the catch (a round with humorous or bucolic words) and the glee (a madrigal-like part-song) were actually intended mainly for public performance, albeit in convivial men's clubs in taverns. Vast numbers of catches and glees were written towards the end of the century, and such was the vogue for them that prizes were instituted for their composition and performance.

above: The Duet by Arthur Devis, 1749
below: The building erected in Green Park for the fireworks display in 1749. For the occasion Handel was commissioned to write his Musick for the Royal Fireworks

The one type of chamber music that was largely confined to the home was the accompanied keyboard sonata, presumably because the keyboard parts were considered the preserve of female amateurs, who did not appear in public. The genre began in England with Giardini's Op 3 (1751) for harpsichord and violin, and rapidly expanded to take in works with two accompanying instruments (violin or flute and cello), three (two violins and cello), or four (string quartet). The accompanying parts can often be omitted without damaging the music and tend to be extremely simple, so that gentlemen amateurs did not need to practise, or so that teachers never outshone their pupils. In many ways, the accompanied sonata is the epitome of 18th-century civilised life: urbane, undemanding, and an expression of the natural order of things. When that 'natural order' was swept away in the democratic ferment of the new century the settled patterns of 18th-century musical life went with it.

A Perspective View of the Building for the Fireworks in the Green Park, taken from the Reservoir.

Printed for R. Sayer opposite Fetter Lane Fleet Street.

8

A Land Without Music?

THE 19TH CENTURY & VICTORIAN ERA

1800–1880

DAVID BYERS

The 1790s mark a great watershed in music in the British Isles, as elsewhere. Patronage of the kind which bound Haydn to Prince Esterházy was coming to an end; more than ever, musicians had to fend for themselves. Increasingly, market-forces determined the ebb and flow of reputations, taste and success during the 19th century.

London was the largest centre for music-making in Europe; the regional centres which had flourished in the 18th century – Edinburgh, Dublin and Bath – were now in decline, more often receiving-venues for touring musicians, like the Irish tenor Michael Kelly and his company of Italian singers. And touring wasn't much fun in those days of stage-coach and packet-boat!

Far from being a land *without* music there were many concerts and opportunities in Britain, particularly for the famous and foreign, but the endless hours of work and travel required just to make a living were enough to strain all but the hardiest of creative talents. Composers like Samuel Wesley and Sterndale Bennett, 40 or 50 years apart, endured endless, exhausting days of teaching, travelling between pupils' houses in difficult conditions, giving lectures, and seeking recognition from an apparently disinterested public.

Samuel Wesley, son of Charles Wesley, the hymnwriter, was one of the most interesting of the composers working in Britain in the first years of the 19th century. His elder brother, Charles, remained an 'obstinate Handelian' but both were brought up in the full knowledge of contemporary

Chapter opener shows,
top right: **Caricatures of Arthur Sullivan and W S Gilbert by Ape and Spy for** *Vanity Fair*
middle left: **Beethoven's Broadwood piano, a donation by the famous British firm, sent to the composer in Vienna in 1818**
bottom right: **Hand-coloured engraving showing Pandean minstrels at Vauxhall Gardens**

above: **William Sterndale Bennett, painted by James Warren Childe**
left: **Samuel Wesley, a portrait by John Jackson**

trends; young Samuel's early symphonies of the 1780s, written for the family's annual series of subscription concerts, show a complete awareness of the Mannheim school – represented in London by J C Bach and Abel, and in Edinburgh by the Earl of Kelly. The 'English Mozart', as William Boyce described Wesley, was often prone to nervous depression, which was said to have been caused by an accident in 1787 when he fell into the cellar of an unfinished house one evening and lay unconscious until the next morning.

In 1784 Wesley had converted to Roman Catholicism, much to the distress of his family. Many of his best works, the Latin motets, were written for the Portuguese Embassy Chapel where Vincent Novello was in charge of the music and where Wesley first experienced the wealth of music for the Catholic liturgy. The attraction of the new-found religious affiliation was musical rather than dogmatic and his wedding in 1793 was a Church of England one. This marriage only lasted two years before a separation, and eventually he set up home with his former house-keeper. She bore him several more children including Samuel Sebastian Wesley – who would become one of the most influential and important 19th-century composers of Anglican church music.

Many of Samuel Wesley's letters have yet to be published – they reveal an often humorous individual with wide interests and a genuinely Romantic nature. His individual style combined contemporary trends with a deep knowledge of baroque and even renaissance music. Three major choral works stand out: the early *Missa de Spiritu Sancto*, written, dedicated and sent to Pope Pius VI in 1784, still awaits a modern recording; the *Ode to St Cecilia* written in 1794, lost and then reconstructed from memory in 1826 (both scores survive!); and his exceedingly fine *Confitebor*, written in 1799 but not performed until 1826 – a work with a rich tapestry of influences. After the early symphonies of the 1780s there's a remarkable B flat major symphony from 1802 which reveals the musical legacy of Haydn's London visits. This is mature Wesley at its best – characterful, strongly classical, and with a definitely English flavour.

These years at the turn of the century marked his own discovery of the music of J S Bach; he spent much time proselytising on behalf of his 'musical Demi-God'. The direct outcome of this is a corpus of organ music, particularly the 12 Voluntaries, Op 6. These absorb the Bach influence and take the 18th-century voluntary by the scruff of the neck and launch it into a new century.

Keyboard music of the period offers a treasure-trove. The leading player and composer was Muzio Clementi, who had been brought from Italy to Dorset at the age of 14 by an eccentric English traveller. Hummel, Dussek, John Cramer and Pinto (much admired by Wesley) were all important figures who developed and exploited the potential of the piano. Their travels and meetings with composers like Haydn and Beethoven kept British music and audiences abreast of developments elsewhere.

When the 13-year-old John Field from Dublin was apprenticed to Clementi he had to demonstrate the pianos in Clementi's piano warehouse in return for lessons. Field wrote the first of his seven virtuosic piano concertos for a concert at The King's Theatre in London in 1799 and three years later teacher and pupil set off on a continental tour, ending up in St Petersburg where 'drunken John' Field settled and was fêted for his playing. In his series of *Nocturnes* he eschewed technical display for a more lyrical and intimate approach – influencing several generations of composers, particularly Chopin and Mendelssohn.

Orchestral music during these years was heard at Subscription Concerts, such as those organised by Salomon for Haydn, and the many Benefit Concerts each season in which players took it in turn to give their services on behalf of one of their colleagues. These concerts, in London as throughout the islands, had mixed programmes, combining orchestral music with vocal numbers and chamber music.

In London in 1813 a number of leading musicians, including Clementi, set up the Philharmonic Society to regularise concert-giving. Mozart, Haydn, Beethoven and Cherubini were the mainstay of the programming; British composers accounted for only one sixth of the works, but the advent of the Society did encourage some

above: A Village Choir by Thomas Webster, exhibited at the Royal Academy in 1847. As a child, Webster sang in the Chapel Royal Choir but turned to painting after the death of George III
left: John Field, a lithograph by Engelbach
below: Cipriani Potter

new music. Clementi contributed six symphonies between 1813 and 1824, fresh and inventive in style, the melodic lines betraying his Italian origins.

The first native-born composer to be represented by a symphony at the Philharmonic Society was William Crotch, Professor of Music at Oxford, whose oratorio *Palestine* had been enthusiastically received in 1812. Like Wesley, his style owed much to Haydn and Mozart, often with a seasoning of the 'ancient' – in his case Handel rather than Bach.

Another of the Philharmonic's founders was Thomas Attwood who, with royal patronage, had studied for a year and a half with Mozart. He wrote some fine songs and glees and he spent the 1790s providing music for the London theatres, often adapting music for the staple diet of musical farces, before turning his attention to church music; he introduced a contemporary musical language into the church though it did not find favour.

Attwood and Crotch both taught the young Cipriani Potter ('Little Chip' to his friends), who spent some months studying in Vienna. There the rather deaf Beethoven read through Potter's Overture in E minor and recommended him to a teacher. 'Botter (sic) has visited me a few times, he seems a good fellow and has a talent for composition', wrote Beethoven. Between 1819 and 1834 Potter wrote at least ten symphonies, only nine of which survive. Their musical language had moved

on from that of Wesley and Crotch, the spirit of Beethoven had been absorbed: Potter's fascination was for short motifs which he worked with bustling confidence and imaginative orchestration.

Potter was also a fine pianist and he gave the first British performances of many Mozart concertos and three of Beethoven's. When the new Academy of Music opened its doors in 1823, Potter became the piano teacher for the male students and Dr Crotch was appointed principal. In 1832 Crotch, having been seen rewarding one of the female students with a kiss for an apparently successful harmony exercise, was forced to resign. Potter succeeded him and remained as principal until 1859. These were difficult years when the (now *Royal*) Academy of Music was beset with funding problems and dominated by a committee headed by the amateur musician Lord Burghersh whose aim seemed to be to secure performances of his own music. All this administration meant that Potter wrote little after his three Shakespeare overtures of the mid-1830s. When Wagner conducted the Philharmonic Society concerts in its 1855 sea-

'A pious Catholic, raving atheist, mad, reasonable, drunk and sober. The dread of all wives and regular families, a warm friend, a bitter foe, a satirical talker, a flatterer... a blasphemer..'

MRS NOVELLO ON
SAMUEL WESLEY

above left: **The 'Moorish-Gothick' orchestra at Vauxhall Gardens, c1840, watercolour by an unknown artist. The pleasure gardens were to remain a national institution until 1859**
right: **Prince Albert playing the organ before Queen Victoria and Mendelssohn at Buckingham Palace in 1842**

son he programmed Potter's G minor Symphony (1832) and referred to its composer as that 'amiable, elderly contrapuntist'.

In the first decades of the 19th century, the environment for the British composer was not an encouraging one. In these years of war with Napoleonic France and of an expanding empire, market-forces demanded easy entertainment. The British stage was dominated by light opera, which tended to be pasticcios and farces like those of John Parry from Wales. There was little opportunity for composers such as Attwood and Henry Bishop to create a national opera even if they had had the will. Mozart's operas reached London in the early 1810s, followed quickly by Rossini's. A new Romantic voice in the guise of Weber's *Der Freischütz* became the fashion in 1824 and Covent Garden responded by commissioning *Oberon*. In 1826 Weber arrived in London for its premiere and died there just a few weeks later.

Another visitor was the 20-year-old Mendelssohn who conducted his Symphony No 1 in C minor at the Philharmonic Society and then travelled to Scotland for his famous visit to Fingal's Cave in 1829, before staying with his friend Attwood. This was the start of a long association with Britain – Mendelssohn's elegant, classical approach to music, along with his love of Handel and Bach, was guaranteed to win him favour. He returned to the Philharmonic in 1833 to conduct his *Italian* Symphony and again in 1834 to conduct *St Paul* at the Birmingham Festival in the newly-completed town hall. In all, he visited

Britain on ten occasions, conducting five Philharmonic concerts in 1844 and the premiere of *Elijah* at the Birmingham Festival of 1846. In a poignant meeting in 1837, the year in which

Victoria became Queen and just weeks before Samuel Wesley's death, Mendelssohn and Wesley heard each other play the organ. 'Oh Sir', said Wesley, 'you have not heard me play; you should have heard me 40 years ago'.

Wesley's son, Samuel Sebastian, spent the 1829 season at the English Opera House, formerly the Lyceum Theatre, experiencing the fashionable German Romantic fare of Weber and Marschner, which coloured the development of his own style. S S Wesley, like his father, was a difficult man; he spent much of his life as a cathedral organist and choirmaster, determinedly fighting to raise the low standards of church music. His output of organ and choral music is crowned by the 12 anthems published in 1853 which combine the rich heritage of cathedral music with all the modern harmonies, the chromaticism and the modulations which were so vital to the 'new' music. Wesley's output declined in his later years, probably due to public indifference and a lack of critical appreciation.

William Sterndale Bennett, from Sheffield,

below: **One of the great Handel festivals at Crystal Palace, 1859**

began to study at the Academy of Music in 1826 when he had lessons from Crotch and then, more importantly, with Potter, who encouraged his love of Mozart. John Field, on his visit home in 1831, heard the young boy play: 'That *little* fellow knows what he's about'. By 1834 Bennett had written four symphonies and the first three of his six piano concertos (the sixth, missing for many years, has recently been rediscovered). He spent the winter months of 1836 in Leipzig and was enthusiastically received by the musical circle which included both Mendelssohn and Schumann. When he played his C minor Concerto (No 3) at the Gewandhaus he won over the hearts of the Leipzigers: 'The audience sat breathless, as though fearing to awaken the dreamer', wrote Schumann. There were two more visits to Leipzig, the last in 1841–42, but after his marriage the amount of teaching Bennett took on to support his family (over 1,650 lessons each year), along with playing concertos and giving recitals, meant that he had little time to compose.

CRYSTAL PALACE CONCERTS

Joseph Paxton's Crystal Palace, originally built in 1851 in Hyde Park for the Prince Albert's Great Exhibition, was re-erected in Sydenham in 1852. The engineer and musical enthusiast, George Grove (1820–1900), secretary of the Crystal Palace company, wanted to inaugurate popular concerts in the palace. The vast spaces could house large audiences, so modest prices could be charged, thus attracting a wider concert audience. The symbol of the scientific, iron-framed palace in the service of enabling ever more people to encounter fine arts typified the post-Exhibition, mid-century philanthropic and educational ideals.

After a modest start, the concerts really got going under the conductor [Sir] August Manns (1825–1907), who, with Grove, inaugurated the Saturday (a working half-day) Popular concerts in 1856. These lasted till their orchestra was disbanded in 1901. The orchestra through regular membership was thus the first permanent London orchestra, as a result of which it reputedly gave the best London orchestral performances.

Manns and Grove masterminded the programmes which pioneered works by Beethoven, Schubert (Grove and Sullivan unearthed the Fourth and Sixth Symphonies and the *Rosamunde* music on a trip to Vienna in 1867), Schumann (Manns' enthusiasm), Brahms, Liszt, Smetana, Dvořák, and promoted works by young British composers such as Parry and Stanford. As a young man in the 1870s, Elgar described his trips from Worcester to the Crystal Palace to hear new works.

The combination of technology, art, material progress and education, were summed up in the remarkable figure of Sir George Grove, who, initially an engineer, became Secretary of the Royal Society of Arts, published a four-volume *Dictionary of Music and Musicians* (1889), and was the founding Director of the Royal College of Music (1883), many of whose still-existing educational ideals derive from the breadth of his mid-Victorian vision.

Roderick Swanston

Bennett's music is still unfairly neglected. It has a strong affinity with Mendelssohn but his style is also informed by Mozart and Beethoven. The solo piano music, the concertos and the concert overtures are the work of a craftsman and a poet, full of charm, delicacy and humour. His late G minor Symphony (1867) and a Sonata Duo for cello and piano deserve to be better known. Bennett belatedly achieved a measure of recognition when he was appointed to the music professorship at Cambridge in 1856. Ten years later he was appointed principal of the RAM, and he was knighted in 1871.

The music of two of Bennett's close contemporaries is also worth exploring. Hugh Pearson was a pupil of Attwood who moved to Germany in 1839 and eventually changed his name to Henry Hugo Pierson. In 1844 he was appointed Reid Professor of Music at Edinburgh in preference to S S Wesley and Sterndale Bennett, but resigned within a year and returned to Germany where his music enjoyed

above: Michael Balfe

much success. Symphonic poems like *Macbeth* and *Romeo and Juliet* inhabit a remarkably modern world, influenced by Berlioz rather than Mendelssohn and Schumann, and therefore not to the British taste of the time. His many songs, often setting classic texts by Shakespeare, Byron, Burns, and others deserve to be heard nowadays.

George Macfarren was a fellow pupil of Bennett at the RAM and succeeded him in 1875 as principal. He wrote nine symphonies between 1828 and 1874 which await revival and reassessment, but Wagner conducted his energetic hunting-music overture *Chevy Chace* (1836) for the Philharmonic and liked it for 'its peculiarly wild, passionate character'. Macfarren was English, but Wagner referred to 'Mr MacFarrinc, a pompous, melancholy Scotsman'! Macfarren's wish was to achieve fame as an opera composer and he had two successes, *King Charles II* (1849) and *Robin Hood* (1860).

National opera had enjoyed a revival when the English Opera House, which had been destroyed by fire in 1830, was rebuilt and re-opened in 1834. Edward James Loder wrote *Nourjahad* for the first season and just a few weeks later John Barnett's *The Mountain Sylph* was produced, an opera which stayed in the repertoire throughout the century. Both composers seemed to promise much, but neither had adequate opportunity to fulfil this potential. Loder combined good orchestration with lyrical warmth – both qualities apparent in his last opera *Raymond and Agnes* (1855); Barnett wrote little else, quarrelled with too many people, and eventually retired.

Neither composer could compete with the great successes of two Irishmen: Michael Balfe and Vincent Wallace. Balfe, a singer himself, took London by storm with *The Siege of Rochelle* (1835), which enjoyed a run of 70 performances with a special one given for the young Queen Victoria after her accession. And there were other triumphs, though none more resounding than *The Bohemian Girl* (1843) which was soon heard throughout Europe and the Americas.

Balfe hoped to establish a tradition of serious opera in English (as distinct from the popular fare of ballad operas) but this proved unattainable. His music followed in the footsteps of Rossini, which was why it was berated by the musical establishment, but his great strength was his ability to

---

ROYAL PHILHARMONIC SOCIETY
Founded in 1813, the Philharmonic Society played a significant role in the revolutionising of London's orchestral life in the 19th century. At its best, the society's orchestra (no longer in existence) set new playing standards. Great names were attracted to appear in one role or another in Philharmonic seasons – Mendelssohn, Liszt and Wagner; Dvořák, Joachim and Tchaikovsky; in this century, the likes of Kreisler, Walter and Bernstein. The commissioning of Beethoven's Ninth Symphony stands as a symbol for the society's commitment to new music, not least by British composers. The occasional loss of the original artistic vision, variable playing standards, periodic cash

crises and most of all, the mushrooming of concert life in the capital, often placed question-marks against the organisation's future. Miraculously it has survived, picking up the 'Royal' title along the way. New niches have been found, whether keeping the Henry Wood Promenade Concerts afloat for a period in the Second World War or, now, a deep involvement in administering awards for emerging young artists.

Concert promotion has continued, featuring new or neglected repertoire by the likes of Walton, Messiaen and Debussy. The RPS's latest cash crisis was solved by the sale (for over £600,000) of a Haydn manuscript – one item in a substantial, under-explored archive. The society's gold medal remains one of the most prestigious international awards to outstanding musicians of the day.

Andrew Green

UNDER THE IMMEDIATE PATRONAGE OF

His Majesty.

PHILHARMONIC SOCIETY.

THIRD CONCERT, MONDAY, MARCH 21, 1825.

ACT I.

Sinfonia Letter T.	Haydn.
Terzetto, "Tutte le mie speranze," Madame CARADORI, Miss GOODALL, and Mr. VAUGHAN (Davide Penitente)	Mozart.
Quartetto, two Violins, Viola, and Violoncello, Messrs. SPAGNOLETTI, OURY, MORALT, and LINDLEY	Mozart..
Song, Mr. VAUGHAN, "Why does the God of Israel sleep," (Samson)	Handel.
Quintetto, Flute, Oboē, Clarinet, Horn, and Bassoon, Messrs. NICHOLSON, VOGT, WILLMAN, PLATT, and MACKINTOSH	Reicha.
Recit. ed Aria, Madame CARADORI, " Per pietà," (Cosi fan tutte)	Mozart.
Overture, Les deux Journées	Cherubini.

ACT II.

New Grand Characteristic Sinfonia, MS. with Vocal Finale, the principal parts of which to be sung by Madame CARADORI, Miss GOODALL, Mr. VAUGHAN, and Mr. PHILLIPS (composed expressly for this Society) - Beethoven.

Leader, Mr. F. CRAMER.—Conductor, Sir G. SMART.

R. D'OYLY CARTE, Proprietor and Manager.

write memorable ballads that caught the public's fancy. Wallace enjoyed a fantastic life as a virtuoso pianist and violinist; he wandered the world from Australia to Peru – as colourfully recounted by Berlioz in *Les soireés de l'orchestre* – and eventually ended up in London in 1845. His opera *Maritana* was produced there that year, its success running *The Bohemian Girl* a close second. Wallace's foreign travels helped colour both the melody and the harmony of his music; his sense of drama and use of strong melody assured performances of the opera throughout Europe.

Such native operatic aspirations proved too difficult to nurture and develop in the heady days of Victorian growth and industrialisation. Other areas of the music market rapidly expanded – there was a vast growth in the number of concerts, orchestras and piano sales. The availability of cheap sheet music, the work of John Hullah and

above: Illustration for *The Mikado* from the programme of the Savoy premiere in 1885

opposite, in box: The programme for an 1825 Philharmonic Society concert introducing to London audiences a 'New Grand Characteristic Sinfonia, with Vocal Finale (composed expressly for this Society)' – in other words Beethoven's Choral Symphony

John Curwen in developing tonic sol-fa, the acceptance of music as part of the school curriculum, and the national rise of large choral societies all contributed to a change in the musical climate. The 1850s brought the Great Exhibition of 1851 and its Crystal Palace, and the Crimean War.

The 1860s introduced a new composer. Arthur Sullivan was born only a year before *The Bohemian Girl* was first produced. At the age of 14 he became the first recipient of the Mendelssohn Scholarship at the RAM where he studied with Sterndale Bennett; then after two years he went to the Leipzig Conservatory (by now a well-worn path for British composers) where his incidental music for Shakespeare's *The Tempest* was written for his final diploma examinations in 1861.

George Grove had become a friend of Sullivan and in his role as secretary of the Crystal Palace, he programmed *The Tempest*. Its instant acclaim helped to launch Sullivan's career.

The new music of Liszt and Wagner had still not made much headway in Britain: Beethoven and Mendelssohn were the linchpins of the repertoire, and Sullivan's music, firmly in the Mendelssohn camp, impeccably crafted, fresh and lively, and not averse to a grand tune, was well received by the public. His Cello Concerto (1866) and the more important Symphony in E minor (1866), sparked into life while he was holidaying in Belfast and later known as the *Irish Symphony*, were amongst the works which consolidated his reputation. Nor was that reputation hindered by his many influential friends, including members of the Royal Family.

Despite this, even Sullivan could not earn a living from his orchestral music and he began to look to opera. Julius Benedict had enjoyed considerable success in 1862 with *The Lily of Killarney*,

above: **The French conductor Louis Antoine Jullien directing one of his promenade concerts in London in 1849, a drawing depicting 'Manners and Custome of ye Englyshe' by Richard Doyle for** *Punch*
left: **Caricature of Gilbert and Sullivan by Alfred Bryan, 1878**

completing the 'Irish Ring' of *The Bohemian Girl*, *Maritana*, and *The Lily*. Sullivan's first theatrical success, *Cox and Box* (1866–67), was much less grand, but it led to his first collaboration with W S Gilbert in 1871, *Thespis* (of which the music is mostly lost), and then the first work commissioned by Richard D'Oyly Carte, *Trial by Jury* in 1874. Thus began over two decades of brilliant collaborations, hampered by troubled relationships. *HMS Pinafore* (1878) was their first full-length work and it established the partnership both at home and in the USA. *Patience* was transferred from the Opéra Comique Theatre to D'Oyly Carte's new purpose-built Savoy Theatre in 1881, and with successes like *The Mikado* and *The Gondoliers* Sullivan's real talents for musical characterisation, deft orchestration and ingenious word-setting were fully exploited in operettas that are still popular throughout the English-speaking world.

The question constantly being asked of Sullivan was whether a composer of his stature should be stooping to write such operettas. His *Overtura di Ballo*, written for the 1870 Birmingham Festival, was a sparkling work which brought together the best of all his worlds. Alongside the operettas he continued to write oratorios and cantatas like *The Golden Legend* (1886). Queen Victoria asked him when he was going to compose a real opera and he responded with *Ivanhoe* (1891) which ran for 160 performances and still merits occasional revival.

In the course of the century, the whole fabric of musical life and concert-giving had changed. The theatre audience still liked its comic operas, the general audience for instrumental music still preferred the German classics; light-hearted extracts were appreciated. But there was now a growing audience which wanted something more substantial and searching. Sullivan was not the composer to deliver that – the changing face of British music was to be provided by another generation.

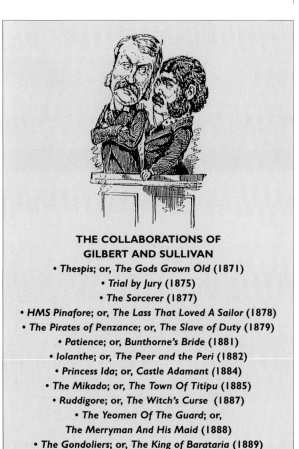

THE COLLABORATIONS OF GILBERT AND SULLIVAN
- *Thespis; or, The Gods Grown Old* (1871)
- *Trial by Jury* (1875)
- *The Sorcerer* (1877)
- *HMS Pinafore; or, The Lass That Loved A Sailor* (1878)
- *The Pirates of Penzance; or, The Slave of Duty* (1879)
- *Patience; or, Bunthorne's Bride* (1881)
- *Iolanthe; or, The Peer and the Peri* (1882)
- *Princess Ida; or, Castle Adamant* (1884)
- *The Mikado; or, The Town Of Titipu* (1885)
- *Ruddigore; or, The Witch's Curse* (1887)
- *The Yeomen Of The Guard; or, The Merryman And His Maid* (1888)
- *The Gondoliers; or, The King of Barataria* (1889)
- *Utopia, Limited; or, The Flowers Of Progress* (1893)
- *The Grand Duke; or, The Statutory Duel* (1896)

Dates refer to first performances

9

PROMETHEUS UNBOUND

THE BRITISH MUSICAL RENAISSANCE

1880–1914

MICHAEL KENNEDY

The main significance of the 1880s for British music is that seven Gilbert and Sullivan operettas were first performed during that decade. *Sevillana*, a short piece by a Worcester violinist, Edward Elgar, introduced this provincial composer's name to London at the Crystal Palace concerts in 1884 and in 1888 he composed the perennial charmer *Salut d'amour* which, had he not sold it outright to a publisher for just over two pounds, would have made him a not so small fortune. These are all works which are still heard; yet most surveys of what is (conveniently rather than wholly accurately) called 'the English musical renaissance' take 1880 as a starting-point because a work of which few people today

Chapter opener shows, *top right:* Sir Henry Wood in a stained glass window dedicated to the conductor in St Sepulchre Without Newgate Church, London *middle left:* Advertisement for an early gramophone *bottom right:* Sir Edward Elgar, photographed in 1933, toasting his 76th birthday

below: **Sir Charles Villiers Stanford, a portrait by William Orpen**

know a note. The *Scenes from Shelley's Prometheus Unbound* by Hubert Parry had a moderate success at that year's Gloucester Festival. In the recent Parry revival which has led to recordings of two complete sets of the five symphonies and of several of the choral works, no one has felt impelled to revive *Prometheus Unbound*. The vintage year of the decade for Parry was 1887 when his Miltonic choral ode *Blest Pair of Sirens* was first heard, a work Elgar was later to describe as 'one of the noblest works of man' and Vaughan Williams as 'my favourite piece of music written by an Englishman'.

Nevertheless, it still seems fair to inaugurate this period with Parry and Charles Villiers

Stanford since they were major influential figures in British music for almost half a century as composers, conductors, teachers, administrators and scholars. Stanford, an Irishman, conducted the first performance of *Blest Pair of Sirens* and also of Parry's Second Symphony (the *Cambridge*) in 1883. That shrewd critic Bernard Shaw saw through the pious barricade of oratorios and cantatas and the Brahmsian façade of the seven symphonies to the real Stanford and declared, after Gilbert had quarrelled with Sullivan, that the librettist would find an ideal substitute collaborator in Stanford. Shaw perceived that even if Stanford idolised Brahms, his gifts were more akin to Dvořák's and that his real musical nature was expressed in the Irish rhapsodies, the part-songs and such choral works as the *Songs of the Fleet* where his lyrical melodies, allied where appropriate to a genuine flair for orchestral tone-colour, have a Sullivanesque charm, wit and fluency.

If Britain at this time had possessed a real opera tradition, Stanford might have developed into a different composer. In his Dublin youth he was stagestruck, spending his time at operas and plays. He studied in Germany, where he heard more opera, including the first *Ring* cycle at Bayreuth in 1876 (though he remained resistant to the Wagner virus). His first two operas were performed in

Germany in 1881 and 1884 but had no success in England. He wrote four more between 1896 and 1919, but although in his teaching at the Royal College of Music he laid stress on the importance of opera and often conducted student performances, it is undeniable that he was discouraged at a crucial point in his career as a composer and switched his attention to church music (the Service in B flat of 1879 is a marvellous example), to incidental music for plays by Tennyson and to the choral works and symphonies which the British festivals required of him.

Parry, too, attended the first Bayreuth Festival. Although his music betrays few traces of it, he was a passionate Wagnerian, to the dismay of his teacher George Macfarren, Principal of the Royal Academy of Music, who wrote to him on the eve of his departure for Bayreuth that 'an earthquake would be good that would swallow the spot and everybody on it'. Parry's personal and musical character is almost as complex as Elgar's in its radicalism conflicting with an innate conservatism and the effect of social mores on his career – he rejected religion and was, for the time, on the Left in politics, to the dismay of his father. Whereas Elgar was of lowly birth, Parry belonged to the Gloucestershire squirearchy. He studied music against family wishes and for a three-year period abandoned it to work at Lloyd's. *Prometheus Unbound* was the work – regarded as 'advanced' – with which he moved into the forefront. It led to the inevitable commissions for oratorios, hence *Judith* (1888) and *Job* (1892), both of which attracted Shaw's savage scorn. Although neither work is as bad as Shaw made out, one cannot avoid the deduction that Parry was fulfilling a duty in response to public demand. The choral Parry is more truly represented by his Tennyson

above: **Sir Edward Elgar, Sir Dan Godfrey, Sir Alexander Mackenzie, Sir Charles Villiers Stanford (seated) and Sir Edward German and Sir Hubert Parry (standing), pictured at the Bournemouth Centenary Festival in 1910**
left: **Sir Hubert Parry**

setting *The Lotos-Eaters* (1891-2) in which he surrenders to a luxuriant, hedonistic sensuousness all too rare in his work. But if we except *Blest Pair of Sirens* and the majestic glories of the 1902 Coronation anthem 'I was glad', the greatest of Parry's choral works are probably the *Invocation to Music* (words by Robert Bridges) of 1895 and the *Ode on the Nativity* (William Dunbar) of 1912, in both of which he combined a more overtly operatic declamation with a tight motivic structure.

It is wrong to suppose that the pre-Elgar British composers were unknown outside their native country. As already mentioned, Stanford's operas were performed in Germany. Both Parry and Stanford were championed by the illustrious Austro-Hungarian conductor Hans Richter, who

COBBETT AND CHAMBER MUSIC

At the turn of the century, according to the businessman and patron Walter Wilson Cobbett (1847–1937), British chamber music was in the doldrums.

So, encouraged by Stanford and the Worshipful Company of Musicians, he set up a series of musical competitions. With them he forged a link with the Elizabethan and Jacobean *Fancies* for viol consort, in stipulating that his *Phantasies* should be in a short single movement of contrasting sections.

The first competition, for a string quartet *Phantasy*, was held in 1905. There were 67 entries: winner, William Hurlstone, runners-up, Frank Bridge and Haydn Wood. The *Phantasy* Piano Trio competition two years later was won by Bridge. Then followed a Violin Sonata competition, a series of 10 Cobbett commissions for various chamber ensembles, and two more competitions after the First World War for *Folk-Song Phantasies*.

The Cobbett prize lives on at the Royal College of Music. Benjamin Britten and Malcolm Arnold are among its distinguished winners. Countless *Phantasies* have been composed over the last 90 years. In the hands of Stanford, Bridge, Howells, Ireland, Moeran and Britten, it became a distinctive musical form.

Cobbett's legacy is in the fine British music he inspired and in the *Cyclopaedic Survey of Chamber Music* which he funded and edited in the 1920s.

Paul Hindmarsh

first came to London in 1877 with Wagner. He returned yearly thereafter, established his own concerts, became conductor of the Birmingham Festival and of the Hallé Orchestra of Manchester from 1899 to 1911. He conducted Parry's Piano Concerto in 1879 and the symphonies thereafter. In Vienna he was rapped over the knuckles by the

critic Eduard Hanslick for turning the Vienna Philharmonic concerts into 'a little English colony'. Stanford's *Irish Symphony* (No 3) was given its first performance under Richter in 1887. It was then performed in Hanover, Berlin, Brussels, Rome, Bologna, New York and Boston and was in the programme of the concert which opened the new Concertgebouw in Amsterdam in 1888. The Fourth Symphony was first performed in Berlin. Yet neither Parry's nor Stanford's were the most popular British symphonies of their time. This distinction belonged to the six composed by Frederic Cowen between 1870 and 1897. They included the *Scandinavian* (No 3, first performed in Vienna in 1882), the *Welsh* (1884) and the *Idyllic* (No 6, first performed in Leipzig in 1898). Cowen also wrote operas, songs and light pieces such as *The Butterfly's Ball*. His music is now almost forgotten and his fame rests on his reputation as a conductor: he was probably the first really effective British conductor before the advent of Henry Wood and Thomas Beecham.

Shaw in 1888 declared that the symphony as a musical form was 'stone dead'. He is only one of many false prophets of doom for the symphony over the past 100 years. One of the most enterprising champions of British composers ever to work regularly with an orchestra was Sir Dan Godfrey at Bournemouth from 1893 to 1934. Lewis Foreman's recently published list shows that between 1899 and 1914 he conducted symphonies, or parts of symphonies, by 32 British composers, most of them completely forgotten today. For example, the First Symphony (1889) of Frederic Cliffe, a piano professor at the Royal College of Music who wrote two symphonies, was declared a masterpiece by the *Daily Telegraph* critic. 'It may be doubted', he added, 'whether musical history can show on any of its pages the record of such an Opus 1.' Godfrey conducted it seven times between 1902 and 1910. He conducted symphonies by Edgar Bainton, W H Bell, Ernest Bryson, William Wallace, and the two by Edward German, of which the Second (*Norwich*) is occasionally and deservedly revived. But what became of Edith Swepstone, whose Symphony in G minor had its first performance in Bournemouth on 3 February 1902?

A leading musician who did not compose a symphony was the Scotsman Alexander Campbell Mackenzie who was Principal of the Royal

below: **Sir Henry Wood in the ruins of the bombed Queen's Hall in 1941**
far below: **1912 London Transport poster showing the interior of the Queen's Hall**

THE PROMS

The first season of Queen's Hall Promenade Concerts was launched in 1895 by Robert Newman, manager of the hall, and the young conductor Henry Wood. They intended that these summer concerts should be cheap and popular, but should gradually aim to make the best music available to the widest audience. Wood, who conducted almost every item for nearly fifty years, showed extraordinary dedication in raising standards and introducing the music of modern composers, both British and foreign, to London; it is largely due to his pioneering work that the Proms have evolved over a century into a unique international music festival.

In 1927, following the death of Newman, the BBC took over the running of the Proms. The concerts were now broadcast, and the Queen's Hall Orchestra formed the nucleus of the BBC Symphony Orchestra. When the Queen's Hall was destroyed in 1941, the Proms moved to their present home, the Royal Albert Hall. After Henry Wood's death in 1944, the conducting of the Proms was divided between a number of fine musicians; the

BBC SO provided the backbone of each season, but during the 1950s other British orchestras also made regular appearances.

In the early 1960s the BBC Proms entered an exciting period of renewal and expansion whose effects continue to be felt today. Over the past decades there has been a great increase in the number

of different performers (many from abroad), and a significant widening of repertory: more adventurous programming has introduced much rarely-heard music, as well as performances of complete operas, early music, jazz and ethnic music. Each modern Prom season, running from July to September, contains around 60 concerts, half of which are given by the BBC orchestras. They feature the best of the classical repertory alongside an enormous variety of other music, including new works specially commissioned each year by the BBC.

Andrew Huth

left: **A silhouette of Sir Alexander Mackenzie on a postcard to which the composer has added a message to Edward German, an umbrella and a bird!**
below: **Hamish MacCunn as a dandy in John Pettie's 1887 painting 'Two Strings To Her Bow'**

Academy of Music from 1888 to 1924, parallel with Parry's era as Director of the Royal College of Music from 1894 to 1918. Mackenzie went at the age of ten to study for five years at Sondershausen Conservatory before entering the Royal Academy of Music in London for three years. For 14 years he worked as a violinist and conductor in his native Edinburgh and then lived in Florence for ten years. He composed five operas. His oratorio *The Rose of Sharon* (1884) and cantata *The Dream of Jubal* (1889) achieved success, but today's audiences would probably prefer his Violin Concerto and the *Scottish Concerto* for piano and orchestra, premiered by Sarasate and Paderewski respectively. However it was an early choral work, *The Bride*, introduced at the Worcester Festival in 1881, which impressed one of the orchestral violinists, Edward Elgar. Writing 50 years after the event, Elgar recalled that 'here was a man fully equipped in every department of musical knowledge, who had been a violinist in orchestras in Germany. It gave orchestral players a real lift'.

Among other Scottish composers was Hamish MacCunn, a prickly personality who complained to his teacher Parry that during his time at the Royal College of Music 'I had not met one man, bar yourself, who had acted to me, during the most ordinary intercourse common to society, with the remotest vestige of a supposition that *possibly* I might *be* a gentleman!' (Parry's reply was that he would be glad if the English language could do without the word gentleman. He hated the term, in contrast to Elgar who once said he would like to be known as 'Edward Elgar, gentleman'). MacCunn wrote one orchestral work that survives, the tuneful overture *Land of the Mountain and the Flood*. His opera *Jeanie Deans* had a 20-year vogue and has once been revived since 1914. He later taught composition, directed the opera class at the Guildhall School of Music and concentrated on conducting (he conducted the first performance sung in English of Wagner's *Tristan and Isolde*). His compatriot John McEwen was also involved in academic work (he was Principal of the Royal Academy of Music 1924-36). His *Three Border Ballads* (*Grey Galloway*, *Coronach* and *The Demon Lover*) (1905-8), as a recent recording has shown, are strongly orchestrated and

HOPE AND GLORY?

EDWARD ELGAR 1857–1934

DIANA McVEAGH

At the turn of the century there came to maturity a composer of overmastering power, true creative vitality, and distinctive voice.

Edward Elgar was born in 1857, an outsider in almost every way. He was a provincial, the son of a small tradesman. He left school at 15, and had no academic musical training. As a Catholic, he would have found no traditional organ loft open to him. He forged his way slowly, picking up skills where he could. The village of his birth, Broadheath, gave him country freedom and the noble outline of the Malvern Hills. In Worcester, where the family moved when he was two, he had the run of his father's music shop, of St George's Church where his father (and then he) was organist, and of the Cathedral. He took part in local activities, playing the bassoon in a boys' wind quintet, the piano for choral groups, the violin for the Three Choirs Festival and then in Birmingham; and conducting amateur orchestras whenever he could.

He composed for all these combinations. From the start he had a turn of phrase that was immedi-

above: **The Elgars' cottage at Broadheath, now the Elgar Birthplace Museum**
left: **Edward Elgar with his first bicycle, 'Mr Phoebus', around 1900**

ately recognisable – 'Elgarian'. He matured slowly: after his death, his 1890s works were rarely played, and it came to seem that the *Enigma Variations* of 1899, when he was already 42, had sprung fully formed, Minerva-like. Since then, the revival of his earlier works has shown his steady progression, through the opportunities available to him in the provincial festivals. His overture *Froissart* was commissioned for the 1890 Worcester Three Choirs; then came choral works: *The Black Knight* (1893), *King Olaf* (1896), *The Banner of St George* (1897), *Caractacus* (1898). All are set in far-off times and have chivalrous, romantic subjects. If the inspiration in them is fitful, their energy and eloquent melodies are irresistible.

The final chorus of *Caractacus* shows a strand, a genuine celebration of patriotism, that was to make Elgar the nation's troubadour, leading to the five *Pomp and Circumstance* marches and the official compositions for great state occasions. The love-music in *Olaf*, the Severn-side dawn music in *Caractacus* show a lyrical pastoral strain – 'what the reeds were singing' – which found ultimate expression in the *Falstaff* interludes and became a symbol of the next world for *The Dream of Gerontius*. Sombre passages – Ironbeard's death in *Olaf*, Caractacus's Lament 'O my warriors' – reveal an Elgar capable of profound introspection.

Coming to maturity at the zenith of British imperialism, Elgar was bound to share that age's optimism, and his music glows with colour and opulence. But Constant Lambert's comment in 1933 on the music's 'almost intolerable air of smugness, self-assurance and autocratic benevolence' has too often been cited without his qualifying … 'through no fault of its own', and 'for the present generation'. Reaction against the period's excesses made for reaction against Elgar. But temperamentally Elgar was sensitive and melancholic, and his own life was a struggle. There is on occasion an over-wrought or over-protesting note from which one may flinch. But the pull between outward certainty and inward despondency is what makes his mature music endlessly fascinating and rewarding; often the conflicting feelings are found in the same work, within bars of each other, even fused in the same passages. Yeats spoke of Elgar's 'heroic melancholy'; and under his grandest music runs the refrain 'Lest we forget – lest we forget!'.

The *Enigma Variations*, a landmark in British music, was first performed (St James's Hall, London, 19 June 1899) by Hans Richter, one of the many foreign-born musicians who promoted and encouraged Elgar. Elgar's choice of a set of variations as his first major orchestral essay, one no longer shaped by a text, shows his acute self-knowledge, particularly as the work was not commissioned. Each variation is a gem, independent in mood and style yet linked to its mysterious source. Beecham's dismissal of the Variations as ballet music, though scornful, was not imperceptive. Ashton's deeply touching ballet, showing Elgar in relationship to the human characters known to have inspired the work, is as fine and subtle a commentary as any written words.

Enigma is the first of Elgar's private puzzles, in which he publicly paraded a coded confidential message. The enigmatic dedication of the Violin Concerto is another, and some knowledge of Elgar's life and music is needed for full appreciation of the self-referential *Music Makers*. Another paradox is that this secretive man allowed his dutiful, devoted wife to hoard every sketch, letter, press-cutting, indeed scrap – unlike, say, Hardy (with whose career Elgar's has something in common), who destroyed all he could.

As part of his rigorous self-education Elgar had spent holidays in Germany, at Leipzig as early as 1883, then during the 1890s, hearing as much Wagner as he could. When he decided to set Cardinal Newman's *The Dream of Gerontius* for the 1900 Birmingham Festival, he was able to call on a practised leitmotif technique and widely-varied harmonic resources. His earlier *Light of Life* (1896) had shown the way: in Newman's poem Elgar found a universal subject that touched his own most serious concerns. The death of an old man and his rebirth in the next world can be taken as Christian doctrine and as allegory or myth. From the remote, austere opening to the tenderness of the Angel's 'Softly and gently' Elgar carries Gerontius through judgment to fulfilment in music of astonishing intensity. His fluid chromaticism mirrors every shudder and pang.

'The first progressivist in English music'

RICHARD STRAUSS ON ELGAR, 1902

below: In November 1931, Sir Edward Elgar opened the new Abbey Road recording studios by conducting the London Symphony Orchestra in *Falstaff*. Among the guests was George Bernard Shaw (on staircase)

The great choruses have a majestic spread. Gerontius's 'Firmly I believe and truly' has a Verdian drive, but the side-slipping chords express doubt as well as belief. A fine performance of *Gerontius* is at once a lacerating and an enobling experience.

The two linked oratorios that followed, *The Apostles* (1903) and *The Kingdom* (1906), were composed to Biblical words assembled by the composer. Even more elaborate and ambitious than *Gerontius*, they contain sublime stretches, but others that depend too much on the sanctity of the words to carry less distinguished music.

In 1905 Elgar accepted a professorship at Birmingham university which entailed his giving eight public lectures, the first called *A Future for English Music*; these caused him anxiety and created public controversy. It was his only academic appointment, and his only attempt, apart from freelance teaching in his early days, and some conducting, to earn money except by composing.

For years he fought shy of a symphony. The overture *In the South* (1904) is in length a tone-poem, and one of his sunniest, most ebullient works. The *Introduction and Allegro* for strings (1905) is an intricate, poetic piece, so original as to be unclassifiable. The symphony, when it came in 1908, was a remarkable success, immediately

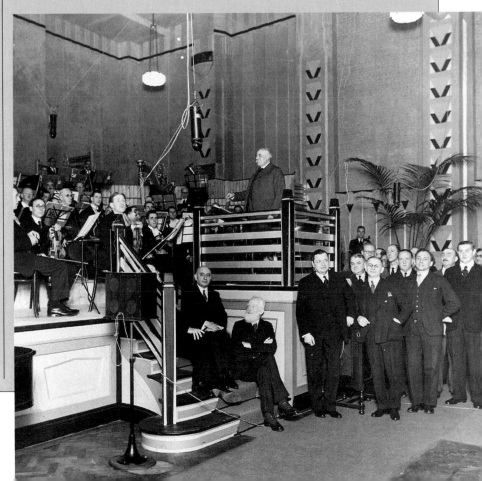

played all over Britain, on the continent, and in the United States. Elgar proved that he had the grasp and stamina for a long, complicated work. His command of tonality is such that modulations are powerful and far-reaching. The orchestration is gorgeous, but the scoring is never applied: the thought is in the sound. Thematically, the music is allusive. The influence of the grand motto-theme is dramatic, and the rundown of the scherzo-tune to form the passionate adagio is shown step-by-step, but many other internal references are fleetingly revealed, and they give the whole work depth and cohesion.

The Second Symphony (1911) bears the Shelley quotation 'Rarely, rarely, comest thou, Spirit of Delight!'. It is perhaps the most layered of Elgar's works, seeming at times to hold two opposing feelings at once which creates strong tensions. The vaunting themes strive for exultation, but from time to time energy ebbs away and there are unnerving glimpses of wraiths and anxieties. These assume nightmare strength when a theme from the first movement batters its way into the third. The symphony's final pages unforgettably mingle delight, regret, and acceptance.

Between the symphonies came the Violin Concerto (1910), a work which for all its elaboration and virtuosity has the nature of a confessional. The impulse partly to reveal, partly to conceal, lies at the heart of this music, with its compelling mixture of passion and inhibition. Elgar dedicated the concerto to Kreisler, who gave the first performance and declared it the greatest violin concerto since Beethoven's. Ernest Newman found that 'human feeling so nervous and subtle as this had never before spoken in English orchestral or choral music'. In 1913 came the symphonic study *Falstaff*, a masterly one-movement score, though possibly it tells as much about its composer as about Shakespeare's character.

Throughout his career Elgar composed slighter pieces. Some were in the salon genre of his period, with a soft, pretty sentiment that found its perfect home in his ballet *The Sanguine Fan*. Others looked back

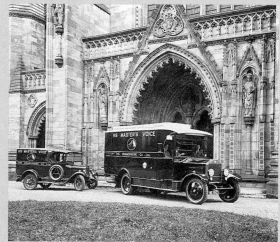

above: **HMV recording vans outside Hereford Cathedral for the 1927 Three Choirs Festival**
below: **Cover design for the score of Elgar's *Cockaigne Overture***

nostalgically to childhood, with such evocative titles as *Dream Children, The Wand of Youth*, and *The Starlight Express*.

Elgar's marriage to an Indian Army major-general's daughter in 1889 brought him great domestic and a little financial stability, but understandably his wife had social ambitions for him. These he sometimes endorsed, sometimes mocked, but the effort added to his insecurities and his touchiness. He was an uneasy man, driven to extremes of jocularity and depression, but one who made and kept close friends – his spontaneous letters make compulsive reading. The Elgars lived first in Malvern, then Hereford, and in 1912 established themselves, by now honoured and fêted, in London; but the war blighted their life there. A cottage in Sussex provided an escape, in which he composed chamber music; and the Cello Concerto (1919), shorter than the Violin Concerto and the symphonies, but the more haunting – harrowing, even – for its constraints. Its elegiac note is so strong that some have heard in it a requiem for the Edwardian age, or for the war dead; or maybe a sensitive man mourning his passing life.

In 1920 Lady Elgar died, and – though he had sometimes looked for romantic inspiration elsewhere – he found the loss incapacitating. Going home to Worcestershire, he more and more adopted the life of a country gentleman; a third oratorio, a third symphony, and an opera after Ben Jonson to be called *The Spanish Lady* were left incomplete. His notable work of these last years was to record, for a percipient HMV Gramophone Company, most of his music – an incomparable testament. In 1933, the year before his death, he flew to Paris to conduct his Violin Concerto with the young Menuhin, and visited Delius – a moving tribute between two composers with little in common except their age.

Much of Elgar's music is idealistic. His riverside, his orchards, his romantic aspirations, his regal *nobilmente*, his land of Cockayne, his spirit of England, his dream of 'strange refreshment' – all this was created by his imagination, and was ever threatened by his own vulnerability. But in his music he gave permanence to his visions.

colourful pieces, as is the *Solway Symphony* of 1911. He composed 17 string quartets between 1893 and 1947, reaching No 6 (*Biscay*) by 1913. His music no more deserves to be forgotten than does that of the Irishman Charles Wood, a Stanford pupil who later taught Vaughan Williams and whose three string quartets and *Dirge for Two Veterans* (1901) have an individual flavour.

Another celebrated British name began by being more familiar in Germany than England. Ethel Smyth entered Leipzig Conservatory in 1877 and was encouraged by favourable reactions to her chamber music from Brahms, Grieg, Dvořák and Tchaikovsky. A *Serenade in D* was performed in London in 1890 and she had a major success in 1893 with her Mass in D (1891), conducted in the

right: **Dame Ethel Smyth pictured with canine friend**
below: **Front cover of *The March of the Women*, the work which became the Suffragette's battle hymn. On one occasion described by Beecham, Ethel Smyth famously conducted it with a toothbrush from her Holloway Prison cell window**

Royal Albert Hall by Joseph Barnby. The audience might have been more than a little surprised had they known that this music had been inspired by Smyth's passion for Pauline Trevelyan, its dedicatee. Even more remarkable was that the performance was a direct result of Smyth's having sung sections of the Mass to Queen Victoria at Balmoral in 1891! Also present was Napoléon III's widow, Empress Eugénie, a friend of Smyth. She insisted on Barnby fixing a date for the performance and paid for the work's publication. Despite such patronage, it was not performed again until Adrian Boult revived it in Birmingham in 1924, but it has lately enjoyed a vogue and has been recorded by Americans in a performance which revels in the music's vitality and contrasts.

Like Stanford, Smyth's inclinations were to opera and her first two, *Fantasio* and *Der Wald*, were produced in Weimar (1898) and Berlin (1902) respectively. She wrote the German libretto of *Fantasio* and, believing that her third opera was likely to be produced in France, wrote the libretto in French – *Les naufrageurs*, better known as *The Wreckers*, a tale of love and smuggling on the Cornish coast. In fact its premiere was in Leipzig in 1906 as *Strandrecht*. In London Beecham and Bruno Walter conducted it in 1910. Because of her outsize personality and her later imprisonment as a suffragette, Ethel Smyth overshadowed other women composers of her day. She was certainly the first in Britain to invade male territory with operas, concertos and a Mass, though one must not forget Edith Swepstone's Symphony mentioned earlier. But whereas Smyth's music is known by a dedicated minority, the *Indian Love Lyrics* (including 'Pale hands I loved beside the Shalimar') of Amy Woodforde-Finden and the song-cycle *In a Persian Garden* of Liza Lehmann reached and retained a wider audience. Smyth's nearest feminine rival was Dora Bright, composer of three operas and of two piano concertos in which she played the solo part.

Dedicated to THE WOMEN'S SOCIAL AND POLITICAL UNION.

VOTES FOR WOMEN

THE MARCH OF THE WOMEN
(Popular Edition in F...To be sung in Unison)
By ETHEL SMYTH, Mus.Doc.
Price: One Shilling & Sixpence net.

To be had of THE WOMAN'S PRESS, 156, Charing Cross Rd, London W.C. and BREITKOPF & HÄRTEL, 54, Gt Marlborough St, London W.

During the 1890s another name had been gaining prominence at provincial festivals: Edward Elgar composed an overture *Froissart* for the 1890 Worcester Festival, a 'choral symphony' *The Black Knight* for Worcester Choral Society in 1893, an oratorio *The Light of Life* for the Worcester Festival in 1896 and, in the same year, *King Olaf* for the North Staffordshire Festival at Hanley. Finally, in 1898, *Caractacus* (dedicated to Queen Victoria who had celebrated her diamond jubilee the previous year) was performed at the Leeds Festival. June 1899 saw the premiere of the *Enigma Variations* in London and, just over a year later, came *The Dream of Gerontius*. The years from 1900 to 1914 were dominated by Elgar with two more oratorios, two symphonies, the symphonic study *Falstaff*, a violin concerto, the *Pomp and Circumstance* marches and a series of other works that are now regarded as national treasures.

Where Elgar differed from Parry and Stanford

above: **Nipper and a gramophone, the famous logo of 'His Master's Voice'**
below: **Cecil Sharp collecting a folk-song from Edwin Clay of Brailes in Warwickshire**

and why he admired Mackenzie was that he was a practical musician. Through playing, and through excursions to London to hear important operas and concerts, he knew a lot of music and he developed a style which is highly personal although compounded of the influences of Schumann, Wagner and Brahms and French composers such as Bizet and Saint-Saëns. The *nobilmente* element in his music, which we should now identify as 'Elgarian', can be traced to Parry – and Parry returned the compliment by composing *Jerusalem*.

Elgar's supremacy is all the more remarkable when one considers the extraordinarily rich background of British composition between 1900 and 1914. He himself had encouraged the Anglo-African Samuel Coleridge-Taylor, whose *Hiawatha* trilogy was more popular than any choral work by Parry, Stanford and even Elgar. Only in the early years of the century did British audiences become gradually aware of the Bradford-born composer

---

CECIL SHARP AND FOLK-SONG

In 1898 the Folk-Song Society was founded and the following year started to issue its journal containing transcriptions of the latest finds. The craze for noting down (or in Percy Grainger's case recording) folk-songs from the singing of elderly country people of the day was in full flood until the First World War, though some collecting persisted until the 1930s. It is undoubtedly true that many tunes were thus saved from oblivion.

Cecil Sharp (1859–1924) at first a collector of folk-dances collected folk-song from 1903, and was the most persistent, eventually collecting nearly 5,000 tunes in England and the USA. It has now been shown he made a very

considerable income from his activities. Very quickly Vaughan Williams, Holst, Balfour Gardiner, George Butterworth and other composers collected tunes and incorporated them into their music in a conscious search for a personal style in rebellion against the prevailing Germanic musical culture.

First successes included Holst's *Somerset Rhapsody* (1906–7, dedicated to Sharp, who collected the tunes) and Vaughan Williams' *Norfolk Rhapsody* No 1 (1906).

The folk-song movement's coup was the acceptance of their arrangements as a staple diet of school music, thus cementing the tunes in the nation's musical consciousness.

Lewis Foreman

S. COLERIDGE-TAYLOR

left: **Samuel Coleridge-Taylor, soon after the popularity of** *Hiawatha's Wedding Feast*
right: **Frederick Delius later in his life, pictured in a wheelchair, with his wife Jelka and Percy Grainger at Grez-sur-Loing**
below: **Sir Granville Bantock in oriental costume**

Calydon (1911). Symphonic poems and a trilogy of operas brought temporary fame to Joseph Holbrooke, but the music of the composer-conductor-pianist Hamilton Harty has lasted better, with a violin concerto and *Irish Symphony* especially attractive. Cyril Scott was another who studied in Germany. His First Symphony was premiered in Darmstadt while Henry Wood conducted his Second in 1903. York Bowen wrote three piano concertos between 1904 and 1908 and a symphony in 1912. A former cellist in Richter's Hallé, John Foulds was an experimenter ahead of his time, but such works as the *Celtic Suite* (1911)

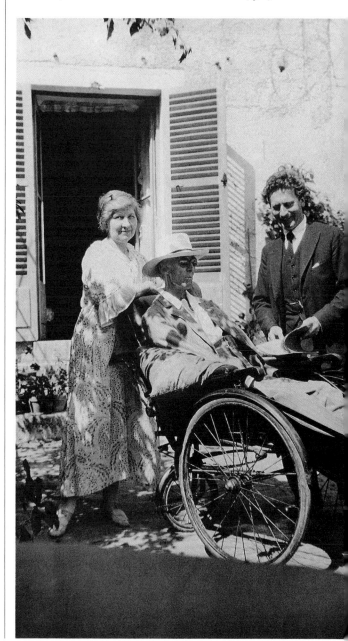

Frederick Delius, who lived in France after a spell managing an orange-grove in Florida and was well known in Europe where Mahler, Strauss, Grieg and Bartók were among his admirers. A concert of his music in London in 1899 had made little impression and it was not until after 1907, when the conductors Wood and Beecham took up the Piano Concerto, the English rhapsody *Brigg Fair*, the tone poems *Paris* and *In a Summer Garden* and the choral works *Sea-Drift* and *A Mass of Life* (a better work than Mahler's Eighth Symphony in my opinion), that the advent of a major creative figure was fully recognised. In the creation of a nostalgic reverie for the days that are no more, Delius had few equals. His finest opera, *A Village Romeo and Juliet* (1900–1), first performed in Berlin in 1907, was conducted by Beecham at Covent Garden in 1910.

Delius was also championed by Granville Bantock, himself a versatile composer of six tone poems which reflect enthusiasm for Tchaikovsky and Strauss. Yet his best music is to be found in the ambitious *Omar Khayyám* (1906–9), a setting of the whole of Edward FitzGerald's English version, and the unaccompanied choral symphony *Atalanta in*

show a less recondite side of his art.

Several composers whose music was heard in the first 14 years of the century created their most significant work after 1914 and belong to the next chapter – Arnold Bax and Havergal Brian come into this category. But Ralph Vaughan Williams had by 1914 composed works that would still have secured him a place in British musical history if he had been killed when he enlisted in the Army on the outbreak of war. Most of these were written after a brief period of study with Ravel in 1908 and include the Housman cycle *On Wenlock Edge*, the *Fantasia on a Theme by Thomas Tallis* for strings, *A Sea Symphony* which was the sensation of the 1910 Leeds Festival and *A London Symphony*, the last English masterpiece to have a first performance before the First World War. Before 1908 Vaughan Williams was known chiefly for some splendid songs and for his work as folk-song collector and hymn-book editor, aspects of his

right: **Painting by Henry Allinson of Sir Henry Wood conducting at the Queen's Hall, the scene of many important musical occasions until it was bombed in 1941**
below: **Bernard Hepton, who played Elgar, and David Pownall, author of the Radio 3 play *Elgar's Third*, pictured with the bound fragments of the Third Symphony at the British Library**

sense of civic duty to the musical community. He was a pupil of both Parry and Stanford. The latter was an irascible, discouraging teacher, but his pupils adored him and they included Gustav Holst, whose short opera *Savitri*, anticipating Britten's church parables by 50 years, belongs to 1908 (though not performed until 1916); John Ireland, mainly known for his chamber music in this period; Herbert Howells; and Frank Bridge, later to be Britten's teacher, whose works up to 1914, such as *The Sea* (1910), were in a romantic idiom far removed from his later style.

Bridge also wrote several chamber works in the old English 'Phantasy' form favoured by the industrialist-patron W W Cobbett who in 1905 instituted a prize for chamber music.
The first winner was another Stanford pupil, William Y Hurlstone, with Haydn Wood, later a successful composer of lighter music, as a runner-up. Hurlstone's early death snuffed out a precious talent, as his piano concerto testifies. What he might have achieved is as unguessable as what might have been achieved by the victims of the 1914–18 War, George Butterworth, whose moving rhapsody *A Shropshire Lad* was conducted by Nikisch at the 1913 Leeds Festival, Ernest Farrar, Denis Browne and, most tragic of all, Ivor Gurney, a song-writer and poet of extraordinary potential who ended his days in an asylum. Had they lived, the future of music in this country would almost certainly have been different.

ELGAR'S THIRD SYMPHONY
During the last two years of his life Elgar worked on a third symphony, a commission by the BBC which Bernard Shaw had engineered. If he had lived to complete it, the work would have totally changed our view of his last creative phase. It is generally felt that Elgar achieved little after the Cello Concerto, yet the abundant sketches for the symphony in both short and orchestral score are of a quality to suggest that 12 years after the Cello Concerto Elgar was once more on firecreatively. W H Reed's description of the composer's passionate involvement in their violin and piano sessions on the work supports this view. As it is, however, the symphony has been discounted, leaving many in the belief that the sketches rely lamely on old ideas and are too fragmentary to be linked in a convincing symphonic discourse.

Unfortunately, the composer's will forbade any 'tinkering' with the symphony or any attempts at a completion, reflecting, no doubt, his depression at being out of fashion and his fear of being posthumously devalued. This has prevented the performance of realisations of the sketches, mine included, which might have revealed the truth; but work on the material has convinced me that the Third Symphony would have been a masterpiece, displaying a concentration and a range of emotion new to his work. There was to be an adagio of muted agony and noble resignation, and an intermezzo in the composer's lighter vein, while the outer movements, represented by substantial unbroken sections, evince a powerful grandeur. It is tragic that this music seems destined not to be heard.

Anthony Payne

10

Heirs and Rebels

The Wars and Between

1914–1945

Lewis Foreman

Arnold Bax once referred to 'that sinister carnival time, the London summer of 1914'. Until the outbreak of war British musical life – in London, in particular – saw unprecedented brilliance and originality, throwing the months after August into sharp contrast. British works first heard included the second opera of Joseph Holbrooke's Wagnerian trilogy *The Cauldron of Anwyn – Dylan* – produced in Hammerstein's ill-fated initiative at the New London Opera House, and Sir A C Mackenzie's opera *The Cricket on the Hearth*, at the Royal Academy of Music. In the concert hall Sir Charles Villiers Stanford's Fourth *Irish Rhapsody* and Delius's *On Hearing the First Cuckoo in Spring* and *Summer Night on the River* were well received. However, the new music was not all understood: the chromaticism of Frank Bridge's *A Dance Poem* for example, with its arresting opening fanfare motif, was rejected as 'ultra-modern in its cacophony'. However, Bridge's tone poem *Summer*, to be premiered in 1916, appeared very much of its time, evocative nature music with a wide-spanning oboe tune.

This turning-point in British music was signalled by the first performance of Vaughan Williams' *A London Symphony*, its atmospheric

Chapter opener shows, *top left:* Portrait of Sir William Walton by Michael Ayrton, 1948 *middle right:* Ralph Vaughan Williams *bottom middle:* Sketch of Gustav Holst working, by his pupil Clare Mackail

above: Sir Arnold Bax painted by Vera Bax *left:* Frank Bridge

textures looking to France rather than Germany. There were many talented newcomers and while a few would be casualties of the war, by 1920 a strikingly new generation had emerged.

Other works dating from 1914 included Holst's 'Mars' from *The Planets*; Bax's wide-spanning, romantic Piano Quintet, and his extended orchestral song cycle *The Bard of the Dimbovitza* (not performed until 1921); Cyril Scott's exotic [first] Piano Concerto (performed in 1915); and John Ireland's mysterious *The Forgotten Rite*, described by the composer as a 'prelude for orchestra', in reality an evocative nine-minute tone poem. Still awaiting rediscovery today is the large-scale Piano Concerto in C minor (the first of two) by the 21-year-old Herbert Howells, described by a contemporary critic as 'magnificent ... worthy of ranking with those of Rachmaninov'.

The initial reaction to the outbreak of war was the cancellation of musical arrangements. The choral festivals at Birmingham, Worcester, Cardiff, Norwich and Sheffield were aborted, effectively ending an era, for they never regained their influence; that at Birmingham was not to be revived for over 50 years. However, the Promenade Concerts continued, though there was a virtual ban on modern German music which eliminated not only Richard Strauss and Schoenberg but inhibited Sir Henry Wood's growing interest in Mahler.

From the novelties performed at the wartime Proms we might pick out in 1914 Frank Bridge's vigorous earlier *Dance Rhapsody*, a piano concerto by Kathleen Bruckshaw played by the composer, the young Eugene Goossens' Straussian tone poem *Perseus*, while Percy Grainger's soon-to-be popular *Handel in the Strand* was heard in an orchestral arrangement by Wood himself. Grainger, of Australian birth and upbringing, left for the USA in September 1914.

By 1915 the amount of British music being played was unparalleled. The Proms included Haydn Wood's Piano Concerto and Frank Bridge's heartfelt *Lament* for string orchestra 'in memory of Catherine, aged nine' who with her family had been drowned when the Lusitania was sunk. Bridge, whose music would be haunted by war horrors for the next 20 years, wrote it in a single day.

Musicians had opposing reactions to the outbreak of war: a quick rallying to the colours, or bewildered pacifism. Bliss remarked: 'The crash of a European war on our very beaches sucked me into its undertow without me ever probing the consequences.' Sir Hubert Parry blamed Prussian militarism for fouling the wellsprings of the spirit in Germany. Parry's humanism is reflected in three wartime works: the warmly expressive orchestral diptych *From Death to Life*, the a capella choral cycle *Songs of Farewell*, and the cantata *The Chivalry of the Sea*, intended to applaud selfless bravery rather than unthinking patriotism. Yet Parry endures from the war, with his instinctive ability to find the wider public with a big tune, in *Jerusalem* and also *England*, a setting of John O'Gaunt's famous speech from Shakespeare's *Richard II*.

Even so, Elgar is remembered as the wartime voice of England. He reacted to reports of atrocities in Belgium with theatrical flair in the recitations *Carillon*, *A Voice in the Desert* and *Le Drapeau Belge*. Inevitably their first impact is now lost. Elgar's enduring wartime work – and his last great choral piece – was *The Spirit of England*, setting poems from Binyon's *The Winnowing Fan* which included the familiar words 'They shall not grow old, as we that are left grow old'.

Although one might argue that the viola as a solo instrument produces the most characteristically *English* sound, with particularly expressive sonatas by Arnold Bax and Rebecca Clarke, a number of composers made their most personal reactions to the war with violin sonatas. Probably Bax was the first with his Second Sonata, its scherzo headed 'The Grey Dancer in the Twilight'. Thomas Dunhill's Sonata in F also has affinities with the war, made clear in its *adagio lamentoso* with its hint of tolling drums in the accompaniment. Yet it was John Ireland's Sonata in A minor, also his second, which found a great popular success when first performed by Albert Sammons in March 1917. Edwin Evans remarked that 'it was as if the music had struck some latent sentiment that had been waiting for the sympathetic voice to make it articulate. Never in the

right: **Delius by Sir Herbert James Gunn. Delius was to die in 1934 within months of his friend Norman O'Neill, Elgar and Holst**
below: **John Ireland and EJ Moeran in the 1920s**

DELIUS

In chronicling the reception of Frederick Delius by the British musical public, the sequence of the music's composition is only of limited assistance. Although many of Delius's works had actually been heard before the First War, for many people the production of the operas *A Village Romeo and Juliet* and *Koanga* in the 1930s presented what for them were new works. Even a now familiar score such as *A Mass of Life* was treated as a new and challenging score whenever it reappeared. Delius's reception by the British public was sealed by the Delius Festival at Queen's Hall in 1929, with the paralysed composer present in his wheelchair, an image reinforced by Gunn's portrait which was widely reproduced. This was later underlined by the events of the composer's death and reburial at Limpsfield, and by the publication of Eric Fenby's vivid story of how he took down Delius's last works by dictation, in *Delius as I Knew Him*. The recording of Delius's music on the Delius Society 78s, conducted by Sir Thomas Beecham, was as important in promoting Delius as the parallel series of Sibelius recordings had been in consolidating the Finn's reputation. Delius's first champion was Sir Henry Wood, and although his most consistent champion was, of course, Beecham, between the wars other conductors such as Geoffrey Toye were active.

Lewis Foreman

FILM MUSIC

The sound film arrived in 1928 with Al Jolson. In the UK it was the panache of Bliss's music for *Things To Come* (1935) which in its day was epoch-making. There were other composers, of course, and the most active was Arthur Benjamin, whose films included *The Man Who Knew Too Much* (1934). When Hitchcock re-made it in 1956, Bernard Herrmann incorporated Benjamin's 'Storm Clouds Cantata' for the concluding Albert Hall sequence. In 1937 Benjamin wrote the music for the first British colour feature, *Wings of the Morning*.

The experimental documentary films of the 1930s should be remembered, particularly those by the GPO Film Unit – Benjamin Britten's music for its film *Night Mail* is probably the most familiar.

But the most successful composer was Walton. His Elisabeth Bergner films, including *Escape Me Never* (1935) and *As You Like It* (1936), led on to his first wartime feature *The First of the Few*, and the *Spitfire Prelude and Fugue* from the film was soon recorded. Walton's biggest success in the cinema came with Laurence Olivier's *Henry V*, first shown in November 1944.

A host of British composers who made substantial reputations in the cinema during and after the Second World War included Richard Addinsell, William Alwyn, Hubert Bath, Bax, and Francis Chagrin. Vaughan Williams' first film score was *49th Parallel*, a story of Nazi infiltration into Canada, released in 1941, followed by *Coastal Command* in 1942, but his chief contribution came later in *Scott of the Antarctic*, subsequently elaborated into his *Sinfonia Antartica*.

Film composers from the 1940s included Alwyn, Berners, Frankel, Lambert, Rawsthorne, Ireland (with *The Overlanders*), and Brian Easdale whose music for the ballet film *The Red Shoes* contains the first use of the ondes martenot by a British composer. In the 1950s Walton, Rawsthorne, Alwyn and others had further films but most successful and prolific was a new name, Malcolm Arnold, whose 120 films included *The Sound Barrier* (1952), *Hobson's Choice* (1953), *The Bridge on the River Kwai* (which won him an Oscar) and *The Inn of the Sixth Happiness*.

Lewis Foreman

annals of British chamber music was success so immediate.' It is notable that within a very few years it was followed by sonatas by Elgar (1918), Howells (No 1, 1917; No 2, 1918; No 3, 1923), Moeran (1923), Rubbra (No 2, 1931) and Bridge (1932).

During the war programmatic associations became inescapable in a number of pieces. Thus George Butterworth's rhapsody *A Shropshire Lad* was not intended descriptively, but its fourth performance, at a Prom in September 1917 following the composer's death, invoked evocative associations of an idealised rural England. When Butterworth's friend F S Kelly, also soon to be killed, wrote his *Elegy* for string orchestra and harp in memory of Rupert Brooke, immediately after burying him on the Greek island of Skyros, the quaver and semiquaver passagework evoked the olive tree that bent over the grave. There were many memorial pieces, for example Howells' *Elegy* for viola, string quartet and strings, written in memory of a viola-playing College friend 'Bunny' Warren, and first heard at the Mons Memorial Concert in 1917. Stanford's Second Organ Sonata, completed in August 1917, concerned itself with the western front, the outer movements 'Rheims' and 'Verdun' separated by a solemn Funeral March; his orchestration of the second and third movements achieved a shortlived celebrity.

After the war, Arthur Bliss and Lord Berners exemplified the spirit of the new, soon underlined by William Walton's *jeu d'esprit*, the entertainment *Façade* in 1923. Bliss withdrew his earlier music, written in a style not unlike early Howells, and produced what he called 'essays in the exploration of sound' soon compared to the music of Les Six. In *Madam Noy* (1918), *Rhapsody* (1919), *Conversations* and *Rout* (1920), the invigoratingly noisy incidental music for *The Tempest* (1921) and a Concerto for piano with a tenor vocalise (1920 – revised as the Concerto for two pianos) he explored the possibilities of the instrumental use of voices and small ensembles. By 1922 with *A Colour Symphony* he had arrived at a mature voice which informed his life's work, and its first performance created a sensation.

Lord Berners, an eccentric aristocrat and in many ways a dilettante, had been a student of Stravinsky and Casella in Rome in 1916 while on diplomatic service. His aphoristic wartime works, including songs and piano pieces such as the *Trois petites marches funèbres*, led Stravinsky to hail him a leading British composer.

During the war, Bax, a composer in far more luxuriant style, enjoyed his most consistent run of composition while at the peak of his form. He thus appeared after 1918 with successive new works quickly establishing him a leading name. These 'brazen romantic' scores included the evocative tone poems *The Garden of Fand*, *Summer Music*, *Tintagel*, *November Woods* and the massive autobiographical *Symphonic Variations* for piano and orchestra. He would soon launch on his cycle of seven symphonies.

It was only near the end of the war that the Ballets Russes returned to London. Between September 1918 and 1929 the Diaghilev company appeared regularly, bringing both pre-war ballets and new ones, including Falla's *Le Tricorne* and, in November 1919, *Parade* with music by Satie and décor by Picasso. The critic Edwin Evans assisted Diaghilev to commission 'symphonic interludes' for the ballet, and Bax, Goossens, Howells, Berners and later Walton, appeared in the programmes with short colourful pieces.

Two generations' varied orchestral treatment of folk-song had developed almost simultaneously before the war – the early *Irish Rhapsodies* of Stanford contrasting strongly with various works of Vaughan Williams, Holst and Grainger. However, by 1917 Stanford's fifth *Irish Rhapsody* surely shows the influence of his pupil Vaughan Williams.

While the influence of folk-song may be felt in the music of Holst, Vaughan Williams and others in the inter-war years, it is largely assimilated, felt as modal colouration and in the cast of melody. E J Moeran in his rhapsodies, although writing folk-sounding tunes, only once was tempted to incorporate the opening phrase of an actual folk-song, though between 1921 and 1926 he had collected 150 songs from the country people of Norfolk. Bax, in his *Phantasy* for viola and orchestra admitted to quoting an Irish folk-tune, though in his *The Truth About the Russian Dancers* he concealed the traditional tune 'To the Maypole Haste

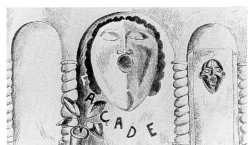

opposite top: **The studio recording of Walton's score for** *Hamlet* **with Laurence Olivier on screen, 1948**
opposite bottom: Night Mail **poster designed by Pat Keely**

above: **The curtain (painted by Frank Dobson) behind which the first performance of** *Façade* **took place. Edith and Osbert Sitwell recited the entertainment through sengerphones positioned in the mouths of the masks**
right: **William Walton, photographed by Cecil Beaton**

Away'. Even in his later music Holst still made occasional use of folk material, as in the finale of the *Fugal Concerto* of 1923, where the tune 'If all the world were paper' is made a subject of a double fugue.

Philip Heseltine once remarked about Vaughan Williams' *Pastoral Symphony* that 'it's all just a little too much like a cow looking over a gate'. Constant Lambert also spoke in this vein, and Elisabeth Lutyens in her lecture notes referred to 'the cowpat' school, a quite inaccurate generalisation, but unfortunately unforgettable and regularly quoted by lazy journalists.

In the first half of the 1920s, Bax, Berners, Bliss, Goossens, Holst, Howells, Ireland and Moeran established themselves, while Vaughan Williams continued to build on his growing reputation. In 1919 Stanford's Second Piano Concerto was given its UK premiere by Benno Moiseiwitsch, to a rapturous reception, but much

EARTHLY THINGS ABOVE
GUSTAV HOLST 1874–1934

DAVID GALLAGHER

Holst is impossible to pin down, which is one of the things that makes him so fascinating. With every piece he wrote, he seemed to want to try something new, learn something new, say something new. 'I may do something quite different tomorrow,' he told his friend, the composer W G Whittaker in 1917. Where *is* the real Holst? He published no orchestral symphonies, no string quartets, no full-length operas: no convenient pigeonholes. He preferred suites, sets of pieces. But he wasn't a miniaturist either: the depth of those pieces is out of all proportion to their length.

Fortunately we have *The Planets*. Holst's best-known music is also his biggest: among his concert works, only the *Choral Symphony* and *The Cloud Messenger* rival *The Planets* in length, size of orchestra, or kaleidoscopic range of moods. The order Holst chose for his *Planets* and musical echoes between them make this seven-movement Suite a kind of two-symphonies-in-one: Allegro, Adagio, Scherzo, Allegro, Adagio, Scherzo, Andante. Each movement, he said, encapsulates one 'constituent of our spirit', corresponding to that planet's astrological character. The seven sides of Gustav Holst?

above: **Vaughan Williams' sketch of Gustav Holst astride his trombone, 1895**
below: **Holst in his room at Barnes in 1911 painted by Millicent Woodford**

1. Mars, the Bringer of War
So shatteringly does *Mars* bring to mind the relentless, implacable horror of mechanised war, that it comes as something of a shock to discover Holst wrote it before the First World War broke out in 1914. His setting of Walt Whitman's *A Dirge for Two Veterans*, written around the same time, shares this terrible vision. Holst the pacifist? Well, not quite: like so many others in 1914 he tried to join up, but was rejected on medical grounds (short-sight and inflamed nerves in his right arm). But Holst the idealistic socialist, certainly; inspired in his twenties by both Whitman and the equally idiosyncratic socialism of William Morris. Morris's ideas – the artist as artisan, art for all, 'part of the daily life of everyone' – shaped Holst's lifelong devotion to music-teaching, even when he no longer needed the money; most famously at St Paul's Girls' School and Morley College for Working Men and Women. *Elegy (In Memoriam William Morris)*, the slow movement of Holst's *Cotswolds* Symphony (1899–1900), is one of the first musical inklings of his maturity; like *Mars*, it is founded on a rhythm repeated incessantly on one note. Such ostinatos are a Holst trademark; he used to joke that they saved wear and tear on his painful arm! But for him, rhythm was the seed of all music. Unusual rhythms are another trademark: *Mars* has five beats to the bar, but characteristically Holst makes it sound completely "right". He was already experimenting with five- and seven-beat bars at the age of 20: they grew out of his constant search for what he called 'the (or a) musical idiom of the English language'. Letting the words take their natural stress, he shaped his rhythms around them. The crucible in which Holst first forged all these elements into his individual voice was the Sanskrit *Rig Veda* – from which he set over 20 hymns, in his own English translations, between 1907 and 1912. Not vintage Holst, perhaps, but a fascinating foretaste.

2. Venus, the Bringer of Peace
The first slow movement of the *Planets* double-

symphony is the perfect antidote to the barbarism of *Mars*. Holst is often accused of being cold and unemotional: *Venus* shows him in another light. This is the Romantic who 'wrote a new love-song every week' for golden-haired, blue-eyed Isobel Harrison, the youngest soprano in his Hammersmith Socialist Choir. And who, a decade after he married Isobel in 1901, finished 40 minutes of heartfelt music despatching *The Cloud Messenger* with an affirmation of love to a wife far away.

There are other premonitions of *Venus* in *The Mystic Trumpeter* (an earlier Whitman setting from 1904); and in 1911 in the imaginative Oriental Suite *Beni Mora*, based on music Holst heard on a cycling holiday in Algeria – financed by his great friend Vaughan Williams who (unlike Holst) had a private income – and the dreamy *Invocation* for solo cello and orchestra. *Venus* has her heirs, too: the equally sensuous *Lyric Movement* with solo viola from the very end of Holst's life, and the distilled beauty of the Seven Partsongs and *A Choral Fantasia* (words by Robert Bridges, another friend). But the peace of *Venus* is most closely echoed by the Four Songs for voice and violin, inspired one summer evening in 1916, when Holst wandered into the Church in the tranquil Essex village of Thaxted and heard a woman singing and improvising her own accompaniment on a violin.

3. Mercury, the Winged Messenger
A truly mercurial scherzo: quicksilver, wing-heeled. No British composer of his time could touch Holst's fleetness of foot (he bequeathed it to Benjamin Britten). With light vitality and suggestions of more than one key and metre at once, *Mercury* darts forward into Holst's future. In *A Fugal Overture* of 1922, Holst's inquiring mind discovered neo-classicism (he would never have dreamt of using the term himself) before Stravinsky or Hindemith. He followed it up with two lithe double concertos; the gossamer scherzo of his *Choral Symphony* (to words by Keats); and his last completed work, a *Scherzo* intended for a symphony, not to mention the amazing *Terzetto* for flute, oboe and viola, each playing in a different key!

above: **Holst and Vaughan Williams on a walking tour in September 1921, probably photographed by W H Whittaker who was with them**

4. Jupiter, the Bringer of Jollity
According to his daughter Imogen, Holst intended *Jupiter* to be 'buoyant, hopeful and joyous' – which is where Vaughan Williams went wrong when he said the famous big tune in the middle didn't really 'fit'. Forget 'I vow to thee my country': Holst set it to that tune reluctantly, years later when he was too overworked to think of a new one. With the buoyant speed, orchestration and articulation Holst asks for in *Jupiter* (but conductors rarely give him!) the tune is no overblown patriotic statement, but a truly joyful, even jovial, outburst. Up and up it goes across nearly three octaves, growing from the same rising three-note phrase which is the germ of all the themes in *Jupiter*.

Holst loved a good tune, too. Vaughan Williams introduced him to folk melodies and he made many arrangements of them, both for voices and – in his beautiful *Somerset Rhapsody* – for orchestra. But he also wrote plenty of his own: in the orchestral *Songs without words*, his Suite No 1 for wind band, or his lovely carol *In the bleak midwinter*.

Carols point to another Holstian mood near the joy of *Jupiter*. Holst's religion was decidedly unorthodox, but he hit it off with the vicar at Thaxted, Conrad Noel, 'a socialist with a great sense of humour'. Through him, Holst discovered the words of the old Cornish carol 'Tomorrow shall be my dancing day'. Captivated, he wrote a joyous tune for them (*This have I done for my true love*) and searched for other texts expressing religious ecstasy through dance. A year later 'Divine Grace is dancing' in one of his greatest visionary masterpieces, *The Hymn of Jesus*.

5. Saturn, the Bringer of Old Age
The second slow movement, Holst's own favourite *Planet*, expresses his own philosophy: the march of old age is tragic, but inevitable, and it should be accepted calmly, even gladly. A life beset by ill-health confirmed Holst in a credo shaped by his early immersion in the Sanskrit *Bhagavad Gîta*: take everything as it comes. Personal property is worthless: Holst treasured only Beethoven's tuning-fork (a gift) and the key to his soundproof music room at St Paul's School, where he wrote almost all his music after 1913. 'Our only sure possession'

is Death – in the words of his astonishingly original and moving chamber opera *Savitri*, his first masterpiece, written in 1908. As well as in *Saturn*, Holst recaptures this mood in two Whitman settings – his haunting *Ode to Death* and the 'sad procession' of *A Dirge for Two Veterans*.

March; procession: another Holst hallmark. He loved walking. In his student days at the Royal College of Music he would save money by walking home the 97 miles from London to Cheltenham; later his favourite holidays were walking tours, often with Vaughan Williams or Whittaker. 'Walking always sets me thinking of new tunes,' he said – and bass lines throughout his music echo with his steps, unhurried but sure, taking everything as it comes, pain or pleasure.

6. Uranus, the Magician

The Planets' second scherzo could hardly be a greater contrast to its first, but Holst is here too: that raucous opening brass summons even spells out (in German) the musical letters of his name, GuStAv H – G, E flat, A, B. The orchestration throughout – including a completely new effect, an organ glissando – is as brilliant as anything in Stravinsky's magical ballets, as the galumphing magician rollicks around, noisily failing to find the spell he wants. Sometimes he seems to be sending up *Saturn* – a medieval alchemist, perhaps, searching hopelessly for the elixir of life.

This is the mood of *Folly's Song* in the scherzo of Holst's *Choral Symphony*, or the scherzo of his *Hammersmith* for wind band. It's Holst at the pub: the George in Hammersmith Broadway where he entertained friends with 'large steaks and draught beer in tankards'. Or *At the Boar's Head* – his one-

'"*Those who can do*"– *those who teach also do. Teaching is doing. Teaching is an art.*'

GUSTAV HOLST'S RETORT TO BERNARD SHAW'S FAMOUS JIBE

above: Holst conducting the Whitsuntide Singers in the gardens of Bishop's Palace, Chichester in 1931

act opera which 'wrote itself': one rainy day in 1924 he spotted that an old English tune fitted a speech of Falstaff's in Shakespeare's *Henry IV*, so he set all the play's tavern scenes to traditional tunes. Then there are the Chaucerian sexual shenanigans of his brief last opera, *The Wandering Scholar*. All *very* far from Holst the student, a teetotal vegetarian! To make ends meet he played trombone in theatre and dance bands: the magical effect of an unaccustomed glass of champagne once led him accidentally to play the piccolo part in the next dance! No mean trombonist, obviously: like *Uranus'* cousin, the equally incompetent Wizard in Holst's opera (and rip-roaring ballet music) *The Perfect Fool*.

7. Neptune, the Mystic

Holst himself is often called a mystic, and it's all too easy to deduce he lacked humanity, his gaze fixed on higher things, 'very near the snow line', as Arthur Bliss put it. One section of *Neptune* follows another without any return to earlier music, stretching out into eternity. But Holst said two of his most deeply mystical experiences were 'the wonderful feeling of unity with one's pupils when teaching, a feeling of contact with their minds other than the contact occasioned by speech' and 'the similar feeling of unity between musical performer and audience'. Mysticism rooted in the seemingly mundane activities of everyday life and work: another reason why teaching meant so much to Holst. Uniquely for a major composer, he spent most of his life not only teaching children and amateurs – 'real people', he called them – but writing music for them. The *St Paul's* and *Brook Green* Suites for the Girls' School string orchestra (and any winds who happened to turn up), the two wind band Suites, *A Moorside Suite* for brass band and countless works with chorus are among his warmest, most immediately appealing pieces.

Holst always had one foot firmly on the ground, even when his questing imagination explored the most rarefied regions: beyond time – as in the *Ode on a Grecian Urn* of his *Choral Symphony* – or beyond space – in *Neptune* or the still more distant song of *Betelgeuse* – or into infinity from the Dorset moorland of his friend Thomas Hardy, in what is perhaps the most perfect and individual of all his works, *Egdon Heath*.

of Parry's and Stanford's music rapidly faded from view.

The 1920s has been called the jazz age, and many musicians and their audiences were variously shocked or delighted by the influence of jazz and popular music. This is particularly found in the use of rhythm (evident in Bliss and Walton), the blues (particularly characteristic in Lambert), and the use of instruments associated with jazz (Ireland in his Piano Concerto in E flat specifies dance band mutes for the trumpets, with their characteristic plangent timbre). Indeed, interviewed before

the last night of the 1994 Proms, conductor Andrew Davis suggested that even Walton's *Belshazzar's Feast* is essentially a '20s' work when he remarked, 'one can almost see the flappers waiting in the wings'. Another '20s' effect is that of the chorus vocalising in a kind of reverie underlining the emotion of a climax. Probably deriving from Ravel's *Daphnis and Chloe* its best known use is in Vaughan Williams' utterly individual masterpiece *Flos Campi* for solo viola, chorus and orchestra, but also used, gloriously, by Bax in *Walsinghame* and by Howells in *Sine Nomine*.

The second half of the 1920s saw a number of more radical scores such as Bridge's *Enter Spring* and his chamber music which looked more to Vienna than Paris, Holst's orchestral evocations *Egdon Heath* and *Hammersmith* and Lambert's *Music for Orchestra* which contrast with the bold tunefulness of Warlock's arrangements in his *Capriol Suite*. Each is quite distinctive.

Walton soon appeared as a new voice, first with *Portsmouth Point*, a Diaghilev 'Symphonic Interlude' in June 1926, followed in November by *Siesta*. In December an orchestral suite from *Façade* appeared as an interlude in Berners' ballet *The Triumph of Neptune*. So when his Viola Concerto was acclaimed a work of genius in 1929, Walton had in fact prepared the path. It was, however, a remarkable rise to fame as an orchestral composer.

Not all the music written was heard, however. By 1930 the BBC was the principal patron of new music, and their anonymous selection panel

left: **Sir Eugene Goossens driving a Canadian train – locomotives were one of his passions**
below: **Cover design by Claude Lovat Fraser for the score of Arthur Bliss's** ***Rout***

became a major source of frustration to many. Typical is John Foulds, whose striking orchestral music made little headway. However, now that he is recorded we may appreciate what was lost, including the powerful *Dynamic Triptych* for piano and orchestra, and the striking suite *Hellas* for double string orchestra, harp and percussion, remarkable for its sonority and effect. In a letter to Adrian Boult, Foulds wrote 'Within the last two years I have submitted four works to the BBC....In each case they were rejected...[so] while my principal serious works have received the approval of some of the greatest names in the musical world, and also of practical conductors...any serious work

ROUT BY ARTHUR BLISS

For Pianoforte, Four Hands

GOODWIN & TABB, LTD.

of mine has a poor chance of winning approval...'. Composers as varied as Frank Bridge and Havergal Brian wrote similarly.

Concertos, particularly piano concertos, appeared from many leading composers. John Ireland's was probably the most successful, but Howells, Vaughan Williams, Walton, Foulds, Bax, Bridge, Rubbra, Alan Bush and Bliss all produced big works for piano and orchestra. Of particular interest is Lambert's blues-inflected Concerto with an accompaniment of just nine instruments. Benjamin Britten, by 1938 becoming well-established, was seen playing his own brilliant concerto at a Promenade concert, the publicity stressing his desire to break down the divisions of music, between light and serious.

There were fewer concertos for the violin. In 1921 Vaughan Williams' *The Lark Ascending,* although written before the war, was first heard with orchestral accompaniment. In 1925 his violin concerto was surprisingly neo-classical in style. Immediately after the Elgar there were few extended British concertos except for the Delius in 1919 (quickly followed by his Double Concerto and that for Cello). Those of Moeran, Walton and Bax were heard during the Second War, as was Britten's

below: **Sir Kenneth Clark, Director of the National Gallery, conducting a rehearsal of the *Toy Symphony* in January 1940. Among the soloists were Myra Hess and Joyce Grenfell**

Violin Concerto of 1939. Julius Harrison's *Bredon Hill,* a latter day *Lark,* briefly evoked a rural idyll of the west, of Bredon and Severn, that the British arts establishment targeted at a wartime audience at home and abroad.

The only immediate successor to Walton's Viola Concerto was Arthur Benjamin's *Romantic Fantasy* for violin, viola and orchestra. Engagingly romantic, it took its theme from an early work of Bax. Possibly the most affecting and highly charged concerto of the 30s was not acknowledged at the time. This was Bridge's *Oration* for cello and orchestra, subtitled 'concerto elegiaco'. Completed in 1930 it was twice broadcast in 1936, and then forgotten for 40 years. Here Bridge makes his great cry, grieving his inability to reconcile his wartime feelings of loss and despair, in what is surely one of the most eloquent works of its time.

Other concertos include Goossens' Oboe Concerto, written for his brother Léon, and Eric Fogg's engaging Bassoon Concerto, while Leighton Lucas's *Sinfonia Brevis* for horn and chamber group is of note for its gamelan-like use of xylophone which disconcerted Benjamin Britten at the first London performance. Light-music composers also addressed concerto writing, and Eric Coates'

THE NATIONAL GALLERY CONCERTS

When war was declared, in September 1939, all concert halls, cinemas and theatres in London were closed. Realising that people needed music more than ever before, the pianist Myra Hess obtained permission to organise concerts of chamber music in the empty National Gallery. More than 1,000 people queued for the first concert, which was given by Hess herself 'in case the whole thing should turn out to be a failure'. Sir Kenneth Clark, the director of the Gallery, wrote, 'The moment when she played the opening bars of Beethoven's *Appassionata* will always

remain for me one of the great experiences of my life: it was an assurance that all our sufferings are not in vain.'

The concerts took place every weekday from October 1939 to April 1946, and they included a vast range of music: the chamber music of Beethoven, Mozart and Brahms, Schubert songs, choral music by Byrd and Gibbons, Bach cantatas, and music by living composers such as Bliss, Vaughan Williams and Poulenc. Hess's own concerts included Mozart's complete Piano Concertos. Among the regular performers were Moiseiwitsch, Irene Scharrer and Denis Matthews, the Griller,

Stratton and Menges Quartets, and the singers Elena Gerhardt, Astra Desmond and Maggie Teyte. The concerts attracted large

audiences throughout the war, and even when the gallery was bombed they continued without interruption in a basement room. They came

to symbolise the survival of artistic values, and Myra Hess herself was admired internationally for her achievement.

Robert Philip

Saxo-rhapsody of 1936, written for the
famous virtuoso Sigurd Rascher bridged
light and serious styles, in contrast to
Haydn Wood's *Philharmonic Variations* for
cello and orchestra, very much the heir of
Tchaikovsky's *Rococo Variations*.

As the 1930s drew to a close, Bliss's
Music for Strings and Britten's *Variations on
a theme of Frank Bridge* underlined the virtuosity of British music to European audiences. New names continued to emerge,
the most striking being Alan Rawsthorne
and Michael Tippett. Rawsthorne's lithe
Symphonic Studies were first heard at the
1939 ISCM Festival in Warsaw only weeks
before Hitler's onslaught, and Michael
Tippett's *Concerto for Double String
Orchestra*, completed in June 1939,
was remarkable not only for its
energy, rhythm and memorable
invention, but also for its radiant
optimism, quite amazing when one
considers the time of its composition.

The period 1914 to 1945 is framed by
two significant British symphonies:
Vaughan Williams' *A London Symphony*
and Michael Tippett's First Symphony,
first performed in Liverpool on 10
November 1945. Between these two
there were written more than 70 symphonies of
stature by some 40 British composers (listed on
page 96). Of these symphonies a significant number achieved immediate recognition, while 37 have
now been commercially recorded, with more in
preparation. This is an astonishing achievement
for a period of 30 years and a supposedly out-
moded artistic form. It is also interesting that
some symphonies from this period were not
performed at the time, such as the first five of
Havergal Brian's eventual 32, while others were
only properly appreciated with modern recordings.

During the First World War only three
symphonies were written by British composers, by
Sir Granville Bantock (whose programmatic
Hebridean Symphony was performed in Glasgow in
1916), Thomas Dunhill and the teenage William
Baines. Yet Vaughan Williams' *Pastoral Symphony*
was evolving in its composer's mind while he was
serving in France. It was heard in 1922, the same

above: **Constant
Lambert conducting;
and the ballet prod-
uction of *The Rio Grande*
with Margot Fonteyn,
Walter Gore and
Beatrice Appleyard at
Sadler's Wells, 1935**

year as were the first symphonies of Bax and Bliss,
and Dunhill's was performed in Belgrade.

Between 1930 and 1934 Bax was the leading
British symphonist with four new symphonies.
But in 1935, the year of his Sixth, Walton's First
and Vaughan Williams' Fourth, both thought
aggressively modern, challenged his position and
were widely played and both soon recorded.

There were also choral symphonies, ranging
from Bernard van Dieren's *Chinese Symphony*, in
eight movements with words taken from Hans
Bethge's *Die chinesische Flöte* (Mahler's source for
Das Lied von der Erde), and Holst's *Choral
Symphony*, setting poems by Keats, to Bliss's
Morning Heroes. Cyril Rootham's Second, with a
choral finale, where women's voices sing 'There
shall be no more death' (from the Revelation of St
John), is dwarfed by the finale of Havergal Brian's
Gothic, a massive epic setting of the Te Deum.

After Holst the only true choral symphony,
using chorus and orchestra through four conventional movements, is Armstrong Gibbs' *Odysseus*,
doubtless inspired by Vaughan Williams' *A Sea
Symphony*, yet personal in invention and choral
writing.

The choral tradition continued, but Elgar's

Spirit of England apart, there were few lasting war-related works, though Sydney Nicholson, Alan Gray and Harold Darke might be remembered, and Cyril Rootham's *For the Fallen* has been issued on CD. Bridge's *A Prayer*, setting words by Thomas à Kempis, was not performed until 1919, and was not widely known until the Chelsea Opera Group's 1982 recording.

Although the days of the great choral festivals had passed, festivals continued at the Three Choirs (revived at Worcester in 1920) and the Norwich Triennial, revived in 1924. A remarkable choral repertoire was written between the wars, though a few scores dominate. The earliest was Holst's *The Hymn of Jesus*, first performed in 1920, receiving an ecstatic reception. Donald Tovey, not an easy man to please, wrote: 'it completely bowls me over. If anybody doesn't like it, he doesn't like life.' Nine years later Constant Lambert's *The Rio Grande*, had another tremendous reception. 'Jazz changed into music of genius' read one headline.

Also well received from its premiere in the autumn of 1930 was Bliss's 'symphony' *Morning Heroes*, his tribute to his brother Kennard and

above: Havergal Brian (right) with Hugh Maguire, leader of the BBC Symphony Orchestra, and the conductor Norman Del Mar at the first public performance of Brian's Twelfth Symphony at the 1966 Proms
left: **Michael Tippett listening to a rehearsal of *A Child of our Time* in 1945**
right: **Gerald Finzi in 1933**

their comrades from the trenches, taking words from *The Iliad*, Whitman, Li-Tai-Po, Wilfred Owen and Robert Nichols, with the significant innovation of orator rather than sung solo.

But the pivotal score was Walton's *Belshazzar's Feast* (words arranged by Osbert Sitwell from the Old Testament). This dramatic and revolutionary piece revitalised the choral tradition and dominates the period, rejuvenating the form with its blazing conviction and compact drama, first heard in 1931. Later John Ireland's *These Things Shall Be* and Vaughan Williams' *Dona Nobis Pacem* had an immediate response from a public concerned with impending war and rumours of war.

Against this repertoire Michael Tippett's oratorio *A Child of Our Time*, first performed in 1944, struck a new note, both for its contemporary relevance and for the composer's inspired use of negro spirituals in the manner of chorales. Tippett's concern is at once specific and universal. *The Times* report of its premiere noted 'Tippett has succeeded to a quite remarkable extent in creating a powerful work out of a contemplation of the evil abroad in the world of yesterday and today'.

Vaughan Williams' highly individual and surprisingly varied art underlines a characteristic feature of British choral music between the wars, and after: the way in which texts were assembled as anthologies from the great span of English literature, often juxtaposing poets born hundreds of years apart. Vaughan Williams was a master at this, a skill underlined in his *Thanksgiving for Victory*, afterwards *A Song of Thanksgiving*. Here he juxtaposes the Old Testament, Shakespeare's *Henry V* and Kipling's *Puck of Pook's Hill*, a miscellany assembled with a flair touched with genius.

Requiems for victims of war triggered powerful emotions, and it is easy to understand how Delius's *Requiem*, completed in 1914 but not performed until 1922, was rejected owing to its pagan sentiments. Not heard again until a New York performance in 1950 (given in German), Sir Charles Groves' revival in November 1965 was the first time most music lovers could make any realistic assessment of it. In contrast John Foulds' *A World Requiem*, on words ranging from Bunyan to the Hindu religious poet Kabir, was briefly a tremendous success on Armistice Night. To an emotional packed Albert Hall in 1923, it was presented by massed forces. Despite a ten-minute ovation, it was not a critical success, and it has since been forgotten.

The opposite problem dogged Havergal Brian's visionary *Gothic Symphony* which, although published in 1932, remained unperformed until 1961, and only came fully to life when massed forces were conducted by Sir Adrian Boult

below: **Rehearsing MacNeice's *Christopher Columbus* in 1942, with the BBC Symphony Orchestra and the BBC Chorus conducted by Boult and a cast headed by Laurence Olivier**

at the Albert Hall in 1966.

Other choral works now successfully revived include those by Bax, Moeran and Lambert's large-scale *Summer's Last Will and Testament*. Of the choral works of Sir George Dyson three stand out: *In Honour of the City*, a short setting of Dunbar's words perhaps better known from Walton's treatment; *The Canterbury Pilgrims*, his masterpiece, first heard in 1931 and *Nebuchadnezzar* (1935), eclipsed by the blaze of Walton's *Belshazzar*, but crowned by an ecstatic setting of the Benedicite.

The years from 1914 to 1945 saw a great flowering of songwriting. While Ivor Gurney's haunted settings were not recognised until later, Peter Warlock, John Ireland, Gerald Finzi and Armstrong Gibbs were particularly active, while a

RADIO MUSIC

Early in the history of broadcasting, producers became aware of the dramatic potential of the new sound medium, and developed new studio techniques for radio-genic productions of classic drama with newly composed incidental music, or completely through-composed pieces specifically for radio, combining orchestra, singers and actors.

Britten's music for Edward Sackville-West's *The Rescue* (1943), was the 'ne plus ultra' of this type. The music performs a function on air like scenery and even action in the theatre; it supplies a background mood, by skilful use of leitmotifs warns of the arrival of characters, and by its gestures describes unseen actions. Many composers aspired to the fusion he achieved; significantly, of the hundreds of scores produced from the 1930s to the 50s, Britten's are some of the few to

have been revived.

The list of composers reads like a *Who's Who* of the times: Vaughan Williams, Walton and Ireland, William Alwyn, Bliss, Britten, Lambert, Elizabeth Poston (whom Churchill engaged to send coded wartime messages in music) and Alan Rawsthorne. Much of this work became incorporated into major free-standing works. For example Vaughan Williams' 1942 radio version of *The Pilgrim's Progress* (with Sackville-West, and starring John Gielgud) was his fourth work based on Bunyan, prior to the opera.

Later came the great refugees, Roberto Gerhard, Walter Goehr, and Berthold Goldschmidt whose music for Shelley's *The Cenci*, eventually found its way into his prize-winning opera, *Beatrice Cenci*.

Walter Goehr was prolific throughout the 1940s and 50s. Gerhard contributed many pieces with a Latin flavour,

among them *Christopher Columbus*, celebrating the 450th anniversary of the Discovery of America. One of his most significant scores was the 1942 *Don Quixote* starring Ralph Richardson. Gerhard's music became part of his ballet, *Don Quixote*, evidence of how the BBC was able to underpin a composer's livelihood.

William Alwyn was a major contributor throughout the same period. His serious music is becoming available on CD, and his reputation as a man more associated with film and radio needs to be reassessed in the light of it.

Louis MacNeice played a crucial part in radio drama. Alwyn was among the many composers who collaborated

with him. Walton wrote the music for his renowned *Christopher Columbus* (also in 1942!). And Alan Rawsthorne provided music for *Trimalchio's Feast*, MacNeice's adaptation of Petronius' *Satyricon*. Among Rawsthorne's most ambitious scores was a 1941 production of *The Golden Cockerel*.

Christopher de Souza

TOWARD THE UNKNOWN REGION

RALPH VAUGHAN WILLIAMS 1872–1958

ALAIN FROGLEY

More than most, Vaughan Williams' life and music are riven with extraordinary paradoxes. Here was the honorary high-priest of the pastoral cult who could be utterly enraptured by his first sight of New York City. A stubborn agnostic and great-nephew of Charles Darwin, he nevertheless wrote some of the greatest Christian hymn-tunes of all time ('For all the Saints' and 'Come down, O Love Divine' to name just two). Scion of the professional, privileged elite he became a lifelong socialist, and although his music is regarded as quintessentially English, it was admired by Ravel, Rachmaninov, Bartók, Sibelius, and Bernstein among others.

Some of the contradictions are typical of the late-Victorian era in which the composer grew up; others are highly idiosyncratic. Some are primarily the invention of critics and image-makers. The deeply misleading co-option of Vaughan Williams' music and person into the service of the narrow view of English national identity – pastoral, parochial, and emotionally buttoned-up – that was so strong from the 1920s to the 1950s, and remains a persistent force even today, has been decidedly double-edged. It contributed to the critical acclaim and popularity Vaughan Williams experienced during his lifetime, but guaranteed a strong back-lash against his music during the anti-Establishment years of the 1960s. The pendulum has swung back towards the centre now, but,

below: **Ralph Vaughan Williams with the American conductor Leopold Stokowski in 1957**

although popular with audiences and record-buyers, Vaughan Williams has still to receive his due in terms of balanced critical appraisal.

Part of the problem is that, in the main, we hear only a small selection from a very extensive output. Works such as *The Lark Ascending*, *Serenade to Music* and the *Fantasia on a Theme by Thomas Tallis* are indeed beautiful (and also remarkably original, something which is often overlooked). Yet they represent only one side of the composer's work. As with his American contemporary Charles Ives, some of the paradoxes in Vaughan Williams' musical and personal nature stemmed from an unusually broad-minded and affirmative attitude to both life and music. This 'extraordinary ordinary man', to use Michael Kennedy's telling phrase, encompassed in his music a wide range of experience, worked in a huge variety of genres (everything from folk-song arrangements to film music), and continued to experiment right up to the end of his long life, which spanned the period from Wagner to Boulez. To take just the nine symphonies, the backbone of the Vaughan Williams *oeuvre*: here we encounter an enormous range of subject matter and style, stretching from the soaring vocal lines and passionate Elgarian opulence of the *Sea Symphony*, first performed in 1910, to the jagged contours and kaleidoscopic orchestration of the bleak *Sinfonia Antartica* (based on the music Vaughan Williams wrote for the 1948 film *Scott of the Antarctic*).

The path to artistic maturity was long and hard. After rigorous academic study with Parry, Stanford and Wood, at the Royal College of Music and at Cambridge (where he also read History), Vaughan Williams reached his early thirties still feeling that he had no sure sense of direction as a composer. The biggest problem was the lack of a well-established native tradition, British music having been in the doldrums for much of the 19th century. His close friend Gustav Holst wrote to him: 'Don't you think we ought to victimize Elgar? Write to him first and then bicycle to Worcester and see him *a lot*?' Yet although Elgar

offered symbolic inspiration, as an English composer who had found an individual voice and had achieved recognition both at home and abroad, his music did not ultimately offer a real way forward for these two restless young men.

The breakthrough for Vaughan Williams came with his discovery of English folk-song, and the highly individual imprint this left on his own music. When he heard 'Bushes and Briars' sung by an Essex labourer in December 1903, it was a revelation. He straightaway set about collecting folk-songs in the field, and celebrated his discoveries in works such as the three orchestral *Norfolk Rhapsodies* (two were later withdrawn) and, a little later, the *Five English Folk-Songs*, published in 1913, perhaps the composer's most imaginative and individual folk-song arrangements. He also adapted a number of folksongs for *The English Hymnal*, the editorship of which he took on in 1904. Both folk-song and hymn-tunes were crucial to Vaughan Williams' search for a musical language that was fresh and direct in expression, particularly in the area of melody, and that was also in some way distinctively English. It is striking that throughout his life he always referred to his compositions, even large-scale works such as symphonies and operas, as 'tunes'.

Nevertheless, the folk-song influence on Vaughan Williams' music has often been exaggerated: it was usually a matter of emulating certain abstract attributes rather than quoting a tune. Another important stimulus to his development was British art music of earlier centuries. He learned much from the contrapuntal methods and harmonic language of the great Tudor composers, and from the vigorous word-setting of Purcell. But foreign influences were equally essential to Vaughan Williams' development: the music of his beloved J S Bach, the techniques of development and transition perfected by Brahms and Wagner, the utopian and metrically adventurous poetry of Walt Whitman, and, finally, the refined orchestral mastery of Debussy and Ravel.

As with all great artists, though, the unmistakable voice of Vaughan Williams can always be heard, whatever the influence. In 1908, after three months of study with Ravel, this voice began to ring out loud and clear, and in the *Fantasia on a Theme by Thomas Tallis* (1910) one senses that rare and supreme joy of genius at last finding the

means and confidence with which to express itself fully and in its own unique terms. The rapt contemplation of the opening is gradually animated by a ground-swell that builds to a searing climax; the masterly, unforced manner in which movement grows out of stasis set a distinctive model for Vaughan Williams' mature art. This is one of the great masterpieces of early 20th-century music. In terms of Vaughan Williams' overall artistic philosophy, however, the key work of this period is *A London Symphony*, first performed in 1914. True to his credo that the composer must 'make his art an expression of the whole life of the community', *A London Symphony* not only reflects the sights and sounds of the capital, with its hansom-cab bells and street vendors' cries, but also seems to comment, sometimes in celebration, but often darkly and painfully, on the social and spiritual state of the nation.

below: **Portrait of Vaughan Williams by Gerald Kelly**

The creative spring tide that had begun around 1908 was dammed by the outbreak of the Great War. Vaughan Williams saw active service in both the artillery and ambulance corps. By a great good fortune, though, he suffered neither serious physical injury nor the debilitating psychological damage that wrecked his pupil Ivor Gurney, along with so many others.

To many young English composers his music seemed to have brought back to life, and so to have made creatively accessible once again, a native tradition submerged since the end of the 17th century. As well as lecturing, editing, and adjudicating competitions, he taught composition at the Royal College of Music during the 1920s and 30s. Even more importantly, though, he led by example in a stream of large-scale and innovative works. Although only two of the symphonies were written during this period, together they give an idea of his expressive range. The Fourth, a product of the early 1930s, is violent and tumultuous; its

below: John Piper's original designs for the Sadler's Wells production of *Job* based on William Blake's drawings, revived recently by the Royal Ballet

creator said of it, 'I don't know whether I like it, but it's what I meant'. *A Pastoral Symphony*, composed almost a decade earlier, is muted and restrained. But cold winds and dark clouds cross the landscape. The composer revealed in later years that the origins of the work went back to the war-torn landscape of northern France, not the peaceful Cotswolds with which many early critics associated it.

Vaughan Williams' pastoral vein is nearly always shot through with a painful sense of loss, and of man's ambivalent place in a fallen world. But his music also looks continually beyond this world. He viewed art as something that opens 'the magic casements' to worlds beyond, and, although an agnostic, he most often chose to express this vision in terms of the Christian, and particularly biblical, imagery with which he had grown up. The symphonies have unfortunately tended to overshadow other

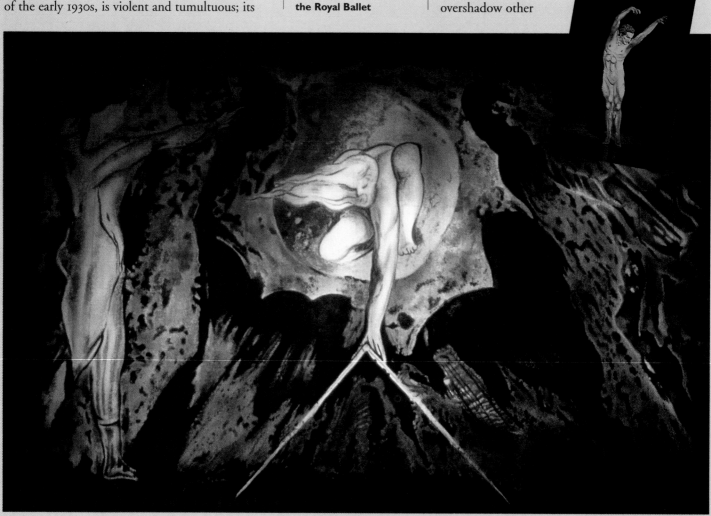

major works from the inter-war years. The oratorios *Sancta Civitas* and *Dona Nobis Pacem* (the latter strikingly anticipating Britten's *War Requiem*), along with the riotously earthy *Five Tudor Portraits*, show the strength and variety of Vaughan Williams' approach to the large-scale choral work. In the instrumental field the *Concerto Accademico* and the fascinating Piano Concerto in C major suggest parallels with certain continental contemporaries, particularly Bartók. The ballet score *Job*, inspired by William Blake's illustrations of the biblical story, is one of Vaughan Williams' greatest masterpieces. Its haunting luminosity captures with uncanny precision the dream-like quality of Blake's vision, and the composer conjures an almost unbearable sense of paradise lost. The musical symbolism used to dramatize the opposition of Good and Evil went on to resonate throughout Vaughan Williams' later music.

But the most deeply buried treasure is to be found in the five completed operas. They very rarely receive professional productions, but they reveal an inexhaustible well of supple lyrical expression (the composer's first operatic effort, *Hugh the Drover*, is full of marvellous tunes) and – contrary to much critical opinion – a fine sense of theatre and of musical drama. Of his operatic progeny, it is surely *The Pilgrim's Progress* that Vaughan Williams would most have wanted to survive. Bunyan's moral fervour and sense of spiritual quest were central to Vaughan Williams' own philosophy, and he worked intermittently for over 40 years on setting this classic religious allegory, completing it only in 1951. Yet arguably his greatest opera is also his bleakest. *Riders to the Sea*, first performed in 1937, is a virtually word-for-word setting of J M Synge's play, a Hardy-like tale of stoic resignation in the face of implacable Nature and of Fate. The brooding, unrelenting atmosphere intensifies in masterly fashion as the opera approaches its tragic and inevitable outcome.

Some of the musical terrain touched upon in these operas is also explored in the two symphonies written around the years of the Second World War. The radiantly affirmative Fifth Symphony, first performed in 1943, shares musical material with the Bunyan stage work and inhabits a similar emotional world. The Sixth, premiered

above: **Penguin Dance, drawing made by Ursula Vaughan Williams during recordings of the** *Sinfonia Antartica.* **'There were so often breaks in recording sessions at the Kingsway Hall while underground trains rushed beneath us – and I am a doodler … but how Adrian Boult managed to preserve this, and give it, with other papers, to the British Library, I do not know'.** below: **Vaughan Williams' sketch of himself perched on a pipe, in a letter to Holst, 1895**

four years later, pushes even further than *Riders to the Sea* along the dark side of the composer's expressive spectrum, progressing from an opening of terrifying ferocity to a finale of exhausted desolation, a course that critics – but not the composer – were quick to link to the war and its aftermath.

Vaughan Williams enjoyed an Indian summer in the last few years of his life, and was enormously prolific for a composer in his eighties. Some of the impetus no doubt came from the happiness of his second marriage, to the poet and writer Ursula Wood, which began in 1953 (his first wife had died in 1951). The composer's apparently unflagging energy was conspicuous during his third and final trip to the USA, made in the autumn of 1954. He lectured and conducted from coast to coast, and was feted enthusiastically wherever he went. The widespread view that Vaughan Williams' music is too English for export is dramatically refuted by its popularity in America; this was at its height in the 1950s, and star conductors such as Mitropoulos, Szell and Stokowski competed hotly for the premieres of the last three symphonies. The compact and subtle Eighth Symphony, often mistaken for a light work, was a runaway success in the US.

This late harvest also includes the fine Violin Sonata, *An Oxford Elegy*, the Christmas cantata *Hodie*, and the Tuba Concerto (two major works, a cello concerto and the opera *Thomas the Rhymer*, were left in draft at the composer's death). The music of Vaughan Williams' last decade has been consistently underrated. Here he effected a complex synthesis of the extreme expressive polarities that had earlier set at odds works such as the Fifth and Sixth Symphonies, creating a world of ambiguous and constantly shifting emotional perspectives. Although there are 'dark sayings' in this post-Hiroshima music, despair is not allowed to have the final word. The apparent glimpse of heaven with which the Ninth Symphony ends is a leap of faith – it is not the inevitable, expected outcome of the sombre and troubled course which the work has followed up to this point. Yet within the uncompromising integrity of Vaughan Williams' vision, this affirmation of hope hardly seems like an easy way out. Here is surely a message that can speak to us all.

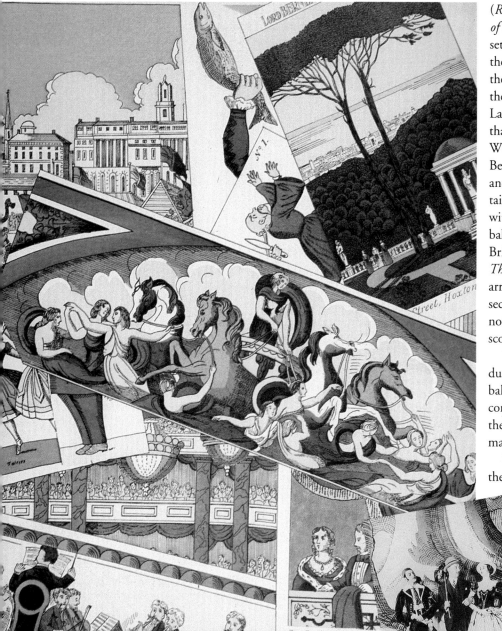

(*Romeo and Juliet*) and Lord Berners' *The Triumph of Neptune*, with book by Sacheverell Sitwell and set inspired by the celebrated Pollock's model theatre. Diaghilev's death left a vacuum which, in the UK, was filled by the Carmargo Society, soon the Vic-Wells Ballet, under the direction of Lambert. They presented a succession of works that quickly assumed classic status – Vaughan Williams' *Job*, Gavin Gordon's *The Rake's Progress*, Berners' *A Wedding Bouquet*, Bliss's *Checkmate*, and Lambert's own *Horoscope*. The ballet maintained momentum during the war, though often with two pianos rather than orchestra, when new ballets had music by Bliss, Lambert, Berners, Britten and Walton, the last with the unsuccessful *The Quest*, at the time upstaged by his own Bach arrangements, *The Wise Virgins*. In 1944 Bliss's second major ballet, *Miracle in the Gorbals* was notable for its contemporary setting and arresting score.

There were other touring ballet companies during the war, and, in Scotland, Erik Chisholm's ballet *The Forsaken Mermaid* was conducted by its composer with Anglo-Polish Ballet. After the war there would be an explosion of creativity with many new ballet scores.

The loss of the Covent Garden seasons during the First War stimulated the development of British opera. Between 1914 and 1918 new operas included Liza Lehmann's *Everyman*, Stanford's *The Critic* and Ethel Smyth's *The Boatswain's Mate*. While these are comparatively unknown, they have been revived since the war. Now totally forgotten is J E Barkworth's *Romeo and Juliet*, first given in 1916.

At Glastonbury, Rutland Boughton's festival persisted from 1914 until 1927, featuring his own operas, but also others such as Edgar Bainton's *Oithona* and Clarence Raybould's *The Sumida River*, the latter based on a Japanese No-play, anticipating Britten's *Curlew River*. Boughton's *The Immortal Hour* had a record-breaking run in London after the war, while his nativity opera, *Bethlehem*, often performed, precipitated a scandal when presented in modern dress in 1926. In 1924 Boughton's *Alcestis* appeared at Covent Garden and *The Queen of Cornwall* at Liverpool in 1927.

recent CD collection reminds us that Howells also wrote delightfully. His *In Green Ways* is particularly effective with orchestral accompaniment. In 1936 Britten's *Our Hunting Fathers* made virtuoso demands on the orchestra, followed by *Les Illuminations* and the *Serenade for tenor, horn and strings* in 1943. With string orchestra, the striking personal voice of Finzi's intoxicating *Dies Natalis* was heard in 1940, though some of the songs dated from 1926.

Diaghilev commissioned two British composers to produce ballets: the 19-year-old Constant Lambert

above:
Front cover of the piano score of Berners' ballet *The Triumph of Neptune* (1926)
above right: **Lord Berners with dancers Serge Lifar and Alexandra Danilova on the set of *The Triumph of Neptune***

In London in the 1920s new British operas included Gustav Holst's *The Perfect Fool* (at Covent Garden), Armstrong Gibbs' comic operas *The Blue Peter* (at the RCM) and *Midsummer Madness* (at the Lyric Hammersmith), Ethel Smyth's *Entente Cordiale* (at the RCM) and in 1929 Eugene Goossens' harmonically taut one-acter *Judith*.

Vaughan Williams remained a thread running through British opera and *The Shepherd of the Delectable Mountains* (later incorporated in *The Pilgrim's Progress*), *Hugh the Drover*, and *Sir John in Love* were all staged, followed in the 1930s by *The Poisoned Kiss* and *Riders to the Sea*.

However, quite a few new British operas were produced outside London, several overseas. Delius's *Fennimore and Gerda* was staged in Frankfurt in 1919; it would not be seen in the UK until 1968. Stanford's last opera *The Travelling Companion*, newly published under the Carnegie publication scheme, was seen in Liverpool and in 1930 was the only opera chosen by Michael Tippett for the Barn Theatre, Oxted. It was given a full production by Sadlers Wells in April 1935. Other overseas productions included Lord Berners' comedy *Le Carrosse du Saint-Sacrement* in Paris in

above: Rutland Boughton
below: First staged in Birmingham in 1924, Granville Bantock's *The Seal Woman* wove 20 of Marjorie Kennedy-Fraser's *Songs of the Hebrides* into a charmingly original chamber opera. The photograph shows Bantock, Adrian Boult, Kennedy-Fraser (who also took the title role), designer Paul Shelving and Barry Jackson

1924, Cyril Scott's sorcerer's apprentice story *The Alchemist*, composed during the war and produced in Essen in 1925 and Albert Coates' *Samuel Pepys* in Munich in 1929. Later when Coates' *Pickwick* was seen at Covent Garden in 1936 it was of particular interest for the symphonic interludes, their style surely paralleling Shostakovich's *Lady Macbeth of Mtsensk* which Coates had recently produced for the BBC.

Between 1930 and the outbreak of war the number grew, though none has commanded the stage in the longer term. The most successful were comic operas, including Thomas Dunhill's *Tantivy Towers* which ran for nearly six months in 1931, and Walter Leigh's bubbling *The Pride of the Regiment* (1931) and *Jolly Roger* (1933). Other comic operas included Alfred Reynolds' *Derby Day*

WOMEN COMPOSERS

The comparative success of women composers before the First World War continued after 1914. Bournemouth, where Dan Godfrey had given 24 performances of scores by eight women between 1893 and 1913, was reinforced as a centre of influence when the Belgian composer Juliet Folville, professor at the Liège Conservatoire, settled there as a refugee. Her piano concerto was produced in 1916 and on three further occasions. Between 1914 and 1934 when he retired, Godfrey gave a further 97 performances of orchestral works by 25 women. Over the succeeding half-century the totals would be tiny.

In April 1924 Godfrey gave the first ever concert of orchestral works by British women composers, including Smyth, Susan Spain-Dunk, Dora Bright, R Fox-Reeve, and Dorothy Howell. Apart from Dame Ethel few of the composers Godfrey played are known today, even as names, though several were also featured by Sir Henry Wood at the Proms. Most successful was Dorothy Howell, whose *Lamia* had been 'a very great success' at Liverpool in 1919 and was soon followed by the ballet music *Koong Shee* and her piano concerto in 1923.

Later other women composers emerged, notably Elizabeth Maconchy, Grace Williams, Ruth Gipps, Phyllis Tate and Elisabeth Lutyens. Maconchy went abroad with a travelling scholarship in 1929, and the Prague Philharmonic, with Erwin Schulhoff as soloist, gave her piano concerto, afterwards taken up by Harriet Cohen. In 1930 Wood gave her suite *The Land* at the Proms. Other works followed with performances at ISCM festivals and elsewhere.
Lewis Foreman

(words by A P Herbert), and Arthur Benjamin's one-acter *The Devil Take Her*, a great success at the RCM in 1931. Lighthearted though spare was Holst's *The Wandering Scholar*. Less successful were grand operas such as Tovey's static *The Bride of Dionysus* (Edinburgh, 1931), and Lawrance Collingwood's *Macbeth* at Sadler's Wells in 1934. Again Frank Bridge was not appreciated at the time, but his nativity opera *The Christmas Rose*, coloured by his later harmonic idiom, is affecting.

In the summer of 1935 *Iernin* by the 21-year-old George Lloyd appeared from nowhere and had a short successful run at London's Lyceum Theatre. The BBC 1986 revival, now on CD, gave a good feel for its magic. Three years later Lloyd's opera *The Serf* was seen at Covent Garden before touring to Liverpool and Glasgow. Eugene Goossens' *Don Juan de Mañara* was produced at Covent Garden soon after the Coronation in 1937. One critic dubbed it the opera without tunes, but this is unfair and a 1959 BBC revival underlined the work's dramatic command.

Havergal Brian's *The Tigers*, a satire on army experiences in the First World War (the Tigers are a regiment of conscripts), was written between the last years of the war and the early 1930s and

below: Poster for the original run of George Lloyd's Celtic opera, *Iernin*

requires a huge cast and elaborate staging. Considered for production in Dresden, Fritz Busch's interest evaporated with the Nazis. The full

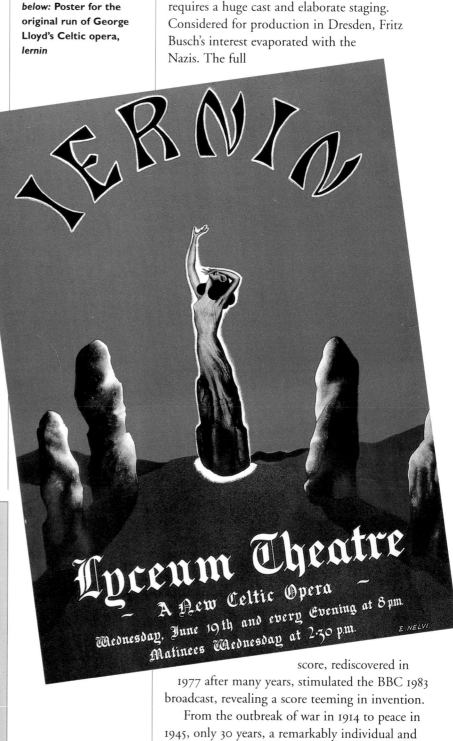

score, rediscovered in 1977 after many years, stimulated the BBC 1983 broadcast, revealing a score teeming in invention.

From the outbreak of war in 1914 to peace in 1945, only 30 years, a remarkably individual and varied repertoire was created by a wide range of composers who established personal idioms now recognised world-wide as English. Only when viewed from the end of the century is it possible to appreciate the scale of their achievement, an appreciation facilitated by a large library of recordings mostly made between the 1970s and today.

BRITISH COMPOSERS OF SYMPHONIES BETWEEN 1914 AND 1945	
William Baines	Thomas Dunhill
Sir Granville Bantock	George Dyson
Stanley Bate	Armstrong Gibbs
Sir Arnold Bax	Ruth Gipps
W H Bell [South African]	Eugene Goossens
Arthur Benjamin	Victor Hely-Hutchinson
Lennox Berkeley	Joseph Holbrooke
Arthur Bliss	Gustav Holst
Rutland Boughton	John Ivimey
York Bowen	George Lloyd
Alexander Brent-Smith	John McEwen
Havergal Brian	Frank Merrick
Benjamin Britten	E J Moeran
Alan Bush	R O Morris
Adam Carse	Edmund Rubbra
Erik Chisholm	Bernard Stevens
Hubert Clifford [Australian]	Michael Tippett
Christian Darnton	Sir Donald Tovey
	Bernard Van Dieren
	Arnold van Wyk [South African]
	Ralph Vaughan Williams
	William Walton
	Stanley Wilson

II

BACK TO THE FUTURE

MUSIC AFTER THE SECOND WORLD WAR

1945–1963

STEPHEN JOHNSON

Germany surrendered on the 7th of May 1945; Japan followed three months later. Immediately the *Daily Express* announced a competition to find a musical work worthy to celebrate the allied victory. The winner was *A Symphony of Liberation* by the 29-year-old Bernard Stevens, a confident, thematically-memorable work, as its recent revival on CD has shown. But after that it is hard to find any kind of British concert work on the subject of the War. Vaughan Williams' turbulent Sixth Symphony could be cited (though the composer rejected the 'war' tag), as could Britten's Canticle III, *Still Falls the Rain*, a setting of Edith Sitwell's famous meditation on Christ's sufferings amid 'the fires of the world, – dark-smirched with pain'. And then there is the Violin Concerto 'in memory of the six million' (1951) by Benjamin Frankel, an enigmatic but deeply felt work, surprisingly neglected. Otherwise it was not until Britten's *War Requiem* (1961) and Tippett's opera *King Priam* (1961) – both premiered during the 1962 festivities for the opening of the new Coventry Cathedral – that British composers appeared ready to confront the horror of war directly. Even then, neither Tippett nor Britten refers specifically to the Second World

**Chapter opener shows,
top right: Act III of the
original production of
Tippett's *King Priam*
middle left: Tippett and
Britten on the former's
60th birthday in January
1965
bottom right: Costume
design by Kenneth Green
for the first production
of *Peter Grimes***

***right:* Poster for the
Festival of Britain in
1951
left: Rehearsal for the
world premiere of
Britten's *War Requiem*
in Coventry Cathedral
in 1962**

War: Britten's use of poems by Wilfred Owen shifts the focus more towards the 1914–18 War, and Tippett's plot is based, if somewhat loosely, on Homer's *Iliad*.

This may seem less surprising if one considers the general mood in Britain in the immediate post-war years. Understandably, people appear to have wanted to put the memory of strife and devastation behind them as quickly as possible and set their faces hopefully towards the future. In 1945 the country voted in a new Labour Government, which quickly set in motion a housing programme, large-scale industrial nationalisation and the creation of the National Health Service. The Arts Council of Great Britain was set up in 1945, and the forward-looking, celebratory Festival of Britain

followed in 1951; and the crowning moment – literally – of this new determined optimism came in 1953 with the Coronation of Elizabeth II, for which Walton wrote his opulent neo-Elgarian March *Orb and Sceptre*. There was talk of a 'new Elizabethan age', with Britain once again at the head of nations.

The question of how British music might move forward after the War exercised several writers. A book published in 1946, *British Music of Our Time*, ends with a chapter entitled 'What Now?' Its author, Robin Hull, selects eight British composers whom he considers suitably 'forward-looking', and attempts to identify the specific challenges they face. 'The revolt against late romanticism has entered upon a second, consolidating phase.' The first phase, represented by Schoenberg's rejection of tonality and championing of the equal treatment of the 12 notes of the chromatic scale is, says Hull, over and done with. Far from changing the traditional musical language irrevocably, Schoenberg enriched it, increasing the possibilities open to the modern composer, who is most likely to choose a 'middle course' between Schoenbergian 12-tone serialism and traditional major-minor tonality.

As an anticipation of what was to come in this country, Hull's chapter is strikingly prescient. It also outlines – unconsciously this time – the vast gulf that separated musical Britain from the progressive mainstream on the continent. In France, Germany, even in Italy, post-Schoenbergian serialism had entered an even more radical phase. For the young Pierre Boulez for instance it offered the possibility of systematic control of all the dimensions of music and the 'annihilation of the will of the composer'. And for many, Boulez very much included, it had acquired a new political dimension (undreamed of by Schoenberg himself), associated with the intellectual wing of the extreme left.

below: **Andrzej Panufnik with his daughter Roxanna, now also a composer**
small picture: **Roberto Gerhard in 1954**

Post-war Britain also saw the rise of a generation of composers with radical left-wing beliefs: Bernard Stevens was one, Ronald Stevenson and Robert Simpson are two more striking examples, and there was the veteran communist composer Alan Bush, whose music had been temporarily banned by the BBC during the war on account of his political affiliations (the ban was lifted when Vaughan Williams protested vigorously on Bush's behalf). But of these four highly contrasted composers, only Stevens attempted any kind of consistent engagement with Schoenbergian 12-note serialism (Simpson, for one, found it abhorrent), and in Stevens' case the results are still recognisably tonal. Hindemith and the more emotionally

IMMIGRANT COMPOSERS

The political turmoil of the 1930s and 40s uprooted many prominent or rising European composers. Some went to America, others found Britain secure but closer to home. These composers often found that Britain could be surprisingly neglectful. Before he defected from Communist Poland in 1954, Andrzej Panufnik was his country's star composer, but – as one Polish writer put it – 'he went from No 1 in Poland to no-one in Britain'. The modernist 1960s and 70s were the low point for Panufnik, but over the last decade interest has grown steadily. In some ways works like the choral *Universal Prayer* (1969), the intense, boldly theatrical *Sinfonia Sacra* (1963) and the exquisite choral miniature *Song to the Virgin Mary* (1964) anticipate the currently fashionable 'Faith Minimalists' – John Tavener, Henryk Górecki and Arvo Pärt – though Panufnik's emotional and

technical resources are far greater, and his achievement may turn out to be more lasting.

Roberto Gerhard, Spanish-born but of French-Swiss descent, came to Britain after the Spanish Civil War in 1939. He too was neglected in the 1950s, but at the same time he seems to have experienced an artistic rebirth, in which ideas of his teacher Schoenberg are developed with tremendous energy and imagination. The First Symphony (1953) is a major landmark, looking forward to such astonishingly exuberant late masterpieces as the *Concerto for Orchestra* (1965) and the 'astrological' chamber works *Gemini, Libra* and *Leo* (1966, 1968 and 1969).

The German-born Berthold Goldschmidt fled Berlin in 1935. His Jewish ancestry and the Nazis' branding of his controversial opera *Der gewaltige Hahnrei* ('The Magnificent Cuckold') as *Entartete Kunst* (Degenerate Art) made staying impossible. At first Goldschmidt attracted attention in this country; his opera *Beatrice Cenci* won him an Arts Council Prize at the Festival of Britain in 1951. But neglect and creative near-silence were to follow. It is only with the recent revival and recording of *Der gewaltige Hahnrei* that Goldschmidt's reputation has again begun to rise.

Others survive almost solely as names. The Hungarian Mátyás Seiber, who also came to England in 1935, is mostly remembered as an out-

standing composition teacher, though his Joyce-based cantata *Ulysses* (1947) has been revived with some success. The current neglect of the Austrian Hans Gál, another refugee from the Nazis, is hard to explain. His beautifully crafted, Brahmsian chamber works, deliberately unaffected by Schoenberg, ought to appeal strongly in these modernist-phobic times. Franz Reizenstein, who left Berlin a year before Goldschmidt (1934), had more success here, notably with the choral *Voices of the Night* (1951) and the radio opera *Anna Kraus* (1952). But his most enduring work is the brilliantly funny pastiche *Let's Fake an Opera*, written for the 1958 Hoffnung Interplanetary Music Festival.

Stephen Johnson

charged Ernest Bloch are clearer stylistic influences, as they are on quite a number of British composers at this time. Much the same could be said of the works Benjamin Frankel wrote from the mid-50s onwards, and especially after his First Symphony (1958) – ironically, given that by then he and Stevens belonged to bitterly opposed political camps. But Frankel's exploitation of the tensions between tonality and 12-tone serialism is more explicit – too explicit, some might say, though it can also be dramatically or expressively telling.

Atonal serialists of a true Schoenbergian cast are difficult to find in the post-war period. Two names stand out however. For some musical Britons, Humphrey Searle represented an acceptable face of Schoenbergianism: non-tonal, but like Frankel and Stevens expressive in a broadly familiar, late-romantic manner; on the whole though, Searle's music doesn't seem to have worn well. For Elisabeth Lutyens the reverse has been true. In the 1950s, when she produced some of her most imaginative and technically advanced music, she suffered almost total neglect. Old-fashioned misogyny may have been partly to blame (though the post-war period brought successes for some British women composers, notably Elizabeth Maconchy), as might her notorious outspokenness. But as the composer Anthony Payne puts it, Lutyens' use of 12-note techniques 'seems to have

above: **Robert Simpson**
below left: **Alan Bush in 1975**

been considered almost morally reprehensible by some in England in the 1950s'. Nowadays she is seen by many, especially those on the progressive wing, as a courageous and uniquely inspired pioneer.

From the continental ultra-modernist point of view the feature of British musical life that would probably have appeared most deplorable was the continuing rise of the traditional symphony. In this respect, Britain was showing more in common with the USA, Scandinavia, even the Soviet Union, than with its European neighbours. For Boulez, Stockhausen and their adherents, this hopelessly bourgeois form, with its inescapable romantic-heroic associations, had become at best an irrelevance, at worst an obscenity. But many British composers, encouraged no doubt by the triumphant success of Walton's First Symphony (1935) and of Vaughan Williams' Fourth, Fifth and Sixth (1935, 1943 & 1947), found it a vehicle for their kind of 'forward-looking' thoughts. Walton himself seems to have found his First Symphony a hard act to follow. His long-awaited Second (1960) disappointed many critics at its first appearance, but it has more admirers today, as do the possibly still finer Cello Concerto (1956) and the orchestral *Variations on a Theme by Hindemith* (1963). But while Walton hesitated before tackling the medium again, others were more prolific. The term 'Cheltenham Symphony', often used caustically in the modernist 1960s and 70s, was coined to describe the typical product of the Cheltenham Festival (founded 1945). To many today the label brings unavoidable associations with an orchestral sound redolent of London fogs, austerity menus and the creaky film acting and *mise en scène* so wickedly lampooned by Harry Enfield.

Time may change our perspectives of course, but for today's ears the symphonies of once-important figures such as Peter Racine Fricker, Alan Rawsthorne and even the Schoenbergian Searle can sound fatally dated. Of these Rawsthorne may have the strongest chance of survival. His Third Symphony – written in 1964, but in many ways a late flowering of Cheltenham symphonism (it was premiered at Cheltenham) – illustrates his virtues and flaws well. The first movement and finale gesture awkwardly towards less severe forms of 1950s modernism, but the middle two movements – a darkly atmospheric sarabande and a mysterious, fleeting scherzo – show a high level of inspiration and technical assurance. Rawsthorne is at his most appealing in the Overture *Street Corner* (1944) and the two Piano Concertos (1942 & 1951, the second a Festival of Britain commission), and these are occasionally revived.

Other composers whose symphonies have aroused more recent interest include William Alwyn and the Welshman Daniel Jones, composer of the incidental music for the Italia Prize-winning original 1954 radio production of Dylan Thomas' *Under Milk Wood*. It is the secureness of the symphonic working-out that impresses most, despite a genuine, unforced depth of feeling. Alwyn in particular shows moments of real poetry, sometimes with a more than faintly Gallic flavour, especially in his chamber music. Not everyone agrees that either composer's musical voice is quite distinctive enough but Alwyn is now well represented on CD, and he is certainly worth exploring.

One could hardly accuse the symphonies of Tippett, Edmund Rubbra, Robert Simpson or Malcolm Arnold of a lack of distinctive character. Rubbra has been criticised for his orchestral sound ('mud and porridge' was one choice description),

above: **Daniel Jones in 1951**
right: **Elisabeth Lutyens**
left: **Alan Rawsthorne in 1949**

especially in some of the earlier symphonies. But from the Fifth (1949) onwards, greyness or coarseness increasingly gives way to moments of fine orchestral imagination – soulful clarinet and cold muted horns in the slow 'Canto' movement of No 6 (1955), or the strikingly Mahlerian timbres of oboes, horns and harp in the opening of No 7 (1957). And for many, the deep meditative seriousness of Rubbra's music, with its unselfconscious use of elements from Tudor polyphony and the Elizabethan madrigalists, rewards persistence.

There can be no complaints about Simpson's or Arnold's handling of the orchestra. Both are first-rate technicians, capable of creating unforgettable sonorities. One thinks of Simpson's granite-like wind-chords and quiet, spacious string textures, or Arnold's gorgeous imitation of cocktail lounge *muzak* in the first movement of his Fourth

Symphony (1960). But their originality goes way beyond sound-colour. While both composers strengthened and enriched their techniques in reaction to the modernist tendencies of the 1960s and 70s (with which they felt profoundly out of sympathy), all the basic elements were there from the start. Simpson's first three symphonies (1951, 1956 & 1962) show the freshness, energy and powerful command of symphonic argument that he has developed throughout his career, and the first three quartets (1952, 1953 & 1954) are in their more intimate way equally rewarding.

Where Simpson's style seems grittily single-minded, Arnold's can be cornucopia-like, glancing from Mahler to Sibelius to 50s pop music and Ealing Comedy film-scores with startling quickness. Arnold is a virtuoso at adopting popular

The Tide Will Turn!

THE OPERAS OF BRITTEN, TIPPETT AND WALTON

MICHAEL KENNEDY

The success of *Peter Grimes* 50 years ago spurred a new generation of British composers to regard the opera house as a place where their talents could at last be favourably deployed. Most of those who acclaimed *Peter Grimes* as Britain's first opera (meaning first indisputable masterpiece) also believed it was Britten's first opera and therefore all the more remarkable. But there had been in 1940–1 *Paul Bunyan*, written for students while the composer was living in the United States. It has a racy and topical libretto by W H Auden. Britten's music not only anticipates much of what he was to write later but shows how thoroughly he had absorbed an American idiom reflecting Gershwin, Copland and Kurt Weill.

So, with hindsight, the mastery of *Peter Grimes* does not seem so unexpected. *Paul Bunyan* dealt with a community – of lumberjacks. *Peter Grimes* is about the fishing community of the Borough. Britten was surprised by the success of *Grimes*. He expected its subject-matter would disqualify it – Grimes, a fisherman who might or might not be a sadistic child-abuser, is not a conventional operatic hero – and he was depressed by the bitter schisms within the Sadler's Wells company which its production caused. It was these which led him and

friends to found the English Opera Group to perform new works with the least possible expense and to tour them throughout the country. Initially, Glyndebourne was associated with this venture and Britten's next two operas, both composed for chamber forces, were first produced there, *The Rape of Lucretia* in 1946 and the comedy *Albert Herring* in 1947. In the latter the librettist, Eric Crozier, had transferred a Maupassant story to a Suffolk setting, with characters who might well have been lurking in the background of the Borough in *Peter Grimes* but now took centre stage in a rich parody of village life. Unfortunately he eschewed comedy thereafter, except for parts of *A Midsummer Night's Dream*.

The break with Sadler's Wells was not complete, for when an opera was commissioned from Britten for the 1951 Festival of Britain, the plan was that Sadler's Wells should produce it at the Edinburgh Festival. But *Billy Budd* proved to be beyond its resources and the premiere was given by Covent Garden with the composer conducting. With a libretto by E M Forster and Eric Crozier based on Herman Melville's story, this powerful work took several years to receive the acclaim it deserved. As in *Peter Grimes* and *The Rape of Lucretia* and even to a certain degree in *Albert Herring*, this tale of a conflict between good and evil, with accompanying moral dilemma, on board an 18th-century British man-o'-war shortly after the Mutiny on the Nore, mirrors Britten's preoccupation with the theme of the destruction or corruption of innocence, a theme associated with his own homosexuality which can be discerned as a kind of sub-plot in both *Peter Grimes* and *Billy Budd*.

His next opera, *Gloriana*, was commissioned to mark the Coronation of Queen Elizabeth II in June 1953. Based on Lytton Strachey's *Elizabeth and Essex*, it was deemed by many to be an insult to the young Queen because it showed her predecessor in an unfavourable light. In fact, as revivals have shown, it is a moving portrait of royalty torn

THE TIDE WILL TURN!

between private emotion and public duty. But the savage and spiteful nature of the initial reaction encouraged Britten to turn his back on the metropolitan operatic scene and to concentrate his energies on the Aldeburgh Festival which he had co-founded in 1948. Aldeburgh was where he lived and where his heart was. Nevertheless, his next work was a response to a commission from the Venice Festival of 1954 and is regarded by many as his supreme operatic masterpiece. Since his teens he had known Henry James's *The Turn of the Screw*, about two children in an East Anglian manor house who were 'possessed' by ghosts. He turned to Myfanwy Piper, wife of the artist John Piper, for a libretto. She told the gripping story in a prologue and 15 scenes linked by 16 orchestral interludes in the shape of a theme and 15 variations. In many of his instrumental works Britten had shown himself a master of variation form and his deployment of it for a stage work was a stroke of genius enhanced by evocative writing for a small orchestra. This opera, too, provided yet another aspect of Britten's favourite theme of innocence and corruption with sexual overtones, which no doubt also drew him to Shakespeare's *A Midsummer Night's Dream* (1960) in which the depiction of Oberon as a countertenor and Tytania as a coloratura soprano gives a highly charged sexuality to their quarrel over the 'little Indian boy'.

Britten's operatic work throughout the 1960s was channelled into three short church parables. He returned to the opera house proper in 1970 when the Vietnam War provided a new platform for his lifelong pacifism and he and Mrs Piper dramatised another Henry James story, *Owen Wingrave*, about the scion of a military family who rebels against the family tradition, is disinherited and dies in a haunted room when challenged to sleep there alone by his heartless fiancée. Although written for television, the opera was always intended for the theatre. It remains the least known of Britten's operas and also the least successful, a too obvious tract for the times. His

above: The 1985 Opera North/Scottish Opera co-production of Tippett's *The Midsummer Marriage*
below: Peter Pears as Aschenbach in the Aldeburgh premiere of *Death in Venice* in 1973

last opera (again with Myfanwy Piper) was *Death in Venice*, a setting of Thomas Mann's novella about the German novelist who goes to Venice while suffering from a creative 'block', falls in love with a Polish boy to whom he never speaks and dies during an outbreak of cholera. Here the themes and sub-themes which fed Britten's creative imagination are fused into a painfully personal apotheosis.

When Britten died in 1976, his friend Sir Michael Tippett observed that the triumph of *Peter Grimes* had meant that Britten was 'willing in himself and, indeed, determined to be, within the 20th century, a professional opera composer... One of the achievements for which he will always be remembered in musical history books is that, in fact, he actually *did* it'. Tippett's five operas are the largest significant body of work after Britten's but explore different avenues of approach. His first opera, *The Midsummer Marriage*, was performed, to general incomprehension, at Covent Garden in 1955. It would be inaccurate to ascribe its genesis to impetus from the success of *Peter Grimes* even though he began serious work on it in 1946, because it emerges from his correspondence that he had ideas for an opera as early as 1941. Much as he admired *Peter Grimes*, he regarded it as 'English verismo'. Magic was what interested Tippett and *The Midsummer Marriage* is a curious and ultimately successful amalgam of modern characters

who enter a magic world similar to that of *Die Zauberflöte*, and *A Midsummer Night's Dream*. It is a 'quest' opera, with druidical scenes which suggest that Stonehenge would make an ideal location for it. Tippett has written all his own librettos and these have been criticised, not always unjustly, for a gauche mixture of the vernacular and the pretentiously poetic, sometimes highly effective, sometimes embarrassing and tending to be easily outdated. This matters least of all in *The Midsummer Marriage*, where the music's rapturous lyricism carries all before it in a flood of inspired inventiveness. As also happened with *Billy Budd*, it was a later BBC studio performance (under Norman Del Mar) which led to new and appreciated stagings.

If *The Midsummer Marriage* is Tippett's most attractive opera, perhaps his 'greatest' is *King Priam* (1958–61) in which he investigates the influence of fate on tragic characters. It brought about a change in style, with more dissonance and barer, sparser orchestration (the strings are not used in Act II) and monologues for the principal characters. Tippett's writing for female voices is, on the whole, more operatic than Britten's in the sense that the arias for Hecuba and Helena are nearer to a Verdian model. Investigation of human relationships is extended and deepened in *The Knot Garden* (1966–70), a plotless opera with allusions to the Mozart of *Così fan tutte* and the Shakespeare of *The Tempest*. The couples whose problems are investigated by an analyst include two male homosexuals, one of them black. The score makes atmospheric use of the electric guitar and draws on jazz and rock. Civil rights, racialism, political torture and 'freedom fighting' are part of

above: **Sir William Walton rehearsing *The Bear* for BBC Television in 1969**
below: **A scene from the first production of *Troilus and Cressida* at Covent Garden in 1954**

the plot. The music is a development from *King Priam* in its rapid movement (the scenes are short) and emotional variety. It was followed (1973–6) by *The Ice Break* in which Tippett again confronts contemporary problems, the characters including a released Soviet dissident, a black athlete (Olimpion), and a 'psychedelic messenger' (Astron). It is a short work in which the music starkly contrasts violence and lyricism. The latter predominates in Tippett's last opera, *New Year* (1986–8), in which he returns in some ways to the magical fantasies of *The Midsummer Marriage*. A trainee woman doctor with a tearaway foster brother becomes involved with the pilot of a space ship from the future ... only Tippett could find the apposite music for this kind of plot. In his eighties he remained a child of his time.

The oldest of the trio of major British composers born within the 14 years before the First World War was William Walton. He wrote two operas, the second a one-act 'extravaganza'. Always creatively lit up by the thought of rivalling the success of another composer (*Belshazzar's Feast* following Lambert's *The Rio Grande*, for example), Walton was directed towards an opera by *Peter Grimes* ('I thought it was not a good thing for British opera to have only one opera by one composer'). In 1947 he began work on *Troilus and Cressida*, to a libretto by Christopher Hassall. Composition occupied the best part of six years. His aim was to write a full-blown 19th-century romantic opera within a 20th-century context. Whether he succeeded is still a matter for intense argument between the work's supporters and detractors which the 1995 Opera North production is sure to intensify. What is certain is that the time was out of joint when it was first produced at Covent Garden in 1954. Britten was all the rage and the tide had not yet turned to bring back into general favour such composers as Mahler, Strauss and Elgar. Walton later revised and cut the work and recast the role of Cressida for mezzo-soprano instead of dramatic soprano. Whether these changes were for the better is also arguable. Walton's other opera, a success from the first, was, ironically, first performed at the 1967 Aldeburgh Festival. An adaptation of Chekhov's short story *The Bear*, the music is in Walton's witty parodistic vein. The plot may be slight, but the listener scarcely notices.

'If wind and water could write music, it would sound like Ben's'
YEHUDI MENUHIN ON BENJAMIN BRITTEN

styles, and he has written some of the most enduringly popular music of the post-war period, notably the Overture *Tam O' Shanter* (1955) and the sets of *English Dances* (1950–51). He was also one of several composers listed in this chapter

(including, surprisingly, Humphrey Searle) who made memorably funny contributions to Gerard Hoffnung's three anarchic Hoffnung Music Festivals (1956, 1958 & 1961, the last organized by friends after Hoffnung's death). What makes Arnold's symphonic music thoroughly contemporary rather than merely nostalgic is the rich vein of irony that pervades it. The garishly cinematic big tune in the Fifth Symphony (1961, written in memory of several friends, including Hoffnung) can be moving despite its apparently shameless sentimentality, especially so in the disturbing 'failed' apotheosis at the end. Some words about the slow movement Arnold wrote in a programme note provide a key: 'In times of great emotion we speak in emotional clichés'.

Symphonic music has not been so central to the output of Michael Tippett, but two fine symphonies (some would say his finest) fall into this period. If they are not as well-known as they should be, this may be simply because they are still frighteningly difficult to bring off in concert. The first performance of the Second in 1958 broke down, and the conductor, Adrian Boult, had to apologise and begin again, sporting-ly laying the blame on himself. But as Colin Davis's remarkable record-ing eventually showed, this is an exhilarating, gloriously positive work, echoing the numinous, magical world of Tippett's opera *The Midsummer Marriage* in its slow movement – a world opened up again in the Piano Concerto of 1955.

Tippett's First Symphony (1945)

left: **Edmund Rubbra**
below: **Sir Malcolm Arnold with Julian Bream for whom he composed his Guitar Concerto (1957), one of 18 concertos he has written for particular soloists**

still awaits its champion, but it may turn out to be an even finer work than the Second; its bleak, impassioned slow movement and muscular fugal finale are amongst the finest things he has written. But the two most enduringly popular works of this period, in fact of his career as a whole, are the *Concerto for Double String Orchestra* (1939) and the *Fantasia Concertante on a Theme of Corelli*, also for strings (1953). Nowhere is Tippett's style more technically assured or expressively warm and direct. The Elizabethan contrapuntal and rhythmic freedom that so appealed to Rubbra is here effortlessly, joyously fused with such seemingly incongruous elements as the American Negro Spiritual, quasi-Puccinian lyricism and a highly personal form of baroque ornamentation.

Not every British composer of the post-war period was drawn to the symphony however. Benjamin Britten for instance produced no major orchestral work between the brilliant and deserv-ingly popular *Young Person's Guide to the Orchestra* (1946) and the sombre, almost wilfully *un*-popular *Cello Symphony* (1963). And it may be significant that the rising generation of women composers seem to have shown little interest in the form. The Welsh composer Grace Williams wrote two, though she quickly withdrew the First (1943), and

it is for her lyrical and illustrative music – for example, the *Sea Sketches* (1944) and the folk-inspired *Penillion for Orchestra* (1955) – that she is most likely to be remembered today, though the choral *Missa cambrensis* (1971) also has its admirers. Elizabeth Maconchy composed a *Symphony for double string orchestra* in 1953, but it is her impressive cycle of 13 string quartets (spanning over 40 years and now all available on CD) on which her reputation rests. Bartók was the most obvious influence on Maconchy's style, especially the rhythmic innovations and the marrying of sometimes sharply dissonant harmonies with vestiges of traditional tonality. Maconchy seems to have had an easier time than the more radical Lutyens in getting her music heard in the 1950s, but neglect came later, and it is only recently that interest in her work has begun to grow again. Phyllis Tate is now virtually unheard, but her music, though less forcefully individual than that of Lutyens or Maconchy, can be delicately imaginative and often lucidly textured, especially

right: **Elizabeth Maconchy**
below: **Opening night of the 100th season of the BBC Henry Wood Promenade Concerts – Andrew Davis with the BBC Symphony Orchestra and Chorus, the Philharmonia Chorus and the BBC Singers, 15 July 1994**

in her chamber music and songs. She too deserves reappraisal.

Apart from Tippett's *The Midsummer Marriage* (1952), Walton's *Troilus and Cressida* (1954) and the big works of Britten, almost nothing of the operatic work of the post-war years has survived. Sheer cost, of course, makes revival difficult, and yet reading through the critical writings of the times, it is rare to find an operatic work leaving much of an impression. Perhaps one day we may see the vindication of Lennox Berkeley's *Nelson* (1953) – the music at least was admired by some. Sir Arthur Bliss's *The Olympians* (1949) is another possible candidate, though it was coolly received at the time. Alan Bush's overtly propagandist *Wat Tyler* has its admirers, and it won him one of the four Festival of Britain prizes at its 1951 premiere, but it was from Communist East Germany that

PATRON'S PROGRESS
Innovation and experiment have always had a central place in the BBC's thinking. Its very foundation in 1922 was an act of faith, and music of all kinds was a linchpin from the earliest days of 2LO. In 1927 the Company became the Corporation; and that same year it acquired the Proms from Sir Henry Wood, Gustav Holst became the first-ever recipient of a BBC commission, for *The Morning of the Year*, and the BBC Wireless Chorus (forerunner of the BBC Singers) became a permanent body. The BBC Symphony Orchestra under Adrian Boult was created in 1930.

By 1994 there were over 30 commissions annually: what matter if many of them 'die forgotten, as a dream/Dies at the opening day', provided one or two – Poulenc's Sinfonietta, Tippett's Second Symphony, Harrison Birtwistle's *Earth Dances* – struck gold? The foundation of the Third Programme in 1946, with its avowedly elitist platform, was another act of a supremely confident cultural patron. As, among the conductors, Wood begat Boult begat Sargent begat Davis begat Boulez, or as William Glock begat Robert Ponsonby begat John Drummond as the power behind the scenes, so the BBC's concert programmes (as throughout the Proms' first 100 years) offer a wonderfully accurate barometer of each decade's Zeitgeist.

For performers of all kinds, too, the BBC became the patron *par excellence*. The relationship became symbiotic, difficult to alter. Changes in the Zeitgeist interact with changes in the political, social and broadcasting landscapes (satellites, digital audio, compact discs, new TV and radio networks) and seem to induce an atmosphere of permanent change. In the midst of these assaults, the BBC's arts administrators have a delicate balancing act to perform – as between, say, the needs of the Bach enthusiast on the Clapham Omnibus and the Tippett fan on an Orcadian croft. They must keep their eyes firmly on the future.
Piers Burton-Page

later encouragement largely came, perhaps to his detriment in this country.

The scarcity of enduring choral music is harder to understand; after all, in marked contrast to opera, there was a strongly established British tradition here. Britten's 12-movement *Spring Symphony*, for three soloists, boys' choir, chorus and a large, colourfully constituted orchestra (including a cow horn), is one glowing exception, as, in a more modest way, is Gerald Finzi's *Intimations of Immortality* (1950). Finzi's music is sometimes criticized for a lack of formal backbone, but the radiant lyricism and inspired word-setting carry this work and the fine songs of his last years, and there is a welcome absence of post-war drabness; the same could also be said for the two outstanding concertos, for clarinet (1949) and cello (1955).

There are other fine, surviving choral pieces: liturgical works by Herbert Howells for instance, Vaughan Williams' *Three Shakespeare Songs* (1951), or Walton's *Coronation Te Deum* (1953), and there are signs of growing interest in the church music of Rubbra, which could turn out to be more widely appealing than his symphonic music. However Fricker's spectacular oratorio *The Vision of Judgement* (1958), once compared with Walton's pre-war masterpiece *Belshazzar's Feast*, has sunk without trace.

Fortunately the condition of solo vocal music at this time seems to have been healthier. Finzi's later songs have been mentioned, and there are fine individual solo vocal works by Lutyens, Rubbra and others, as well as several striking song-cycles such as Tippett's *The Heart's Assurance* (1951), Vaughan Williams' *Ten Blake Songs* for voice and oboe (1957), and the beautiful, surprisingly neglected *Four Poems of St Teresa of Avila* for contralto and strings (1947) by Berkeley.

The outstanding composer of solo vocal music in this period was Benjamin Britten. The orchestral song-cycle *Nocturne* (1958) has never been as popular or as critically acclaimed as the earlier *Serenade for tenor, horn and strings* (1943), but it contains music which is just as fine, and as original, for instance the eerie, pseudo-naive 'Midnight Bell' and the powerful, Mahlerian Shakespeare-setting that ends the work, 'When most I wink, then do mine eyes best see.' Also from this period come the second and third

canticles *Abraham and Isaac* (1952) and *Still Falls the Rain* (1954), the *Six Hölderlin Fragments* (1958) and the superb, dark-toned Hardy cycle, *Winter Words* (1953).

The focus of this chapter has been on concert music, but there is another medium that should be mentioned – film. Many of the composers mentioned wrote for the cinema, and although the 'continuous symphony' film score popular before the war (in which almost every stage of the action is supported by music) was on the wane, the amount of extended, sophisticated composition that went into some productions can startle audiences brought up on modern minimalist scores – when they notice it, that is. Arnold, Alwyn, Berkeley, Frankel, Lutyens, Rawsthorne, Stevens and Walton all wrote extensively for the cinema, as

below: **Britten with a squirrel (André Ravasio) at a rehearsal for his setting of the Chester Miracle Play *Noye's Fludde* in 1958**

did three distinguished composers from an earlier generation, Arnold Bax (*Oliver Twist*, 1948; *Journey into History*, 1952), John Ireland and Vaughan Williams. The chief agent (besides money!) in attracting these 'serious' composers to write for what was sometimes considered an ephemeral or sub-artistic medium was Muir Mathieson, musical director first of Alexander Korda's London Film Productions, then at the J Arthur Rank Organization.

Whatever the composers thought of their film work at the time, the industry was a major financial support to many: established, rising, or still struggling. It was probably, along with BBC commissions, the most important consistent source of income at that time. Ironically, this 'ephemeral' medium has been the main reason why some composers' names have not passed completely into obscurity. It may even be that some of the most enduring music of the post-war years is to be found here, rather than amongst the reams of now-forgotten Cheltenham Symphonies. Certainly attitudes to what constitutes 'High' and 'Low' Art (if those terms are allowed at all) have changed enormously over the last three decades.

right: **E M Forster and Britten at the time of their collaboration on** *Billy Budd* **in 1949** *below:* **David Lean's film of** *The Bridge on the River Kwai* **for which Malcolm Arnold wrote the music**

But perhaps we shouldn't write off the Cheltenham Symphonists yet. Rising generations often turn against the products of their parents' times, as for instance did the young composers of the so-called 'Manchester School' – Alexander Goehr, Peter Maxwell Davies and Harrison Birtwistle – whose uncompromisingly post-Schoenbergian early works had already begun to stir up controversy by the beginning of the 1960s. But perhaps we are now far enough away from the late 1940s and 50s to view the art that emerged then with more detachment. Already there are signs that the revival of interest in 20th-century British music, until recently restricted exclusively to the first half of the century, is beginning to reach some of the composers discussed here. Simpson, Arnold, Rubbra, Alwyn, Maconchy, and more recently Stevens and Lutyens, have in differing degrees all found their stars in the ascendant again. One could add more names: Howard Ferguson for instance, whose finely crafted, strongly melodic chamber and instrumental works have been appearing again in recording catalogues, as have a handful of pieces by Arnold Cooke (once labelled 'The English Hindemith') and the symphonist William Wordsworth, a descendant of the poet's brother. The territory is richer and more varied than is often supposed, and posterity may have a few surprises for those who have already reached their verdicts.

12

BETWEEN THE END OF
THE CHATTERLEY BAN AND
THE BEATLES' FIRST LP*

1963 AND BEYOND

ROBERT MAYCOCK

❊ from *Annus Mirabilis* by
Philip Larkin

The story of classical music in Britain is repeatedly set up by events outside. Like the nation's political history it polarises between the sitting occupants, usually the heirs of a previous invasion, and the next generation of incomers whom they resist as single-mindedly as a rumour of rabies. Such waves of invasion therefore break much later than you would expect – about ten years' delay is a useful rule of thumb.

In the last 40 years they have rolled in with ever-increasing frequency. Before the first of these assaults on our island way of life, a preface. Some of the truest originals of the 1960s – John White, Howard Skempton, Gavin Bryars, who combined a simplicity and directness with a quirky turn of phrase – were seen as eccentrics. The brightest light on the experimental scene was Cornelius Cardew, blessed with the mystic touch of Stockhausen. In later years Cardew was to turn against the avant-garde as his Maoist principles led him towards a new simplicity and into his greatest project: the Scratch Orchestra. Open, democratic, mixing its media and its performing spaces, and active through the early 70s the Scratch Orchestra lies behind both subsequent performance art work and radical musical attitudes. But that is to skip ahead: as Macmillan's government collapsed, musically it was Darmstadt and Paris that set the pace as the long-dammed force of 50s innovation, the post-war legacy of Schoenberg and Webern and Messiaen, broke through the bastions of British resistance.

Chapter opener shows,
top right: **The Maltings at Snape**
middle left: **A bar of James MacMillan's orchestral work** *Britannia* **(1994)**
bottom right: **Peter Maxwell Davies in 1968**

above: **Alexander Goehr**
left: **Sir Peter Maxwell Davies**

There had been a few prophets in the wilderness. Elisabeth Lutyens lived on to 1983 and wrote some of her finest pieces in a climate which almost accepted her. Her mix of the fastidious and the intense left an indelible mark on her pupils (of whom Brian Elias, today writing vocal and instrumental scores of powerful refinement, is the most faithful). Like Roberto Gerhard she was championed in the BBC regime of William Glock from 1960 on. The new creative impetus started up among a few inquisitive students in Manchester. Alexander Goehr – always the intellectual leader and later a dominant composition teacher – proclaims in his music loyalty to his father Walter, a Schoenberg pupil, and his own education with Messiaen. Nowadays, some of the most approachable surfaces in any of the Manchester School's works hide an intricacy and subtlety of form that can still be disorientating on a first encounter. By the next piece, Goehr's restless intelligence has often moved on to solving another set of problems. Possible starting-points for the listener new to his work include the song-cycle *Sing, Ariel*, premiered at Aldeburgh in 1990, or the most recent of his not-quite-symphonies (heard at the 1994 Proms), *Colossos or Panic*, where lucidity coexists with lavish sounds in an after-echo of French orchestral traditions, or his stage works which run at a higher expressive temperature.

Sir Peter Maxwell Davies burst on to the scene with the shrieking flamboyance of music-theatre pieces such as *Eight Songs for a Mad King* (1969). Alongside the wildness went a withdrawn, ascetic tendency and a fascination with arcane procedures derived from medieval music. Since he moved to Orkney in the 1970s the prolific rate of composing has continued, while the heat has gradually been supplanted by a strong sense of place. His 1980 opera *The Lighthouse* held drama and austerity in a gripping balance and has been regularly revived. His symphonies and concertos have divided their public: for all their moments of evocative poetry they do not communicate easily to the unpersistent, who will find the essence of the later Max more directly in his shorter instrumental pieces.

With the power of Sir Harrison Birtwistle's music there can be no argument: you take it or you leave it. It has not mellowed with the years. A visionary power has replaced the stridency of his 60s shock-opera *Punch and Judy*, but the stance is

as confrontational as ever. It is immediate in its force – even the humour is elemental – and its complexity lies more in the piling-up of layers of writing to form dense masses than in any structural obscurity. There is spare, spacious writing of an intense beauty. But the poetic visions of orchestral works like *The Triumph of Time* (1972) and *Earth Dances* (1987) are bleak and terrifying. The other side of the coin is timeless, sensuous writing for chorus and a personal way with melodies of vast proportions. Sometimes, as in the recent piano concerto *Antiphonies*, the density defeats Birtwistle's most ardent admirers. Then there will be a *Gawain* (his 1991 opera), in which dramatic directness carries all before it.

Such has been the prominence of these three composers' music that it distracts from the range of what started in the 1960s. Jonathan Harvey emerged on the Europhile tide, but his serial tendencies were underpinned by a spiritual urge, and his music has a more serene, exploratory sound, reflecting an interest in Asian music and philosophy as well as the Christian mystical tradition. Among dramatic works his *Inquest of Love* transcended a list of English National Opera commissions that had preceded it. The same generation included Hugh Wood, consistently terse and forceful (but almost relaxed in his best-known piece, the 1991 Piano Concerto for Joanna MacGregor), and another influential teacher, the quirky and definitely unrelaxed Justin Connolly.

Several of the period's leading figures have gained in stature as they separated themselves from

above:
Harrison Birtwistle surrounded by masks
left: **Birtwistle's opera *The Mask of Orpheus* staged by English National Opera in 1986**

the avant-garde. Nicholas Maw had in 1962 written *Scenes and Arias*, a declaration of continuity with the Romantics in soaring lines for women singers and a glowing orchestra. Never pastiche, always fresh in its sound and its workings, the music now sounds ahead of its time. Along with John McCabe and Robert Simpson he has written some of the finest English music for string quartet since Maconchy. McCabe, independent enough from the start to adapt traditional means to intelligent contemporary ends, has built up a prolific catalogue of dynamic orchestral pieces – with the outcome that few have had their due share of performances. The 60s' most puzzling figure, Richard Rodney Bennett, is overdue for revaluation. Evidence: his Symphony No 3 (1987). Previously the impression had been that he wrote well-behaved scores inflected by study with Boulez (following Lennox Berkeley), and let his hair down in film music and cabaret. That symphony brings the two sides together; the lyrical facility capable of producing his *Murder on the Orient Express* score actually extends the power and range.

Floating up in 1968 through the debut concert of the London Sinfonietta and the Apple record label of the Beatles, John Tavener's *The Whale* had a devotional character that nobody paid much attention to beside its up-to-the-minute wildness and social connections. As Tavener trod the spiritual path towards the arms of Mother Russia, his conviction grew that music lost its way not just in the early 20th century but centuries earlier. By the time of *The Protecting Veil* (1989), his famous meditation for cello and orchestra, his mature voice had been heard in a still-continuing series of big choral works, and most authentically in the alternately austere and joyous *Akathist of Thanksgiving* (1988), which is not just the music for an Orthodox service but the service itself.

Despite folk memories, less radical musicians were not always sidelined. Consider William Mathias and Alun Hoddinott, Malcolm Williamson and Gordon Crosse, Thomas Wilson and Gerard Schurmann and, since his death in 1988, Kenneth Leighton – some have become neglected, yet they were often prolific, and among the leaders of their generation. Williamson, a most fluent and wide-ranging musician with an Australian lack of inhibition about appealing easily, can still surprise – watch for the 1995 BBC commission. Thea Musgrave, composer of vigorous, theatrical concertos and a striking opera *Mary, Queen of Scots* (1977), transferred her main scene of activity to the United States where her language grew bolder and simpler. That parallels

above: **Hugh Wood**
below right: **Film still from *The Piano* for which Michael Nyman wrote the music**
below left: **Nicholas Maw**

the progress of Iain Hamilton, a vigorous presence in the 1950s and 60s who reappeared from America in the early 1980s to present English National Opera with an operatic *Anna Karenina* of unexpected tunefulness. Two notable builders-on-foundations, however, marginalised in the 1960s, have gained enthusiastic followers: Robert Simpson and Andrzej Panufnik.

True to the spirit of the age Michael Tippett was elevated as a new-born modernist with his Concerto for Orchestra (1963). But this was one phase in a rapid move towards eclectic cultural ideas. References in the Third and Fourth Symphonies include electronic sound, rock, Beethoven, and philosophical programmes. *The Mask of Time* (1972–84) is a deliberate culmination of his life's work in its urge to embrace all he knew. The heart of Tippett's late work, though, lies in music for quartet and piano and the Triple Concerto (1979), which renews the lyrical genius of the *Concerto for Double String Orchestra*.

Elizabeth Maconchy and Priaulx Rainier remained among the senior figures. As before, Britten and Walton dominated the scene, the latter despite adding little to his output. Britten had suggested with the Wilfred Owen settings in his

---

NICHOLAS MAW (b 1935)
Beauty is a flexible concept, but in the ravishing sound world of Nicholas Maw it comes close to finding a satisfactory aural definition. *Scenes and Arias*, his first acclaimed work, combines complex harmonic logic with ecstatic and abundant melodic writing. His comic opera *The Rising of the Moon*, the song-cycle *La Vita Nuova* (1979) and the *Life Studies* for strings (1973, 1976), show a diversity of means and purposes but share common ground in their spontaneous melodic utterance and masterly formal

action. Maw's strengths as a composer – combining the best of the English tradition with the lessons of European post-war innovation – reach a sumptuous fulfilment in the orchestral *Odyssey* of 1987, 90 minutes in duration and some 15 years in the making. A violin concerto for Joshua Bell and chamber works including *Ghost Dances* and the exotic *Shahnama* have further extended the scope and complexion of Maw's creative persona.

MICHAEL NYMAN (b 1944)
Many currents are merged in the versatile talent of Michael

Nyman: Baroque scholarship, expertise in the American avant-garde, and experience as performer, arranger and folk-song collector. The composer of music for Jane Campion's *The Piano* and Peter Greenaway's *The Draughtsman's Contract* and *Prospero's Books*, he is a pupil of the distin-

guished teacher Alan Bush and of Thurston Dart, the most lively and original musicologist of his time. Their diverse influence shows in Nyman's own work for The Michael Nyman Band, blending classical styles with rock beats and amplification, and touching a new creative pulse in the *Six Celan Songs* (1990), *Where the Bee Dances* (1991), and *MGV* (1993). He has collaborated with choreographers Siobhan Davies, Shobana Jeyasingh and Lucinda Childs, and explored multi-media projects in *The Fall of Icarus*, devised with the Belgian performance company Plan K.
Nicholas Williams

War Requiem that he was entering a new creative phase. In the Noh-inspired ritual drama of his three Church Parables (*Curlew River, The Burning Fiery Furnace, The Prodigal Son*), the cantata *Phaedra* written for Janet Baker, and the cello music for Rostropovich, solo suites (1964–72) as well as the Cello Symphony, he gave clear confirmation, though illness was to cut the phase short in its prime. His Aldeburgh Festival came of age during this period too, as the new Snape Maltings concert hall inspired an artistic expansion to match the physical upgrading.

The next wave of invasion has had less impact on composing than in America, and more on listening and performance habits. Michael Nyman, for one, has little time for the word 'minimalism', when applied to his own music – and indeed he came from an experimental background, while his harmonies and cycles of repetition have sources in Baroque music. More directly in the American line was an upsurge of systems bands, mostly short-lived; The Lost Jockey endured best. This, however, is to run ahead of the pace of change. The music that still flourished for two decades to come was too mixed in style and origin to describe as a school, but had a certain house style all the same – the Sinfonietta-and-subsidy generation. The house was usually on London's South Bank, where the new Queen Elizabeth Hall and Purcell Room could handle smaller and more varied events than the Royal Festival Hall. Away from home several

above: **John Tavener photographed on Aegina, 1993**
left: **Richard Rodney Bennett with Sir Kenneth MacMillan who choreographed his ballet *Isadora***

performances each year took to the road on the Contemporary Music Network.

It is ironic that for years public subsidy, intended to foster access to art of high quality, was in the new-music field appropriated to create work which appealed less and less to fewer and fewer; ironic too that when works as well as their composers have endured ten or 20 years, they are often more rooted in tradition. A case in point is Paul Patterson, who quickly matured from a Penderecki-like glee in wild sounds to conceive a series of choral works that respect the familiar English tradition they are modernising. Otherwise, though, the reason for survival is often some exceptional individual's commitment. Two key figures on that count are Oliver Knussen and Colin Matthews, not as composers but as practical musicians. Knussen takes up the causes as conductor, Matthews records them on the NMC label, and both occupy influential positions, with performing, promoting or funding bodies. A third is Bayan Northcott, who when not working on his own eloquent, painstakingly wrought music, has

'The composer's function is to give insight into experience in a way that can't be expressed through words or visual imagery.'

PETER MAXWELL DAVIES, QUOTED IN *MAX* BY MIKE SEABROOK

written penetratingly about this generation.

Robin Holloway's music embraces many of the period's enthusiasms and contradictions. It sounds like Romantic music written with modernist techniques; melody and harmony suggest a comforting message that the logic of a piece then undermines. The Second Concerto for Orchestra (1979) is a wild, over-the-top bout of exuberance and intricacy, but its aesthetic holds good for shorter and simpler pieces. Other composers have been more circumspect about mixing a modernist inheritance with a gradual readmission of more consonant elements. Knussen's own music, enjoying Rimsky-like glitter alongside fastidiously polished skills, was at its least self-conscious in his relatively prolific twenties (*Ophelia Dances*; Symphony No 3). Colin Matthews, whose music is more expansive, can generate a frightening momentum through processes that run like machines with a will of their own, and is one of the few – Simon Bainbridge is another – to face up to a love-hate relationship with the American repetitive composers, dissected with amusing results in *Hidden Variables* (1989). Dominic Muldowney, experienced in the theatre, has applied virtuoso composing tricks, particularly in the field of rhythmic relationships, to material often taken from mid-century genres; there's an air of Berlin cabaret about more than his songs.

'Isms' are rarely appropriate for these years. David Bedford has evolved a brightly-scored, clear-cut language with repetitive figuration, but it doesn't 'belong' with anybody else's; sometime membership of a rock group and continuing work in education has kept it uniquely youthful. Nicola LeFanu has given an evocative, East Anglian cast to a tight-knit serial inheritance, though her lyrical leanings have taken a freer direction in stage pieces such as *Blood Wedding* (1993). The craggy, Schoenberg-meets-English-pastoral individuality of Anthony Payne, the orchestral finesse of Martin Dalby, the vocal sensitivity of Alison Bauld, the swirling patterns and evolving forms of Robert Saxton, the deadpan stealth of Jonathan Lloyd: post-modern maybe, but they sound quite different, linked only by needing a mind-set that can accept the 'difficult' alongside the familiar. This was prime time too for electroacoustic music, which developed in something of an isolated world, spinning off the engaging talents of Tim Souster and the American emigré Stephen Montague to make a wider impact.

The fulminating energies and references of Michael Finnissy's music, its uncompromising stance and expressionist immediacy, place it at the far end of an arduous path to realisation. It is a different path from that of Brian Ferneyhough, whose sometimes explosive musical character grows directly out of minutely controlled detail. Intensely concentrated and unrelenting, Ferneyhough's music has attracted more performances in Germany than Britain. James Dillon has been luckier, perhaps because through the teeming surfaces a visionary urgency and anger

left above:
Robin Holloway
right: **Piano Circus, the contemporary ensemble of six pianists**

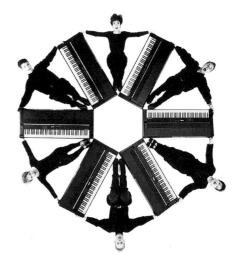

makes itself felt. Towards the other end of the spectrum, David Matthews' distinction lies partly in a lyrical and rhythmic freshness, but more fundamentally in sheer consistent quality of writing, embodied in clearly-wrought works – especially symphonic orchestral pieces, including four symphonies, and string quartets – that make the quality immediately apparent. Like Maw, but unlike Holloway and quite differently from his younger brother Colin, he has made peace with 20th-century musical history and his music radiates confidence in what he accepts and what he leaves behind.

In the 1990s, groups such as Icebreaker, modelled on the Dutch minimalist pattern with hints of heavy rock, the whimsical, Satie-inspired George W Welch, the sextet Piano Circus, or the specialists in the 'new complexity' inspired by Ferneyhough, Exposé, have their own circles of composers. More people are creating music; composition is part of the national curriculum. Instead of a few great spirits the younger generations have

above: **The composer James MacMillan and percussionist Evelyn Glennie discuss the concerto** *Veni, Veni, Emmanuel* **which he wrote for her in 1992**
below left: **Oliver Knussen**
below centre: **Kent Opera's premiere of** *A Night at the Chinese Opera*
below right: **Judith Weir**

many proficient, enjoyable, exciting composers. They are often impatient with the formal atmosphere of traditional concert halls and frustrated by the limitations of churches or theatres – a situation that arts centres outside central London have addressed to their benefit. Pessimists see cultural decay. But if Western civilisation is on the way out, it is taking its leave with a fine display of fireworks and allowing more powerful and confident cultural influences to make their first mark on its art as much as on its restaurants.

Cautious listeners, catching a mood of musical fundamentalism, find solace in the gentle consonances of Howard Skempton and Gavin Bryars. These two are really musical radicals; but they have, in a word, 'heart', when much new music drowns in irony. So does the extraordinary survivor George Lloyd, who in his eighties keeps on writing and conducting orchestras with the energy of a man in his prime. His burgeoning symphonies radiate a between-the-wars Britishness as they race along on a stream of consciousness with prolific melodic fluency towards unstoppable,

OLIVER KNUSSEN (b 1952)
There are few yardsticks with which to measure Oliver Knussen's achievement other than those of his own making. A child prodigy who wrote and directed his First Symphony with the LSO at the age of 15, he is internationally renowned as a composer and conductor. His Third Symphony (1979), a work of virtuosic orchestral technique, has been twice recorded and has received over 70 performances to date. His operatic double-bill on Maurice Sendak stories, *Where the Wild Things Are* (1983) and *Higglety Pigglety Pop!* (1990) has also received worldwide acclaim. Whether childlike and tender or violent and surreal, his music encompasses not only a singular expressive utterance but also a complete sensibility. Recent works have included the *Whitman Settings* (1992) for soprano and orchestra, and a horn concerto for Barry Tuckwell (1994). Knussen has been an Artistic Director of the Aldeburgh Festival since 1983, injecting fresh vigour into this renowned institution.

JUDITH WEIR (b 1954)
It is difficult to conceive of Judith Weir's robust creative personality except in the context of its fruitful interaction with other cultures: Chinese Yuan dramas in *A Night at the Chinese Opera*, Spanish legend in the *Missa del Cid*, and Scottish folk-lore in the Highland music-drama *The Vanishing Bridegroom*. Avoiding pastiche, the pungent harmonies and sharp-edged rhythmic schemes of her music infiltrate familiar ethnic inflections and

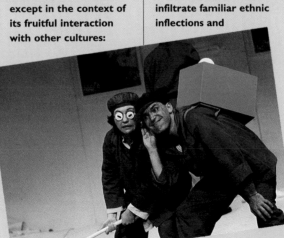

cast a spell of their own that can be both joyful and disturbing. The results are without parallel in British music – and no less so when the context is the medieval world of *Sederunt principes* or the German Romanticism of her recent opera for ENO, *Blond Eckbert*. Distance may be essential to her compositional technique, but her expression of spirit is warm and intimate.

Nicholas Williams

piled-up climaxes, lacking nothing but the deft shaping hand of a good editor.

Younger leading lights have emerged in the established way, setting their sights on BBC and London Sinfonietta commissions. James MacMillan, with *The Confession of Isobel Gowdie* (1990) and a spectacular percussion concerto for Evelyn Glennie, makes such an immediate appeal to the emotions that the sheer sophistication of his technique hasn't always had its due. If he continues as committed to making music not just for its own sake but for humanity's, he will take his listeners where he pleases. So, perhaps, will the equally committed Steve Martland. Emerging from a background of aggressive Dutch minimalism his *Babi Yar*, which appeared on a rock CD label at the end of the 80s, was a milestone in contemporary recording. Without softening he has opened up, and the cumulative lyrical keening of *Patrol* for string quartet (1992) will have drawn in many listeners as it quietly extended his expression and technique.

On the strength of his Thatcher-era opera *Greek*, drawn from Steven Berkoff's East End *Oedipus* play, and titles like *Beating about the Bush* and *Three Screaming Popes*, Mark-Anthony Turnage acquired the image of a rebel. But the music speaks with a cosmopolitan lyrical streak and an eclectic range of rhythmic and harmonic techniques, like an English Henze. Abrasively-scored tuttis and memories of great jazz soloists, as in *Drowned Out* and *Kai*, products of his 90s residency with the City of Birmingham Symphony Orchestra, are only part of the story. The restless tension sometimes seems to come from a struggle

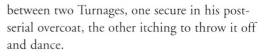

right: **George Benjamin**
below: **Mark-Anthony Turnage**

between two Turnages, one secure in his post-serial overcoat, the other itching to throw it off and dance.

Along with the laconic, direct voice of Judith Weir, these three have acquired high profiles. Among others treading the same path Diana Burrell, modernist by conviction, wants to stretch minds but doesn't resort to obscurantism. Rather she has instilled a sharp, salty sense of place and poetic atmosphere, urban as well as East Anglian (*Landscape*, 1988), and a personal treatment of instruments as though they were animals or birds, sometimes hunting in packs (*Resurrection*). Michael Berkeley, briefly prominent with a passionate anti-nuclear cantata *Or Shall We Die?* (1982), revealed a harsher, discomforting voice in his Clarinet Concerto (1991) and probed English neuroses at greater length in the opera *Baa Baa Black Sheep* (1993). A more quirky musical poet, Benedict Mason, catches fleeting visions, many-layered and barely grasped before they have gone. Given to whimsical

titles and inspirations – *Concerto for the viola section* (1992), *Lighthouses of England and Wales* (1987), *Playing Away* (1994), he pursues the matter with rigour and refinement.

Even more fastidious and unprolific, George Benjamin delivers (eventually) pieces with an unexpected robustness and air of confidence alongside the intricacy and sense of fantasy he has inherited from the example, and the teaching, of Messiaen. His qualities were apparent in his student orchestral piece, *Ringed by the Flat Horizon* (1979–80) which has been widely performed. He has more successfully than most integrated electro-acoustic sounds into live instrumental pieces, as in *Antara* (1987), a larger-than-life fantasy on the timbre of the panpipes. Simon Holt is another whose works are relatively few but elegantly wrought and comprehensible to traditionally inclined ears without sounding 'retro'. More productive, equally polished and increasingly lyrical, John Casken takes advantage of contemporary techniques while retaining an unforced emotional charge, eloquently so in his Cello Concerto (1991), written for the Northern Sinfonia and its cellist-

director Heinrich Schiff, the orchestra to which Casken later became 'composer in association'. Others in this 'open-modern' area of expression include the more down-to-earth John Woolrich, the ultra-fastidious Rupert Bawden, the intensely sensitive David Sawer, and the bright young minds Sally Beamish and Thomas Adès. Martin Butler, whose neatly wrought music often presents easy-going West Coast surfaces, is already along the road to the next wave.

This 'third wave' includes encounters with popular genres and with the classical styles of other cultures. Post-colonial times have seen a more sophisticated willingness to meet distinct musical languages on their own terms, rather than as 'exotic'

right: l to r, Tom McDonnell, Marie Angel, Andrew Burden and Claire Daniels in Opera Factory's 1994 production of Nigel Osborne's *Sarajevo*
below left: Simon Bainbridge
below: Andrew Toovey

objects, though still incorporating them in essentially Western compositions. Nigel Osborne has been one of the more accomplished successors to the European modernist line, but has extended his interests to many lands, most recently with *Sarajevo* for Opera Factory, pursuing a passionate involvement of art and politics. For Keith Gifford the source is Thai music, from which he has borrowed instruments as well as turns of phrase. Giles Swayne and Geoffrey Poole have found relationships with African music, which Swayne embodied powerfully in *CRY* (1980), a creation saga for voices live and amplified. With James Wood, carefully researched rhythmic and melodic patterns from several destinations underlie dynamic, elemental music for percussion and for voices.

More slowly, musicians from outside Europe and America have become composers in the Western sense. No longer does the dominant nation's art appropriate an outside element; instead the techniques of Western composing are used by people of another culture to pursue their own expressive ends. The first role model is the Japanese Tōru Takemitsu, who only sounds European on the surface; the matter of how one note follows another works by a different mentality. Composers with origins in Britain's former colonies eventually appeared. John Mayer and Naresh Sohal introduced an Indian perspective; Param Vir has adhered more to European traditions in staging Indian subjects. The most radical Indian-born composer, Priti Paintal, has worked some of the Western overlay out of her system and rediscovered modal and rhythmic roots, along with a vigorous African influence. Often she uses improvising musicians within a composed structure, as in *Polygamy* (1993) for her ensemble Shiva Nova with jazz marimba, Indian and Western instruments. A similar assertiveness operates in the various nations of the United Kingdom. Most Scottish composers work within

SIMON BAINBRIDGE
(b 1952)
Few composers have absorbed the lessons of minimalism with such originality and discretion as Simon Bainbridge. *Spirogyra* of 1971 and the Viola Concerto of 1978 had already demonstrated a seductive harmonic palette prior to his crucial encounter with Reich's music during a Bicentennial fellowship visit to America in 1978 (he had studied at Tanglewood with Gunther Schuller in the early 1970s). Subsequent works such as *Voicing* (1982) and the *Concertante in Moto Perpetuo* (1983) retained the precisely imagined sound-world while building concise, cogent structures using a personal version of process techniques. Strongly influenced by visual media, Bainbridge has extended his musical arguments into the third dimension, notably in the Fantasia for Double Orchestra (1984) for two interacting instrumental

groups, and in the Double Concerto (1990) for oboe and clarinet. An orchestral *Toccata* of 1992 and a Clarinet Quintet from the following year have further extended the range of his polished, refined art.

ANDREW TOOVEY
(b 1962)
Predominantly fiery, yet also containing a core of radiant tranquillity within its ambit, the music of Andrew Toovey has a dual aspect that looks as much to the school of Cage as to the new complexity of Ferneyhough and Finnissy. Sources of extra-musical inspiration range from the theatre of Antonin Arnaud

and the poetry of e e cummings to the painting of Mark Rothko and Francis Bacon. With the new-music group Ixion, Toovey – a pupil of Jonathan Harvey and Morton Feldman – has created a formidable repertoire of works for small ensemble, including *Adam* (1989) and *Adam Adamah* (1991). Several pieces are 'combines', capable of simultaneous performance together. Stage works *The Spurt of Blood* (1990) and *Ubu Roi* (1992) gained a reputation for scabrous aggression, also reflected in the title of the piano quartet *Fetish Figure (Timid Brute)* of 1993.

Nicholas Williams

the same constraints as English ones, even if they use distinctive material; but a few, notably William Sweeney and Edward McGuire, have taken the further step of deriving forms and techniques from traditional Scottish music.

The chasm between post-60s pop and 'new music' also took a while to bridge. David Bedford seemed out on his own in the 70s; a decade later the Michael Nyman Band had the sound and drive of rock in it, even if the composing was different. Now, Graham Fitkin is writing subtly voiced, propulsive music with the funkiness and invention of a written-out improvisation, Errollyn Wallen has taken the idioms and singing styles of black America and Britain into the ambit of composed concert pieces, Jenny Roditi has developed a cosmopolitan stage style in her opera *Inanna* (1992), written for Odaline de la Martinez and Lontano, who toured it around Britain two years ago. Eleanor Alberga, who also belongs with the

below: **Michael Nyman at work in his study**

previous paragraph's tendencies, has brought Caribbean roots, an African inheritance, a dancer's rhythmic awareness and an ear for down-to-earth idioms to some of the classic European forms.

All the composers in this latest wave give the lie to suggestions that musical originality is thinning out. The most heartening story belongs to Minna Keal, who returned to composing in her seventies and had a symphony performed at the 1989 BBC Proms. It wasn't the same music she used to write 50 years earlier: gritty, dissonant and active, it sounded the work of a composer who couldn't stop developing. Nobody could have predicted it. But in that quality of pure surprise lies the clue to creative energy. The British musical scene, outside the concert hall as well as inside, now includes an unprecedented richness and diversity of styles and sources that have what it takes to keep the energy, and the surprises, flowing.

Chronology of 500 British composers

with other composers and

musical events

Incorporating an index of British composers
mentioned in the main text

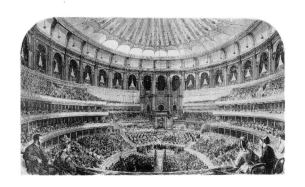

Chronology opener
shows, *top right:* **Fingal's
Cave on the Scottish
island of Staffa which
Mendelssohn portrayed
in his 1830** *Hebrides
Overture.* **This water-
colour was painted by
William Leitch**
middle left: **Late 17th-
century English violin
decorated with the arms
of the Stuart kings**
bottom right: **Opening of
the Royal Albert Hall by
Queen Victoria on
29 March, 1871**

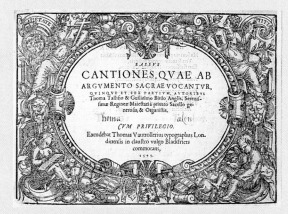

top: **Musicians from a
psalter copied in England
in the second quarter of
the 14th century**
above: **Title page of the**
Cantiones, **published by
Byrd and Tallis under
their new royal patent
for printing music in
1575**

John Christopher Smith
(1712–95) *49*
John Stanley (1712–86)
36, 51, 54
John Alcock (1715–1806) *53*
William Felton (1715–69) *54*
James Nares (1715–83)
Felice de Giardini (1716–96)
56
Carl Friedrich Abel (1723–87)
55, 58
Capel Bond (1730–90) *53*
William Jackson (1730–1803)
Thomas Erskine, Earl of Kelly
(1732–81) *55, 58*
Thomas Linley father
(1733–95)
Benjamin Cooke (1734–93)
53
Johann Christian Bach
(1735–82) *48, 54, 55, 58*
Jonathan Battishill
(1738–1801)
William Herschel (1738–1822)
Michael Arne (c1740–86)
Samuel Arnold (1740–1802)
50, 51
Samuel Webbe (1740–1816)
Joseph Corfe (1741–1820)
Charles Dibdin (1745–1814)
50
James Hook (1746–1827)
50, 53
William Shield (1748–1829)
50
John Stafford Smith
(1750–1836)
Muzio Clementi (1752–1832)
59
John Marsh (1752–1828)
Thomas Linley son (1756–78)
51
John Danby (c1757–98)
Charles Wesley (1757–1834)
58
Michael Kelly (1762–1826) *58*
Stephen Storace (1762–96)
50
Thomas Attwood (1765–1838)
59, 60, 62
John Callcott (1766–1821)
Samuel Wesley (1766–1837)
55, 58–9, 60, 61
Johann Baptist Cramer
(1771–1858) *59*
William Crotch (1775–1847)
59, 60, 61
John Parry (1776–1851) *60*
Thomas Moore (1779–1852)
John Field (1782–1837) *59, 61*
George Frederick Pinto
(1785–1806) *59*
Henry Bishop (1786–1855) *60*
Cipriani Potter (1792–1871)
59–60, 61

John Goss (1800–80)
John Barnett (1802–90) *62*

c1715 Three Choirs Festival
starts

1721 J S Bach's *Brandenburg
Concertos*
1728 Pepusch and John Gay's
The Beggar's Opera

Joseph Haydn (1732–1809)
1732 The first Covent Garden
Theatre opens

1742 Handel's *Messiah*
performed in Dublin

1749 Handel's *Musick for the
Royal Fireworks*

Wolfgang Amadeus Mozart
(1756–91)

Luigi Cherubini (1760–1842)
1762 Gluck's *Orfeo*
1764 Mozart meets J C Bach
in London

Ludwig van Beethoven
(1770–1827)

1776 Charles Burney
publishes his first volume of
History of Music

1785 Mozart's *The Marriage of
Figaro*
Carl Maria von Weber
(1786–1826)
Gioachino Rossini
(1792–1868)
Franz Schubert (1797–1828)
Hector Berlioz (1803–69)

Julius Benedict (1804–85) *64*
John Thomson (1805–41)
Michael Balfe (1808–70)
62–3, 64
Samuel Sebastian Wesley
(1810–76) *58, 61, 62*
John Pike Hullah (1812–84)
7, 63
William Vincent Wallace
(1812–65) *62, 63, 64*
Edward James Loder (1813–65)
62
George Macfarren (1813–87)
62, 67
Henry Hugo Pierson
(1815–73) *62*
William Sterndale Bennett
(1816–75) *58, 61–2, 63*
John Thomas (1826–1913)
John Stainer (1840–1901)
Walter Parratt (1841–1924) *36*
Joseph Parry (1841–1903)
Arthur Sullivan (1842–1900)
61, 63–4, 64, 66
Alexander Campbell
Mackenzie (1847–1935)
68–9, 74, 78
Hubert Parry (1848–1918)
*61, 66, 67, 68, 69, 74, 76,
79, 85, 90*
Charles Lloyd (1849–1919)
Arthur Goring Thomas
(1850–92)
Frederick Corder (1852–1932)
Frederic Cowen (1852–1935)
68
Charles Villiers Stanford
(1852–1924)
*8, 61, 66–7, 68, 73, 74, 76,
78, 80, 81, 85, 90, 94, 95*
Alan Gray (1855–1935) *88*
Maud Valérie White
(1855–1937)
Frederic Cliffe (1857–1931) *68*
Edward Elgar (1857–1934) *8,
36, 61, 66, 67, 69, 70–2, 74,
76, 79, 80, 86, 87–8, 90, 104*
John Barkworth (1858–1929)
94
Ethel Smyth (1858–1944)
73, 94, 95
William Wallace (1860–1940)
68
Amy Woodforde-Finden
(1860–1919) *73*
Frederick Delius (1862–1934)
*8, 72, 74–5, 78, 79, 86,
88–9, 95*
Edward German (1862–1936)
68
Liza Lehmann (1862–1918)
73, 94
Dora Bright (1863–1951)
73, 95
Arthur Somervell (1863–1937)
Florence Ewart (1864–1949)
Learmont Drysdale
(1866–1909)

1805 Beethoven's *Fidelio*
Felix Mendelssohn (1809–47)
Frédéric Chopin (1810–49)

Robert Schumann (1810–56)
Franz Liszt (1811–86)
Richard Wagner (1813–83)
Giuseppe Verdi (1813–1901)
1813 Philharmonic Society
founded

1816 Rossini's *The Barber of
Seville*
1822 Royal Academy of Music
founded
Anton Bruckner (1824–96)
1825 British premiere of
Beethoven's Ninth Symphony
1830 Mendelssohn's Overture
Fingal's Cave
1832 Berlioz's *Symphonie
Fantastique*
Johannes Brahms (1833–97)
Peter Ilyich Tchaikovsky
(1840–93)
Georges Bizet (1838–75)
Antonín Dvořák (1841–1904)
1846 Mendelssohn's *Elijah*
Birmingham premiere

1850 Wagner's *Lohengrin*
1851 Verdi's *Rigoletto*

Leoš Janáček (1854–1928)

1855 Crystal Palace concerts
begin

Giacomo Puccini (1858–1924)
1860 Eisteddfod
re-inaugerated in Wales
Gustav Mahler (1860–1911)
1861 Brahms' First Piano
Concerto

Claude Debussy (1862–1918)

Richard Strauss (1864–1949)

Jean Sibelius (1865–1957)
Carl Nielsen (1865–1931)

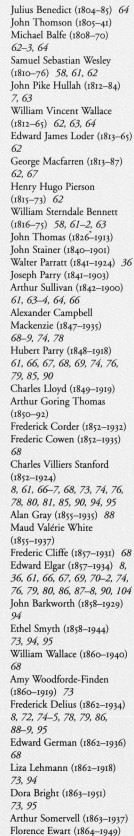

**right: A cartoon of Arthur Sullivan by Linley Sambourne, 1880
below: Gustav Holst at work in his soundproof room at St Paul's Girl's School in 1931**

Edmund Rubbra (1901–86)
80, 86, 96, 101, 105, 107, 108
Freda Swain (1902–85)
William Walton (1902–83)
62, 80, 81, 85, 86, 87, 88, 89, 94, 96, 98, 100, 104, 106, 107, 112
Ralph W Wood (1902–87)
Lennox Berkeley (1903–89)
96, 106, 107, 111
Eric Fogg (1903–39) *86*
Walter Goehr (1903–60) *89, 110*
Berthold Goldschmidt
(1903–) *7, 89, 99*
Richard Hall (1903–82)
Leighton Lucas (1903–82) *86*
Robin Milford (1903–59)
Thomas Pitfield (1903–)
Priaulx Rainier (1903–86)
112
Percy Whitlock (1903–46)
Richard Addinsell (1904–77)
80
Erik Chisholm (1904–65)
94, 96
William Alwyn (1905–85)
80, 89, 101, 107, 108
Francis Chagrin (1905–72) *80*
Christian Darnton (1905–81)
96
Constant Lambert (1905–51)
70, 80, 81, 85, 86, 88, 89, 94, 104
Walter Leigh (1905–42) *95*
Elizabeth Poston (1905–87)
89
Alan Rawsthorne (1905–71)
80, 87, 89, 100–1, 107
Mátyás Seiber (1905–60) *99*
Michael Tippett (1905–)
8, 87, 88, 95, 96, 98, 101, 103–4, 105, 106, 107, 112
Arnold Cooke (1906–)
108
Benjamin Frankel (1906–73)
80, 98, 100, 107
Elisabeth Lutyens (1906–83)
81, 95, 100, 106, 107, 108, 110
Grace Williams (1906–77)
95, 105–6
Imogen Holst (1907–84)
Elizabeth Maconchy
(1907–94) *95, 100, 106, 108, 111, 112*
Howard Ferguson (1908–)
108
William Wordsworth
(1908–88) *108*
Brian Easdale (1909–) *80*
Arwel Hughes (1909–88)
Minna Keal (1909–) *118*
Herbert Murrill (1909–52)
Robin Orr (1909–)
Mansel Thomas (1909–86)
Robert Still (1910–71)

1902 Debussy's *Pelléas et Mélisande*

1903 Janáček's *Jenůfa*

1904 Puccini's *Madama Butterfly*

1905 Debussy's *La Mer*

1905 Strauss's *Salome*

1906 Ives' *The Unanswered Question*
Dmitri Shostakovich (1906–75)
1907 Scriabin's *Poem of Ecstasy*

Olivier Messiaen (1908–92)

Elliott Carter (1908–)

1909 Vaughan Williams' *Fantasia on a Theme of Thomas Tallis*

1911 Mahler's *Das Lied von der Erde*

1911 Strauss's *Der Rosenkavalier*

above: **Sir Edward Elgar and the 17-year-old Yehudi Menuhin at HMV's Abbey Road Studios on the occasion of the famous recording of the Violin Concerto** *below:* **The Scottish composer Thea Musgrave**

Franz Reizenstein (1911–68)
99
Phyllis Tate (1911–87) *95, 106*
Daniel Jones (1912–93) *101*
Stanley Bate (1913–59) *96*
Benjamin Britten (1913–76)
67, 76, 80, 83, 86, 87, 89, 93, 94, 96, 98, 102–3, 104, 105, 106, 107, 112–3
Ronald Center (1913–73)
Cedric Thorpe Davie
(1913–83)
George Lloyd (1913–)
96, 115–6
Wilfrid Mellers (1914–)
Andrzej Panufnik (1914–91)
99, 112
Humphrey Searle (1915–82)
100, 105
Denis ApIvor (1916–)
Bernard Stevens (1916–83)
96, 98, 99, 100, 107, 108
Richard Arnell (1917–)
John Gardner (1917–)
John Addison (1920–)
Geoffrey Bush (1920–)
Peter Racine Fricker (1920–)
100, 107
Malcolm Arnold (1921–)
67, 80, 101/5, 107, 108
Ruth Gipps (1921–) *95, 96*
Antony Hopkins (1921–)
Robert Simpson (1921–)
99, 101, 108, 111, 112
Peter Wishart (1921–84)
Iain Hamilton (1922–) *112*
Madeleine Dring (1923–77)
Stephen Dodgson (1924–)
Anthony Milner (1925–)
Francis Burt (1926–)
John Buller (1927–)
Wilfred Josephs (1927–)
John Joubert (1927–)
Thomas Wilson
(1927–) *112*
Thea Musgrave
(1928–) *112*
Gerard Schurmann
(1928–) *112*
Ronald Stevenson
(1928–) *99*
Alun Hoddinott
(1929–) *112*
Kenneth Leighton
(1929–88) *112*
Christopher Headington
(1930–)
John Mayer (1930–) *117*
David Lumsdaine (1931–)
Malcolm Williamson
(1931–) *36, 112*
Alexander Goehr (1932–)
108, 110
Malcolm Lipkin (1932–)
George Newson (1932–)
Robert Sherlaw Johnson
(1932–)

John Cage (1912–92)

1912 Schoenberg's *Pierrot Lunaire*

1913 Stravinsky's *The Rite of Spring*

Witold Lutoslawski (1913–94)

1915 Sibelius' Fifth Symphony
1916 Jazz achieves wide popularity in America

1917 Salzburg Festival founded
Leonard Bernstein (1918–90)
1918 Bartók's *Duke Bluebeard's Castle*
1919 Elgar's Cello Concerto

1920 Holst's *The Planets*

1921 Prokofiev's *The Love for Three Oranges*

1922 BBC founded
1922 Bliss's *A Colour Symphony*
Iannis Xenakis (1922–)
1923 Walton's *Façade*
1924 Gershwin's *Rhapsody in Blue*
1925 Berg's *Wozzeck*
Pierre Boulez (1925–)
Hans Werner Henze (1926–)

1926 Janáček's *Glagolitic Mass*

Karlheinz Stockhausen
(1928–)

1930 Stravinsky's *Symphony of Psalms*

1930 BBC Symphony Orchestra founded
1931 Walton's *Belshazzar's Feast*

1934 Hindemith's *Mathis der Maler*

1934 Rachmaninov's *Rhapsody on a Theme of Paganini*

Alfred Schnittke (1934–)

1935 Gershwin's *Porgy and Bess*
1935 Prokofiev's *Romeo and Juliet*
1935 Berg's Violin Concerto

1937 Shostakovich's Fifth Symphony

1939 Bartók's Sixth Quartet

1941 Tippett's *A Child of Our Time*

1943 Vaughan Williams' Fifth Symphony

1944 Copland's *Appalachian Spring*
1944 Bliss's *Miracle in the Gorbals*

1945 Britten's *Peter Grimes*

1946 Third Programme begins on BBC Radio

1947 Edinburgh Festival founded

below left: Jonathan Harvey
below: The new Glyndebourne Festival Theatre, opened in 1994

1948 Strauss's *Four Last Songs*

1948 Aldeburgh Festival founded

1949 Messiaen's *Turangalila Symphony*

1951 Stravinsky's *The Rake's Progress*
1951 Vaughan Williams' *The Pilgrim's Progress*

1951 Royal Festival Hall opens

1953 Vaughan Williams' *Sinfonia Antartica*

1954 Britten's *The Turn of the Screw*

1957 Bernstein's *West Side Story*
1957 Poulenc's *Dialogues des Carmélites*

1960 Boulez's *Pli selon pli*

1961 Elliott Carter's Double Concerto
1962 Britten's *War Requiem* and Tippett's *King Priam*

1974 Britten's *Death in Venice*

RECOMMENDED RECORDINGS

During the past 10 to 15 years the repertory of recorded British music has grown enormously, due in part to the CD revolution. The listener interested in this country's classical music now has the choice of hundreds of CDs offering a huge range of works from all periods on many different labels. Chandos and Hyperion in particular have a wealth of British music releases – almost 500 discs between them – but many of the medium and small-scale independent companies such as ASV, Collins Classics, Conifer, Collegium Records, Continuum, CRD, Dutton Laboratories, Gimell, Lyrita, Meridian, Naxos/Marco Polo, Nimbus, NMC, Unicorn-Kanchana, Saydisc and Amon Ra also have fascinating repertoire often not otherwise available. And some of the large companies have exclusively British series (British Composers on EMI; British Pageant on Sony; The British Line on Teldec) or labels with an interesting British repertoire (BMG's Catalyst; Decca's Argo).

This discography (arranged to complement material in the chapters) is an attempt to give the bewildered listener a representative selection of music from the Middle Ages to today. Since the list is limited to around 270 entries, some major works have had to be omitted so that lesser known composers could feature, but all the CDs have been chosen for musical interest as well as for the quality of performance and recording. Together the recommended discs make an excellent introduction to each period of British music.

All the listed CDs were available at the time of this book's publication but deletions do occur and no responsibility can be taken for inaccurate information. The numbers refer to CDs only, although in some cases cassettes may also be available.

1

ENGLISH NATIONAL SONGS
21 Songs from the Elizabethan to the Victorian eras
John Potter, Lucie Skeaping, The Broadside Band/Jeremy Barlow
Saydisc CD-SDL 400

FAIRE IS THE HEAVEN
Music of the English Church from Tallis to Howells and Poston
The Cambridge Singers/John Rutter
Collegium COLCD 107

FROM TAVERNER TO TAVENER
Five Centuries of Music at Christ Church, Oxford
Christ Church Cathedral Choir/Stephen Darlington
Nimbus NI 5328

IN PRAISE OF WOMAN
150 years of English women composers including Smyth, Lehmann, Clarke, Lutyens, Maconchy, Tate
Anthony Rolfe Johnson (tenor), Graham Johnson (piano)
Hyperion CDA66709

LAST NIGHT OF THE PROMS – THE 100TH SEASON
including *Belshazzar's Feast*; *Pomp and Circumstance March No 1*; *Fantasia on British Sea Songs*; *Rule Britannia!*; *Jerusalem*
Bryn Terfel, Evelyn Glennie, BBC Singers, BBC SO & Chorus/Andrew Davis
Teldec 4509-97868-2

SCOTLAND'S MUSIC
An Anthology of Scottish Music from the 9th century to today
Various artists including the BBC Scottish SO
Linn Records CKD008 (2 discs)

TRADITIONAL SONGS OF WALES (CANEUON TRADDODIADOL CYMRU)
23 Songs accompanied by Welsh triple harp, cittern, bagpipe, hurdy gurdy etc
Siwsann George
Saydisc CD-SDL 406

2

COLUMBA, MOST HOLY OF SAINTS
Scottish Medieval Plainchant
Cappella Nova/Alan Tavener
ASV Gaudeamus CD GAU 129

WALTER FRYE
Missa 'Flos Regalis'; *Trinitas dies etc*
The Hilliard Ensemble
ECM 437 684-2

GABRIEL'S GREETING
Medieval Engish Christmas Music
Sinfonye/Stevie Wishart
Hyperion CDA66685

LANCASTER AND VALOIS
English and French Music, 1350–1420
Gothic Voices/Christopher Page
Hyperion CDA66588

THE SERVICE OF VENUS AND MARS
Music for the Knights of the Garter, 1340–1440, by Pycard, Power, Dunstable and others
Andrew Lawrence-King (medieval harp), Gothic Voices/Christopher Page
Hyperion CDA66238

SUMER IS ICUMEN IN
Medieval English songs; Motets; Mass (excerpts); 3 hymns by St Godric
The Hilliard Ensemble/Paul Hillier
Harmonia Mundi HMC90 1154

WORCESTER FRAGMENTS
English sacred music of the Middle Ages
The Orlando Consort
Amon Ra CD-SAR 59

3

ROBERT CARVER
The Complete Sacred Choral Music
Cappella Nova/Alan Tavener
ASV Gaudeamus CD GAX 319
(3 discs, also available separately)

WILLIAM CORNYSH
Stabat Mater and other sacred music
The Tallis Scholars/Peter Phillips
Gimell CDGIM 014

MUSIC FROM THE ETON CHOIRBOOK
by Browne, Cornysh, Davy, Fayrfax, Lambe, Sheryngham, Wylkynson etc
Volume 1: The Rose and the Ostrich Feather
Volume 2: The Crown of Thorns
Volume 3: The Pillars of Eternity
Volume 4: The Flower of All Virginity
The Sixteen/Harry Christophers
Collins 13142, 13162, 13422, 13952
(4 separate discs)

ROBERT FAYRFAX
Missa Albanus; *Aeternae laudis lilium*
The Sixteen/Harry Christophers
Hyperion CDA66073

THE FIELD OF CLOTH OF GOLD
A celebration in music of the 1520 meeting between Henry VIII and François I of France
Musica Antiqua of London/Philip Thorby
Amon Ra CD-SAR 51

NICHOLAS LUDFORD
Missa Videte miraculum; *Ave cuius conceptio*
The Cardinall's Musick/Andrew Carwood
ASV Gaudeamus CD GAU 131

JOHN SHEPPARD
The Church Music of John Sheppard, Volume 1 (11 responsories)
The Sixteen/Harry Christophers
Hyperion CDA66259

SHEPPARD
*Media vita; Christe Redemptor omnium;
Sacris solemnis* etc
The Tallis Scholars/Peter Phillips
Gimell CDGIM 016

JOHN TAVERNER
*Missa Gloria tibi Trinitas; Leroy Kyrie;
Dum transisset Sabbatum*
The Tallis Scholars/Peter Phillips
Gimell CDGIM 004

TAVERNER
*Missa Sancti Wilhelmi; Dum transisset
Sabbatum; Ex eius tumba; O Wilhelme,
pastor bone*
The Sixteen/Harry Christophers
Hyperion CDA66427

TAVERNER
The Western wynde – Mass and song
(with Tallis's *Missa Salve intemerata
Virgo*)
Choir of St John's College,
Cambridge/George Guest
CFP CD-CFP 4654

CHRISTOPHER TYE
*Mass 'Euge bone', Peccavimus patribus
nostris* (with Sheppard's *Libera nos, salva
nos* and other works)
The Clerkes of Oxenford/David
Wulstan
Proudsound PROU CD 126

WESTERN WIND MASSES
by Taverner, Tye, Sheppard
The Tallis Scholars/Peter Phillips
Gimell CDGIM 027

4

AWAKE, SWEET LOVE
Songs and lute solos by Dowland,
Campion, Danyel, Ferrabosco, Ford etc
James Bowman (countertenor),
David Miller (lute), The King's Consort
Hyperion CDA66447

WILLIAM BYRD
*Sacred Choral Music – Masses for 3, 4
& 5 voices; The Great Service, Anthems
& Motets*
The Tallis Scholars/Peter Phillips
Gimell CDGIM 343/4 (2 discs)

BYRD
*Consort and Keyboard Music, Songs
and Anthems*
Rose Consort of Viols with Red Byrd
Naxos 8.550604

BYRD
My Ladye Nevells Booke
Christopher Hogwood (virginals,
harpsichord, chamber organ)
L'Oiseau-Lyre 430 484-2 (3 discs)

BYRD
Motets and anthems
The Cambridge Singers/John Rutter
Collegium COLCD 110

BYRD
*Gradualia – Volume 1: The Marian
Masses*
The William Byrd Choir/Gavin Turner
Hyperion CDA66451

JOHN DOWLAND
Lachrimae, or Sevean Teares
Dowland Consort, Jakob Lindberg
(lute)
BIS CD315

DOWLAND
Second Booke of Songes
Emma Kirkby, Martyn Hill etc, The
Consort of Musicke/Anthony Rooley
L'Oiseau-Lyre 425 889-2

DOWLAND
Dances of Dowland
Julian Bream (lute)
BMG/RCA Julian Bream Edition
09026 61586 2

**ELIZABETHAN CHRISTMAS
ANTHEMS**
Red Byrd with The Rose Consort of
Viols
Amon Ra CD-SAR 46

**ELIZABETHAN & JACOBEAN
CONSORT MUSIC**
by Brade, Byrd, Campion, Coleman,
Holborne, Jenkins, Morley etc
Catherine Bott (soprano),
Michael George (bass), New London
Consort/Philip Pickett
Linn Records CD CKD 011

**FLORA GAVE ME THE
FAIREST FLOWERS**
English madrigals by Morley, East,
Gibbons, Byrd, Weelkes, Wilbye,
Tomkins etc
Members of the Cambridge
Singers/John Rutter
Collegium COLCD 105

MARY'S MUSIC
*Songs and Dances from the time of
Mary, Queen of Scots*
Scottish Early Music Consort/Warwick
Edwards
Chandos CHAN 0529

THOMAS MORLEY
Ayres and Madrigals
The Consort of Musicke/Anthony
Rooley
L'Oiseau-Lyre 436 862-2

THOMAS TALLIS
Lamentations of Jeremiah; Motets
The Tallis Scholars/Peter Phillips
Gimell CDGIM 025

TALLIS
*Spem in Alium; Gaude gloriosa; Miserere
nostri; Salvator mundi I and II etc*
The Tallis Scholars/Peter Phillips
Gimell CDGIM 006

TALLIS
The Complete English Anthems
The Tallis Scholars/Peter Phillips
Gimell CDGIM 007

THE WOODS SO WILD
Lute music by Byrd, Cutting, Dowland,
Holborne, Francesco da Milano
Julian Bream (lute)
BMG/RCA Julian Bream Edition
09026 61587 2

5

ORLANDO GIBBONS
*Music for Prince Charles
Fantasias for the Great Double Bass'*
(with *Fantasies and Fantasy Airs
a 3 and 4* by Thomas Lupo)
The Parley of Instruments/Peter
Holman
Hyperion CDA66395

GIBBONS
Anthems and Verse anthems
King's College Choir, Cambridge,
Philip Ledger with John Butt (organ),
London Early Music Group
ASV Gaudeamus CD GAU123

TOBIAS HUME
*Captaine Humes Poeticall Musicke;
The First Part of Ayres*
Monserrat Figueras (soprano); Paul
Hillier (bass), Hesperion XX/Jordi Savall
Deutsche Harmonia Mundi RD77165

JOHN JENKINS
Lyra Consorts and Fantasia Suites
The Parley of Instruments/Peter
Holman
Hyperion CDA66604

JENKINS
All in a Garden Green – consort music
The Rose Consort of Viols
Naxos 8.550687

WILLIAM LAWES
*For ye Violls – Consort Setts in 5 and
6 parts*
Fretwork/Paul Nicholson
Virgin VC7 59021 2

MARTIN PEERSON
*Private Musicke – Motets, Anthems and
Airs*
Wren Baroque Soloists/Martin Elliott
Collins 14372

PETER PHILIPS
Motets
Winchester Cathedral Choir, The Parley
of Instruments/David Hill
Hyperion CDA66643

PHILIPS
Keyboard Music
Paul Nicholson (harpsichords)
Hyperion CDA66734

**JOHN PLAYFORD'S POPULAR
TUNES**
from the 17th-century publications
entitled *The Dancing Master*
The Broadside Band
Amon Ra CD-SAR 28

THOMAS TOMKINS
*The Great Service (No 3); Anthems;
Organ Voluntaries*
Choir of New College, Oxford/Edward
Higginbottom, David Burchall (organ)
CRD 3467

THOMAS WEELKES
Cathedral Music
Winchester Cathedral Choir/David Hill
Hyperion CDA66477

6

JOHN BLOW
Verse Anthems
Soloists, King's College Choir, Academy
of St Martin in the Fields/David
Willcocks
Decca 436 259-2

BLOW
Venus and Adonis
Soloists, London Baroque &
Choir/Charles Medlam
Harmonia Mundi HMA190 1276

**FOUR AND TWENTY
FIDDLERS**
Music for the Restoration Court band
by Banister, Locke, Grabu, Purcell etc
The Parley of Instruments Renaissance
Violin Band/Peter Holman
Hyperion CDA66667

PELHAM HUMFREY
Verse Anthems
Soloists, Choir of Clare College,
Cambridge, Romanesca/Nicholas
McGegan
Harmonia Mundi HMU90 7053

MATTHEW LOCKE
Anthems, Motets and the Oxford Ode
Soloists, New College Choir, The Parley
of Instruments/Edward Higginbottom
Hyperion CDA66373

LOCKE
Psyche
Soloists, New London Consort/Philip
Pickett
L'Oiseau-Lyre (awaiting release)

**MUSIC OF THE 'CHAPELS
ROYAL'**
Anthems and Motets by Locke, Blow,
Humfrey and Purcell
Soloists, Monteverdi Choir, English
Baroque Soloists/John Eliot Gardiner
Erato 2292-45987-2

HENRY PURCELL
The Complete Anthems and Services,
Volumes I–II
Soloists, Choir of New College, Oxford,
Choir of The King's Consort,
The King's Consort/Robert King
Hyperion CDA66585, 66609, 66623,
66644, 66656, 66663, 66677, 66686,
66693, 66707, 66716
(11 separate discs)

PURCELL
Dido and Aeneas
Janet Baker, Herincx, Clark, Sinclair,
St Anthony Singers, ECO/Anthony
Lewis
Decca 425 720-2

PURCELL
Dioclesian; Timon of Athens
Soloists, Monteverdi Choir, English
Baroque Soloists/John Eliot Gardiner
Erato 4509-96556-2 (2 discs)

PURCELL
The Fairy Queen
Soloists, Schütz Choir of London,
London Classical Players/Roger
Norrington
EMI CDS 5 55234 2 (2 discs)

PURCELL
King Arthur
Soloists, English Baroque Soloists/John
Eliot Gardiner
Erato 4509-96552-2 (2 discs)

PURCELL
Ayres for the Theatre (including
*Chacony in G minor, Suites from
Abdelazer, The Gordion Knot Unty'd* etc)
The Parley of Instruments/Peter
Holman
Hyperion CDA66212

PURCELL
*Come, ye sons of art away, Funeral music
for Queen Mary*
Soloists, Equale Brass Ensemble,
Monteverdi Choir & Orchestra/John
Eliot Gardiner
Erato 4509-96553-2

PURCELL
The Complete Odes and Welcome
Songs
Soloists, Choir of New College,
The King's Consort/Robert King
Hyperion CDS44031/8
(8 discs, also available separately with
different numbers)

PURCELL
Sonatas of 3 Parts etc
Purcell Quartet, Risa Browder
Chandos CHAN 8591, 8663, 8763
(3 separate discs)

7

THOMAS ARNE
Eight Overtures
The Academy of Ancient
Music/Christopher Hogwood
L'Oiseau-Lyre 436 859-2

ARNE
Six Favourite Concertos
The Parley of Instruments/Paul
Nicholson (organ, harpsichord,
fortepiano)
Hyperion CDA66509

**DR ARNE AT VAUXHALL
GARDENS**
Music by Thomas Arne including
*Cantata 'The Morning'; Sigh no more,
ladies* etc
Emma Kirkby (soprano), Richard
Morton (tenor), The Parley of
Instruments/Roy Goodman
Hyperion CDA66237

J C BACH
Six Grand Overtures
English SO/William Boughton
Nimbus NI 5403

J C BACH
*London Symphonies, Op 18 Nos 1, 4, 6,
Op 6 No 6*
Collegium Aureum
BMG/Deutsche Harmonia Mundi
GD77179

WILLIAM BOYCE
Solomon – A Serenata
Bronwen Mills, Howard Crook, The
Parley of Instruments/Roy Goodman
Hyperion CDA66378

BOYCE
Symphonies Nos 1–8
The English Concert/Trevor Pinnock
Archiv 419 631-2

CHARLES DIBDIN
*The Ephesian Matron; The Brickdust
Man; The Grenadier*
Soloists, Opera Restor'd/Peter Holman
Hyperion CDA66608

JOHN GAY/J C PEPUSCH
The Beggar's Opera
Kiri Te Kanawa, James Morris,
Joan Sutherland etc, London Opera
Chorus, National PO/Richard Bonynge
Decca 430 066-2 (2 discs)

MAURICE GREENE
Anthems and Voluntaries
The Choir of New College,
Oxford/Edward Higginbottom
CRD 3484

GEORGE FRIDERIC HANDEL
*Four Coronation Anthems; Musick for the
Royal Fireworks*
Choir of New College, Oxford,
The King's Consort/Robert King
Hyperion CDA66350

HANDEL
Solomon
Soloists, Monteverdi Choir, English
Baroque Soloists/John Eliot Gardiner
Philips 412 612-2 (2 discs)

THOMAS LINLEY (the Younger)
*A Lyric Ode on the Fairies, Aerial Beings
and Witches of Shakespeare*
Soloists, The Parley of Instruments
Choir and Orchestra/Paul Nicholson
Hyperion CDA66613

RULE BRITANNIA
Music by Arne, Clarke, Eccles, Handel,
Purcell, Stanley etc
John Wallace (trumpet), Edmund
Barham (tenor), Leeds Festival Chorus,
English String O/William Boughton
Nimbus NI 5155

JOHN STANLEY
Six Concertos in Seven Parts, Op 2
The Parley of Instruments/Roy
Goodman
Hyperion CDA66338

8

MICHAEL BALFE
The Bohemian Girl
Nova Thomas, Patrick Power,
Jonathan Summers,
National SO of Ireland/Richard
Bonynge
Argo 433 324-2 (2 discs)

**WILLIAM STERNDALE
BENNETT**
Piano Concertos Nos 1 & 3; Caprice
Malcolm Binns (piano), LPO/Nicholas
Braithwaite
Lyrita SRCD 204

STERNDALE BENNETT
*Symphony in G minor; Piano Concerto
No 4; Fantasia in A*
Malcolm Binns (piano), Milton Keynes
CO/Hilary Davan Wetton
Unicorn-Kanchana UKCD 2032

WILLIAM CROTCH
*Sinfonias in E flat and F; Organ
Concerto No 2; Overture in G*
Milton Keynes CO/Hilary Davan
Wetton
Unicorn-Kanchana DKPCD 9126

JOHN FIELD
Nocturnes and Sonatas
John O'Conor (piano)
Telarc CD-80199 & 80290
(2 separate discs)

**THE LONDON PIANO
SCHOOL**
Music by Clementi, Wesley, Pinto,
Field, Cramer, S S Wesley,
Sterndale Bennett
Ian Hobson (piano)
Arabesque Z 6594, 6595, 6596
(3 discs)

CIPRIANI POTTER
Symphonies Nos 8 & 10
Milton Keynes CO/Hilary Davan
Wetton
Unicorn-Kanchana DKPCD 9091

THE ROMANTIC MUSE
English Music in the time of Beethoven
by Pinto, Attwood, Storace, Corfe,
Samuel Wesley and others
Invocation/Timothy Roberts
(fortepiano)
Hyperion CDA66740

ARTHUR SULLIVAN
*Irish Symphony, Overture di Ballo, Cello
Concerto*
RLPO/Charles Groves, Julian Lloyd
Webber (cello), LSO/Charles Mackerras
EMI CDM7 64726 2

SULLIVAN
The Mikado
Welsh National Opera/Charles
Mackerras
Telarc CD-80284

SULLIVAN
The Gondoliers
D'Oyly Carte Opera Chorus &
Orchestra/John Pryce-Jones
That's Entertainment CD-TER2 1187

SULLIVAN
Operatic highlights from *The Mikado,
Iolanthe, The Pirates of Penzance, HMS
Pinafore* etc
Soloists, Glyndebourne Festival Chorus,
Pro Arte Orchestra/Malcolm Sargent
CFP CD-CFP 4238

SAMUEL SEBASTIAN WESLEY
Cathedral Anthems, Volumes 1 & 2
Adrian Partington (organ), Choir of
Worcester Cathedral/Donald Hunt
Hyperion CDA66446 & 66469

SAMUEL WESLEY
Symphonies Nos 3–6
Milton Keynes CO/Hilary Davan
Wetton
Unicorn-Kanchana DKPCD 9098

**VICTORIAN CONCERT
OVERTURES**
by Macfarren, Pierson, Sullivan, Corder,
Elgar, Parry & Mackenzie
English Northern Philharmonia/David
Lloyd-Jones
Hyperion CDA66515

SAMUEL COLERIDGE-TAYLOR
Scenes from The Song of Hiawatha
(complete)
Soloists, Welsh National Opera Chorus
& Orchestra/Kenneth Alwyn
Argo 430 356-2 (2 discs)

FREDERIC COWEN
*Symphony No 3 'Scandinavian'; Indian
Rhapsody, The Butterfly's Ball*
Czechoslovak State Philharmonic/
Adrian Leaper
Marco Polo 8.223273

BENJAMIN J DALE
*Piano Sonata in D minor; Prunella;
Night Fancies*
Peter Jacobs (piano)
Continuum CCD 1044

EDWARD ELGAR
Cello Concerto; Sea Pictures
Jacqueline du Pré (cello), Janet Baker
(mezzo-soprano)
LSO/John Barbirolli
EMI CDC7 47329 2

ELGAR
The Dream of Gerontius (with Parry's
Blest Pair of Sirens & *I was glad*)
Palmer, Davies, Howell, LSO &
Chorus/Richard Hickox
Chandos CHAN 8641/2 (2 discs)

ELGAR
*Enigma Variations; Cockaigne;
Introduction & Allegro; Serenade for
strings*
BBC SO/Andrew Davis
Teldec British Line 9031-73279-2

ELGAR
The Kingdom (with Elgar transcriptions
of Bach and Handel)
Kenny, Hodgson, Gillett, Luxon, LPO
& Choir/Leonard Slatkin
BMG/RCA RD 07863 57862 2
(2 discs)

ELGAR
Symphony No 1; Imperial March
BBC Philharmonic/George Hurst
Naxos 8.550634

ELGAR
Symphony No 2; Serenade for strings
LPO/Leonard Slatkin
BMG/RCA RD 09026 60072 2

ELGAR
Violin Concerto
Nigel Kennedy (violin), LPO/Vernon
Handley
EMI Eminence CD-EMX 2058

THE ELGAR EDITION
Volumes 1–3
*Symphonies Nos 1 & 2; Violin & Cello
Concertos; Falstaff; Pomp & Circumstance
Marches; In the South* etc
conducted by Edward Elgar
EMI CDS7 54560 2; CDS7 54564 2;
CDS7 54568 2 (3 discs each)

HAMILTON HARTY
*With the Wild Geese; In Ireland;
Piano Concerto*
Malcolm Binns (piano), Ulster
Orchestra/Bryden Thomson
Chandos CHAN 8321

**JOHN BLACKWOOD
MCEWEN**
Three Border Ballads
London Philharmonic/Alasdair Mitchell
Chandos CHAN 9241

**ALEXANDER CAMPBELL
MACKENZIE**
*Benedictus; Scottish Rhapsody No 2
'Burns'* & other orchestral works
BBC Scottish SO/Martyn Brabbins
Hyperion CDA66764 (to be released in
March 1995)

**MUSIC OF THE FOUR
COUNTRIES**
by MacCunn, German, Harty & Smyth
Scottish National Orchestra/Alexander
Gibson
CFP CD-CFP 4635

HUBERT PARRY
*Symphonies Nos 1–5; Symphonic
Variations*
LPO/Matthias Bamert
Chandos CHAN 9120–2 (3 discs)

PARRY
*English Suite; Lady Radnor's Suite;
Overture to an Unwritten Tragedy* etc
LSO, LPO/Adrian Boult
Lyrita SRCD 220

ETHEL SMYTH
The Wreckers
Soloists, Huddersfield Choral Society,
BBC Philharmonic/Odaline de la
Martinez
Conifer CDCF 250/1 (2 discs)

SMYTH
Piano Trio; Violin Sonata; Cello Sonata
Chagall Piano Trio
Meridian CDE 84286

**CHARLES VILLIERS
STANFORD**
Symphonies Nos 1–7
Ulster Orchestra/Vernon Handley
Chandos CHAN 9279/82 (4 discs)
(The symphonies are also available
separately, coupled mostly with the *Irish
Rhapsodies*)

STANFORD
Clarinet Concerto in A minor
(with Finzi's *Clarinet Concerto*)
Thea King (clarinet), Philharmonia
Orchestra/Alun Francis
Hyperion CDA66001

STANFORD
*Magnificat for double choir; Three
Motets: Eternal Father* (with Parry's *Songs
of Farewell*)
Choir of Trinity College,
Cambridge/Richard Marlow
Conifer CDCF 155

10

GRANVILLE BANTOCK
Celtic Symphony; Hebridean Symphony;
The Sea Reivers; The Witch of Atlas
Royal PO/Vernon Handley
Hyperion CDA66450

ARNOLD BAX
Symphonies Nos 1–7
LPO, Ulster Orchestra/Bryden
Thomson
Chandos CHAN 8906/10 (5 discs)
(The symphonies are also available
separately with other Bax orchestral
works)

BAX
The Truth about the Russian Dancers;
From Dusk till Dawn
LPO/Bryden Thomson
Chandos CHAN 8863

BAX
Tintagel; The Garden of Fand; November
Woods; Northern Ballad No 1;
Mediterranean
LPO/Adrian Boult
Lyrita SRCD 231

BAX
Choral works: *Enchanted Summer;*
Walsinghame; Fatherland
Soloists, Brighton Festival Chorus,
RPO/Vernon Handley
Chandos CHAN 8625

LORD BERNERS
The Triumph of Neptune; Nicholas
Nickleby; Fantasie espagnole etc
RLPO/Barry Wordsworth
EMI CDM5 65098 2

ARTHUR BLISS
Conversations; Rhapsody; Rout;
Oboe Quintet; Madame Noy;
The Women of Yueh
Elizabeth Gale (soprano),
Anthony Rolfe Johnson (tenor),
Nash Ensemble/Lionel Friend
Hyperion CDA66137

BLISS
A Colour Symphony, Metamorphic
Variations
BBC Welsh SO/Barry Wordsworth
Nimbus NI 5294

RUTLAND BOUGHTON
The Immortal Hour
Anne Dawson, Maldwyn Davies etc,
Geoffrey Mitchell Choir, ECO/Alan G
Melville
Hyperion CDA66101/2 (2 discs)

HAVERGAL BRIAN
Symphony No 1 'Gothic'
Soloists, Slovak Philharmonic Choir
and other choirs, Slovak PO,
Czecho-Slovak RSO/Ondrej Lenard
Marco Polo 8.223280/1 (2 discs)

FRANK BRIDGE
Oration (Concerto elegiaco)
(with Britten's *Cello Symphony*)
Steven Isserlis (cello), City of London
Sinfonia/Richard Hickox
EMI CDM7 63909 2

BRIDGE
Phantasie Trio in C minor, Phantasy in
F sharp minor, Piano Trio No 2
Dartington Piano Trio, Patrick Ireland
(viola)
Hyperion CDA66279

BENJAMIN BRITTEN
Serenade for tenor, horn and strings,
Les Illuminations, Nocturne
Peter Pears (tenor), Barry Tuckwell
(horn), LSO, ECO/Benjamin Britten
Decca 436 395-2

BRITTEN
Piano Concerto, Violin Concerto
Sviatoslav Richter (piano),
Mark Lubotsky (violin),
ECO/Benjamin Britten
Decca 417 308-2

GEORGE BUTTERWORTH
A Shropshire Lad (with Vaughan
Williams' *Ten Blake Songs; Songs of*
Travel etc sung by Robert Tear)
Benjamin Luxon (baritone),
David Willison (piano)
Decca 430 368-2

REBECCA CLARKE
Viola Sonata; Morpheus; Lullaby (with
works by Bax, Britten, Bridge etc –
'English Music for Viola')
Paul Coletti (viola), Leslie Howard
(piano)
Hyperion CDA66687

ERIC COATES
Orchestral Works including *The Three*
Elizabeths; London Suite; The Dam
Busters March; Cinderella; The Three
Bears; Saxo-Rhapsody
RLPO/Charles Groves, LSO/Charles
Mackerras, CBSO/Reginald Kilbey
CFP CD-CFPD 4456 (2 discs)

FREDERICK DELIUS
Paris; In a Summer Garden; Brigg Fair;
The Walk to the Paradise Garden etc
BBC SO/Andrew Davis
Teldec British Line 4509-90845-2

DELIUS
A Song of Summer; Brigg Fair;
Eventyr etc
Hallé Orchestra/Vernon Handley
CFP CD-CFP 4568

DELIUS
Sea Drift; Songs of Sunset;
Songs of Farewell
Bryn Terfel (baritone), Sally Burgess
(soprano), Waynflete Singers, Southern
Voices, Bournemouth SO &
Chorus/Richard Hickox
Chandos CHAN 9214

DELIUS
Appalachia; excerpts from Koanga &
Hassan; On Hearing the First Cuckoo in
Spring; Summer Night on the River;
Songs
LPO, RPO etc/Thomas Beecham
Dutton Laboratories CDLX 7011

GEORGE DYSON
In Honour of the City; At the Tabard Inn;
Sweet Thames Run Softly
Stephen Roberts (baritone), Royal
College of Music Chamber Choir,
RPO/David Willcocks
Unicorn-Kanchana UKCD 2013

JOHN FOULDS
Dynamic Triptych (with Vaughan
Williams' *Piano Concerto*)
Howard Shelley (piano), RPO/Vernon
Handley
Lyrita SRCD 211

ARMSTRONG GIBBS
Symphonies Nos 1 & 3 'The
Westmorland'
National SO of Ireland/Andrew Penny
Marco Polo 8.223553

JOSEPH HOLBROOKE
Ulalume; Bronwen; The Bells;
The Raven; Byron
Slovak Philharmonic Choir,
Czecho-Slovak RSO/Adrian Leaper
Marco Polo 8.223446

GUSTAV HOLST
The Planets; Egdon Heath
BBC SO & Chorus/Andrew Davis
Teldec British Line 4509-94541-2

HOLST
Beni Mora; A Somerset Rhapsody;
Japanese Suite; Hammersmith etc
LPO, LSO/Adrian Boult
Lyrita SRCD 222

HOLST
The Cloud Messenger; The Hymn of Jesus
Della Jones (mezzo-soprano), LSO &
Chorus/Richard Hickox
Chandos CHAN 8901

HOLST
Lyric Movement; Double Violin Concerto;
Fugal Concerto; Brook Green Suite etc
Soloists, ECO/Imogen Holst
Lyrita SRCD 223

HOLST
Savitri; The Dream City (song-cycle orch
Matthews)
Felicity Palmer, Philip Langridge,
Stephen Varcoe, Richard Hickox
Singers,
City of London Sinfonia/Richard
Hickox
Hyperion CDA66099

HERBERT HOWELLS
Hymnus Paradisi; An English Mass
Julie Kennard (soprano), John Mark
Ainsley (tenor), RLPO & Choir/Vernon
Handley
Hyperion CDA66488

JOHN IRELAND
Scherzo & Cortège; Tritons; The Forgotten
Rite; Satyricon; The Overlanders
LSO/Richard Hickox
Chandos CHAN 8994

CONSTANT LAMBERT
Summer's Last Will and Testament;
Aubade Héroïque; The Rio Grande
Sally Burgess, William Shimell, Jack
Gibbons (piano), Leeds Festival Chorus,
Chorus of Opera North, English
Northern Philharmonia/David Lloyd-
Jones
Hyperion CDA66565

E J MOERAN
Symphony in G minor (with Ireland's
Piano Concerto in E flat)
Hallé Orchestra/Leslie Heward
Dutton Laboratories CDAX 8001

ROGER QUILTER
A Children's Overture; As You Like It;
Country Pieces etc
Czecho-Slovak RSO/Adrian Leaper
Marco Polo 8.223444

MICHAEL TIPPETT
A Child of Our Time
Soloists, CBSO & Chorus/Michael
Tippett
Collins 13392

RALPH VAUGHAN WILLIAMS
A Sea Symphony
Felicity Lott, Jonathan Summers, LPO
& Choir/Bernard Haitink
EMI CDC7 49911 2

VAUGHAN WILLIAMS
*A London Symphony, Concerto
Accademico, The Wasps Overture*
LSO/André Previn
BMG/RCA Gold Seal GD 90501

VAUGHAN WILLIAMS
*Symphony No 6; The Lark Ascending;
Fantasia on a Theme by Thomas Tallis*
Tasmin Little (violin), BBC SO/Andrew
Davis
Teldec British Line 9031 73127 2

VAUGHAN WILLIAMS
Sinfonia Antartica
Sheila Armstrong (soprano), LPO &
Choir/Bernard Haitink
EMI CDC 7 47516 2

VAUGHAN WILLIAMS
Piano Concerto; Symphony No 9
Howard Shelley (piano), LSO/Bryden
Thomson
Chandos CHAN 8941

VAUGHAN WILLIAMS
Job – A Masque for Dancing
LPO/Vernon Handley
CFP CD-CFP 4603

VAUGHAN WILLIAMS
The Pilgrim's Progress
Soloists, LPO & Choir/Adrian Boult
EMI CMS7 64212 2 (2 discs)

VAUGHAN WILLIAMS
Hugh the Drover
Soloists, Corydon Singers &
Orchestra/Matthew Best
Hyperion CDA66901/2 (2 discs)

VAUGHAN WILLIAMS
*Serenade to Music; Flos Campi; 5 Mystical
Songs; Fantasia on Christmas Carols*
16 Soloists, Thomas Allen, Nobuko
Imai, Corydon Singers,
ECO/Matthew Best
Hyperion CDA66420

WILLIAM WALTON
*Symphony No 1, Viola Concerto (plus 3
Songs from Façade)*
LSO/Hamilton Harty, Frederick Riddle
(viola), LSO/William Walton
Dutton Laboratories CDAX 8003

WALTON
*Façade; Siesta; Scapino & Portsmouth
Point Overtures*
Edith Sitwell, Peter Pears, English
Opera Group Ensemble/Anthony
Collins, LPO/Adrian Boult
Decca 425 661-2

WALTON
*Belshazzar's Feast; Coronation Te Deum;
Violin Concerto*
Benjamin Luxon, LPO & Choir/Georg
Solti, Kyung Wha Chung (violin),
LSO/André Previn
Decca 440 324-2

WALTON
Henry V – A Shakespeare Scenario
(arr Palmer)
Christopher Plummer (narrator),
Choristers of Westminster Cathedral,
Academy of St Martin in the Fields &
Chorus/Neville Marriner
Chandos CHAN 8892

WALTON
*Suite: The Quest; Sinfonia Concertante;
Music for Children; Capriccio Burlesco* etc
Peter Katin (piano), LSO,
LPO/William Walton
Lyrita SRCD 224

WALTON
*Christopher Columbus Suite; Anon in
Love; The Twelve* etc
Soloists, Westminster Singers, City of
London Sinfonia/Richard Hickox
Chandos CHAN 8824

PETER WARLOCK
The Curlew, 12 Songs, Capriol Suite
James Griffett (tenor), Haffner Quartet,
RPO/Alan Barlow
ASV Quicksilva CD QS 6143

WAR'S EMBERS
Songs by Ivor Gurney, Farrar, Browne,
Kelly, Butterworth
Martyn Hill (tenor), Stephen Varcoe
(baritone), Michael George (bass),
Clifford Benson (piano)
Hyperion CDA66261/2 (2 discs)

HAYDN WOOD
*London Cameos Suite, Rhapsody
Mylecharane, The Seafarer* etc
Czecho-Slovak RSO/Adrian Leaper
Marco Polo 8.223402

WILLIAM ALWYN
Symphony No 3; Violin Concerto
Lydia Mordkovitch (violin),
LSO/Richard Hickox
Chandos CHAN 9187

ALWYN
*Symphony No 4; Elizabethan Dances;
Festival March*
LSO/Richard Hickox
Chandos CHAN 8902

MALCOLM ARNOLD
*Symphony No 2; A Grand Grand
Overture, Concerto for two pianos;
A Carnival of Animals*
Nettle & Markham (piano duet),
RPO/Vernon Handley
Conifer CDCF 240

ARNOLD
Symphonies Nos 3 & 4
LSO/Richard Hickox
Chandos CHAN 9290

ARNOLD
*English Dances; Scottish Dances; Cornish
Dances; Irish Dances; Sarabande & Polka
from Solitaire*
LPO/Malcolm Arnold
Lyrita SRCD 201

ARNOLD
*Film Music including The Sound Barrier;
The Bridge on the River Kwai*
LSO/Richard Hickox
Chandos CHAN 9100

LENNOX BERKELEY
*Symphony No 3; Serenade; Partita;
Canzonetta; Divertimento; Mont Juic*
(written with Britten)
LPO/Lennox Berkeley
Lyrita SRCD 226

**BRITISH FILM MUSIC FROM
THE 1940s AND 1950s**
by Addinsell, Addison, Arnold, Frankel,
Alwyn, Vaughan Williams etc
Various orchestras and conductors,
EMI CDGO 2059

BENJAMIN BRITTEN
Peter Grimes
Peter Pears, Claire Watson, Evans,
Brannigan, Orchestra and Chorus of
the Royal Opera House, Covent
Garden/Benjamin Britten
Decca 414 577-2 (3 discs)

BRITTEN
The Turn of the Screw
Philip Langridge, Felicity Lott,
Aldeburgh Festival Ensemble/Steuart
Bedford
Collins 70302 (2 discs)

BRITTEN
*Four Sea Interludes & Passacaglia from
Peter Grimes; Variations on a Theme of
Frank Bridge; The Young Person's Guide
to the Orchestra*
BBC SO/Andrew Davis
Teldec British Line 9031-73126-2

BRITTEN
*War Requiem; Sinfonia da Requiem;
Ballad of Heroes*
Soloists, Choristers of St Paul's
Cathedral, LSO & Chorus/Richard
Hickox
Chandos CHAN 8983/4 (2 discs)

BRITTEN
The Prince of the Pagodas
London Sinfonietta/Oliver Knussen
Virgin VC7 59578 2 (2 discs)

GEOFFREY BUSH
*A Summer Serenade; A Menagerie;
Farewell; Earth's Bliss* etc
Soloists, Westminster Singers, City of
London Sinfonia/Richard Hickox
Chandos CHAN 8864

THE COMPOSER CONDUCTS
Music by Rawsthorne (*Madame
Crysanthème; Street Corner Overture*),
Addison, Arnell, Bliss, Arnold
Pro Arte Orchestra, Sinfonia of
London, RPO/composers
EMI CDM7 64718 2

HOWARD FERGUSON
Octet; Five Bagatelles; Violin Sonata No 2
(with Finzi's *Elegy*)
Nash Ensemble, Levon Chilingirian
(violin), Clifford Benson (piano)
Hyperion CDA66192

BENJAMIN FRANKEL
Symphonies Nos 1 & 5; May Day
Overture
Queensland SO/Werner Andreas Albert
CPO 999 240-2

ROBERTO GERHARD
Don Quixote; Pedrelliana (En memoria);
Albada, Interludi i Dansa
Tenerife SO/Victor Pablo Pérez
Auvidis Valois V4660

GEORGE LLOYD
Symphony No 5 in B flat
BBC Philharmonic/George Lloyd
Albany TROY 022-2

ELISABETH LUTYENS
Requiescat 'in memoriam Igor Stravinsky';
6 Tempi; Chamber Concerto No 1;
Triolets I & II; The Valley of Hatsu-se;
Isis and Osiris
Jane Manning (soprano),
Jane's Minstrels/Roger Montgomery
NMC D011

ELIZABETH MACONCHY
Clarinet Concertinos Nos 1 & 2
(with *Clarinet Concertos* by Arnold &
Britten's *Concerto Movement*)
Thea King (clarinet), ECO/Barry
Wordsworth
Hyperion CDA66634

MACONCHY
String Quartets Nos 1–4
Hanson String Quartet
Unicorn-Kanchana DKPCD 9080

ANDRZEJ PANUFNIK
Sinfonia Sacra; Concerto Festivo;
Concertino for timpani, percussion and
strings etc
Monte Carlo Opera Orchestra, Soloists,
LSO/Andrzej Panufnik
Unicorn-Kanchana UKCD 2020

PANUFNIK
Tragic Overture; Autumn Music; Heroic
Overture; Nocturne, Sinfonia Rustica
LSO/Jascha Horenstein, Monte Carlo
Opera Orchestra/Andrzej Panufnik
Unicorn-Kanchana UKCD 2016

ALAN RAWSTHORNE
Piano Concertos Nos 1 & 2; Concerto for
two pianos
Geoffrey Tozer, Tamara Cislowski
(pianos), London
Philharmonic/Matthias Bamert
Chandos CHAN 9125

EDMUND RUBBRA
Symphonies Nos 6 & 8 'Hommage a
Teilhard de Chardin'; Soliloquy for cello
and orchestra
Philharmonia Orchestra/Norman Del
Mar, Rohan de Saram (cello),
LSO/Vernon Handley
Lyrita SRCD 234

ROBERT SIMPSON
Symphonies Nos 2 & 4
Bournemouth SO/Vernon Handley
Hyperion CDA66505

SIMPSON
Symphony No 9
Bournemouth SO/Vernon Handley
Hyperion CDA66299

BERNARD STEVENS
A Symphony of Liberation; Cello Concerto
Alexander Baillie (cello), BBC
Philharmonic/Edward Downes
Meridian CDE 84124

RONALD STEVENSON
Passacaglia on DSCH
Raymond Clarke (piano)
Marco Polo 8.223545

MICHAEL TIPPETT
Piano Concerto; Triple Concerto
Martino Tirimo (piano), Ernst Kovacic
(violin), Gérard Caussé (viola),
Alexander Baillie (cello), BBC
Philharmonic/Michael Tippett
Nimbus NI 5301

TIPPETT
Symphony No 2; Suite from New Year
Bournemouth SO/Richard Hickox
Chandos CHAN 9299

TIPPETT
Fantasia Concertante on a Theme of
Corelli; Fantasia on a Theme of Handel;
Symphony No 4
Howard Shelley (piano), Bournemouth
SO/Richard Hickox
Chandos CHAN 9233

TIPPETT
Ritual Dances and Sosostris's Aria from
The Midsummer Marraige; Praeludium;
Suite for the Birthday of Prince Charles
Alfreda Hodgson (contralto), Chorus of
Opera North, English Northern
Philharmonia/Michael Tippett
Nimbus NI 5217

TIPPETT
The Midsummer Marraige
Remedios, Burrows, Carlyle etc, Chorus
and Orchestra of ROH Covent
Garden/Colin Davis
Lyrita SRCD 2217 (2 discs) (to be released
in summer 1995)

WILLIAM WALTON
Troilus and Cressida (scenes)
Soloists, Philharmonia Orchestra,
Orchestra of the Royal Opera House,
Covent Garden/William Walton
EMI CDM7 64199 2

WALTON
Symphony No 2; Partita; Variations on a
Theme of Hindemith
Cleveland Orchestra/George Szell
Sony MPK 46732

GRACE WILLIAMS
Fantasia on Welsh Nursery Tunes;
Carillons for oboe & orchestra; Penillion;
Trumpet Concerto; Sea Sketches
Anthony Camden, Howard Snell, LSO,
RPO/Charles Groves, ECO/David
Atherton
Lyrita SRCD 323 (to be released in spring
1995)

WILLIAM WORDSWORTH
Symphonies Nos 2 & 3
LPO/Nicholas Braithwaite
Lyrita SRCD 207

12

GEORGE BENJAMIN
Ringed by the Flat Horizon; At First
Light; A Mind of Winter
BBC SO/Mark Elder, London
Sinfonietta/George Benjamin
Nimbus NI 5075

RICHARD RODNEY BENNETT
Concerto for guitar and chamber ensemble
(with Arnold & Rodrigo *Guitar*
Concertos)
Julian Bream (guitar), Melos Ensemble/
Malcolm Arnold/David Atherton
BMG/RCA Julian Bream Edition
09026 61598 2

MICHAEL BERKELEY
Clarinet Concerto; Flighting; 'Père du
doux repos...'
Emma Johnson (clarinet), Henry
Herford (baritone), Northern
Sinfonia/Sian Edwards
ASV CD DCB 1101 (single)

HARRISON BIRTWISTLE
Earth Dances
BBC SO/Peter Eotvos
Collins 20012 (single)

BIRTWISTLE
Antiphonies; Nomos; An Imaginary
Landscape
Joanna MacGregor (piano), Radio
Filharmonisch Orkest/Michael Gielen,
BBC SO/Paul Daniel
Collins 14142

BIRTWISTLE
The Triumph of Time; Gawain's Journey
Philharmonia Orchestra/Elgar Howarth
Collins 13872

HOWARD BLAKE
Violin Concerto 'The Leeds'; A Month in
the Country; Sinfonietta
Christiane Edinger (violin), English
Northern Philharmonia/Paul Daniel
ASV CD DCA 905

BRITISH WOMEN
COMPOSERS Volume 1
Music by Lindsay Cooper,
Nicola LeFanu, Elizabeth Maconchy,
Errollyn Wallen
Lontano/Odaline de la Martinez
Lorelt LNT101

BRITTEN
The Prodigal Son
Peter Pears, John Shirley-Quirk etc,
English Opera Group/Benjamin Britten
Decca 425 713-2

BENJAMIN BRITTEN
String Quartet No 3 (coupled with
Tippett's *String Quartet No 4*)
Lindsay String Quartet
ASV CD DCA 608

GAVIN BRYARS
The Green Ray (saxophone concerto,
with Nyman's *Where the Bee Dances*,
Mike Westbrook's *Bean Rows and Blues*
Shots)
John Harle (saxophone), Bournemouth
Sinfonietta/Ivor Bolton
Argo 433 847-2

JOHN CASKEN
Cello Concerto
Northern Sinfonia/Heinrich Schiff
Collins 20062 (single)

PETER MAXWELL DAVIES
The Lighthouse
Ian Comboy, Christopher Keyte,
Neil Mackie, BBC Philharmonic/Peter
Maxwell Davies
Collins 14152

MAXWELL DAVIES
Maximum Max, a compilation
including *Sunday Morning, Farewell to
Stromness, O Magnum Mysterium,
An Orkney Wedding with Sunrise*
Artists include The
Sixteen/Christophers, SCO, RPO, BBC
Philharmonic/Peter Maxwell Davies
Collins 14442

MAXWELL DAVIES
The Martyrdom of St Magnus
Music Theatre Wales, Scottish Chamber
Opera Ensemble/Michael Rafferty
Unicorn-Kanchana DKPCD 9100

MAXWELL DAVIES
Symphony No 2
BBC Philharmonic/Peter Maxwell Davies
Collins 14032

JAMES DILLON
*East 11th Street, Windows and Canopies,
La Femme Invisible*
Music Projects London/Richard Bernas
NMC D004

GRAHAM FITKIN
Hook; Mesh; Stub; Cud
Ensemble Bash, Icebreaker, Delta
Saxophone Quartet, John Harle Band
Argo 440 216-2

**GLYNDEBOURNE WIND
SERENADES**
by Jonathan Dove, Nigel Osborne,
Jonathan Harvey, Stephen Oliver,
Robert Saxton
Members of the OAE & LPO/Jonathan
Dove/Antony Pay/Andrew Parrott
EMI CDC7 54424 2

ALEXANDER GOEHR
The Death of Moses
Soloists, Cambridge University Musical
Society Chorus & Instrumental
Ensemble/Stephen Cleobury
Unicorn-Kanchana DKPCD 9146

JONATHAN HARVEY
Bhakti
Spectrum/Guy Protheroe
NMC D001

ALUN HODDINOTT
*The Heaventree of Stars; Star Children;
Doubles; Passaggio*
Soloists, BBC Welsh SO/Tadaaki Otaka
Nimbus NI 5357

ROBIN HOLLOWAY
Second Concerto for Orchestra
BBC SO/Oliver Knussen
NMC D015M (single)

HOLLOWAY
Violin Concerto; Horn Concerto
Ernst Kovacic (violin), Barry Tuckwell
(horn), Scottish CO/Matthias Bamert
Collins 14392

OLIVER KNUSSEN
*Symphonies Nos 2 & 3; Trumpets,
Coursing; Cantata; Ophelia Dances*
Philharmonia Orchestra/Michael Tilson
Thomas, London Sinfonietta/Oliver
Knussen, Nash Ensemble etc
Unicorn-Kanchana UKCD 2010

GEORGE LLOYD
A Symphonic Mass
Brighton Festival Chorus,
Bournemouth SO/George Lloyd
Albany TROY 100

JAMES MACMILLAN
*Veni, Veni, Emmanuel; ... as others see
us...; Three Dawn Rituals; Untold;
After the Tryst*
Evelyn Glennie (percussion),
Scottish CO/Jukka-Pekka Saraste etc
BMG/Catalyst 09026 61916 2

MACMILLAN
The Confession of Isobel Gowdie; Tryst
BBC Scottish SO/Jerzy Maksymiuk
Koch 3-1050-2

STEVE MARTLAND
Patrol; Danceworks; Principia
Smith String Quartet, Steve Martland
Band/Steve Martland
BMG/Catalyst 09026 62670 2

WILLIAM MATHIAS
*Symphony No 3; Helios; Oboe Concerto;
Requiescat*
David Cowley (oboe), BBC Welsh
SO/Grant Llewellyn
Nimbus NI 5343

COLIN MATTHEWS
Cello Concerto; Sonata No 5 'Landscape'
Alexander Baillie (cello), London
Sinfonietta, Berlin RSO/John Carewe
Unicorn-Kanchana UKCD 2058

DAVID MATTHEWS
Symphony No 4
East of England Orchestra/Malcolm
Nabarro
Collins 20082 (single)

NICHOLAS MAW
Odyssey
CBSO/Simon Rattle
EMI CDS7 54277 2 (2 discs)

DOMINIC MULDOWNEY
Oboe Concerto
Roy Carter (oboe), LSO/Michael Tilson
Thomas
NMC D018S (single)

MICHAEL NYMAN
*The Piano Concerto; MGV
(Musique à Grande Vitesse)*
Kathryn Stott (piano), RLPO,
Michael Nyman Band &
Orchestra/Michael Nyman
Argo 443 382-2

ROBERT SAXTON
*Violin Concerto; In the Beginning; I Will
Awake the Dawn*
Tasmin Little (violin), BBC
SO/Matthias Bamert, BBC
Singers/John Poole
Collins 12832

GILES SWAYNE
CRY
BBC Singers/John Poole
NMC D016

JOHN TAVENER
The Protecting Veil; Thrinos
(with Britten's *Cello Suite No 3*)
Steven Isserlis (cello), LSO/Gennadi
Rozhdestvensky
Virgin VC7 59052 2

TAVENER
We Shall See Him As He Is
Soloists, BBC Welsh Chorus, Britten
Singers, Chester Festival Chorus, BBC
Welsh SO/Richard Hickox
Chandos CHAN 9128

TAVENER
*Ikon of Light; Two Hymns to the Mother
of God; The Lamb etc*
The Sixteen/Harry Christophers
Collins 14052

TAVENER
Akathist of Thanksgiving
Soloists, Westminster Abbey Choir,
BBC Singers, BBC SO/Martin Neary
Sony/Arc of Light SK 64446

MICHAEL TIPPETT
The Mask of Time
Soloists, BBC Singers, BBC SO &
Chorus/Andrew Davis
EMI CMS7 64711 2 (2 discs)

TIPPETT
String Quartet No 5 (with Charles
Wood's *Quartet in A minor, Three
Fantasias* by Purcell; pieces by
R O Morris and Christopher Brown)
Lindsay String Quartet
ASV CD DCA 879

MARK-ANTHONY TURNAGE
*Three Screaming Popes; Drowned Out;
Kai; Momentum*
CBSO/Simon Rattle
EMI CDC5 55091 2

TURNAGE
Greek
Hayes, Suart, Kimm, Charnock, Greek
Ensemble/Richard Bernas
Argo 440 368 2

JUDITH WEIR
*King Harald's Saga; The Consolations of
Scholarship; Missa del Cid*
Jane Manning, Linda Hirst,
Lontano/Odaline de la Martinez, Nick
Herrett, Combattimento/David Mason
Novello NVLCD 109

THOMAS WILSON
*Piano Concerto; Introit (Towards the
Light...)*
David Wilde (piano), Scottish National
Orchestra/Bryden Thomson
Chandos CHAN 8626

HUGH WOOD
Piano Concerto
Joanna MacGregor, BBC SO/Andrew
Davis
Collins 20072 (single)

WOOD
String Quartets Nos 2 & 4
Chilingirian Quartet
Conifer CDCF 239

Recommended Books
AND REFERENCE WORKS

GENERAL

Banfield, Stephen *Sensibility and English Song* (2 volumes; CUP 1985)

Blom, Eric *Music in England* (Pelican, 1942)

Bowden, Anthony *Three Choirs: A History of the Festival* (Stroud, Alan Sutton, 1992)

Boydell, Brian (ed) *Four Centuries of Music in Ireland* (BBC, 1979)

Boyes, Georgina *The Imagined Village: Culture, ideology and the English folk revival* (Manchester University Press, 1993)

Burney, Charles *A General History of Music from the Earliest Ages to the Present Period*, 4 volumes (London, 1776–89; rev edn 1935, repr 1957)

Caldwell, John *English Keyboard Music before the Nineteenth Century* (Blackwell, 1973)

Ehrlich, Cyril *First Philharmonic: A history of the Royal Philharmonic Society* (Oxford, Clarendon Press, 1995)

Fellowes, E H *English Cathedral Music* (London, 1941; rev 5th edition J A Westrup 1969)

Fiske, Roger *Scotland in Music* (CUP, 1983)

Fleischmann, Aloys (ed) *Music in Ireland – A Symposium* (Cork University Press, 1952)

Ford, Boris (ed) *The Cambridge Guide to the Arts in Britain* (9 volumes; CUP, 1988–91)

Fuller, Sophie *The Pandora Guide to Women Composers – Britain and the United States 1629 to the present* (Pandora, 1994)

Norris, Gerald *A Musical Gazetteer of Great Britain & Ireland* (David & Charles, 1981)

Parry, W H *Thirteen Centuries of English Church Music* (Hinrichsen, 1946)

Philip, Robert *Early Recordings and Musical Style* (CUP, 1992)

Purser, John *Scotland's Music* (Mainstream Publishing, 1992)

Routh, Francis *Early English Organ Music from the Middle Ages to 1837* (Barrie & Jenkins, 1973)

Sadie, Julie Anne & Rhian Samuel (eds) *The New Grove Dictionary of Women Composers* (Macmillan, 1994)

Sadie, Stanley (ed) *The New Grove Dictionary of Music and Musicians* (20 volumes; Macmillan, 1980)

Schmitz, Oscar *The Land without Music* (published as *Das Land ohne Musik* in Germany in 1914; English translation by H Herzl, Jarrolds, 1926)

Sharp, Cecil *English Folk Song: Some Conclusions* (1907; 4th edn Mercury, 1965 rev M Karpeles)

Walker, Ernest *A History of Music in England* (Oxford, 1907; rev J A Westrup 1952)

White, Eric Walter *A History of English Opera* (Faber, 1983)

Young, Percy *A History of British Music* (Benn, 1967)

UP TO 17TH CENTURY

Anderson, Nicholas *Baroque Music – From Monteverdi to Handel* (Thames and Hudson, 1994)

Bent, Margaret *Dunstaple* (OUP, 1981)

Brown, David *Thomas Weelkes: A biographical and critical study* (London, 1969)

Burden, Michael (ed) *The Purcell Companion* (Faber, 1994)

Caldwell, John *The Oxford History of English Music*, Volume 1 (Oxford, Clarendon Press, 1991)

Campbell, Margaret *Henry Purcell: Glory of his Age* (Hutchinson, 1993)

Doe, Paul *Tallis* (London, 1968; rev 1976)

Duffy, Maureen *Henry Purcell* (Fourth Estate, 1994)

Fellowes, E H *William Byrd* (London, 1936, 1948)

Flood, W H G *Early Tudor Composers* (Oxford, 1925)

Hand, C *John Taverner: His Life and Music* (London, 1978)

Harley, John *Music in Purcell's London* (Dobson, 1968)

Harris, Ellen T *Henry Purcell's Dido and Aeneas* (Clarendon Paperbacks, 1989)

Harrison, Frank L *Music in Medieval Britain* (London, 1958; 4th edn, Buren, 1980)

Holman, Peter *Four and Twenty Fiddlers* (Oxford, Clarendon Press, 1993)

Holman, Peter *Henry Purcell* (Oxford Studies of Composers) (OUP, 1994)

Holst, Imogen *Byrd* (London, 1972)

Howes, Frank *William Byrd* (London, 1928)

Kerman, Joseph *The Elizabethan Madrigal* (New York, 1962)

King, Robert *Henry Purcell* (Thames and Hudson, 1994)

North, Roger *Roger North on Music* (his writings edited by John Wilson) (Novello, 1959)

Phillips, Peter *English Sacred Music 1549–1649* (Gimell Records, 1991)

Price, Curtis *Henry Purcell and the London Stage* (CUP, 1984)

Spink, Ian *Restoration Cathedral Music 1660–1714* (Oxford, Clarendon Press, 1995)

Spink, Ian (ed) *The Blackwell History of Music in Britain: Volume 3 – The 17th Century* (Blackwell, 1992)

Stevens, Denis *Thomas Tomkins, 1572–1656* (London, 1957)

Stevens, Denis *Tudor Church Music* (London, 1955, 1966)

Stevens, J *Music and Poetry in the Early Tudor Court* (London, 1961, 1979)

Warlock, Peter *The English Ayre* (London, 1926)

Westrup, J A *Purcell* (The Master Musicians, Dent, 1937; rev N Fortune 1979; OUP paperback, 1995)

Wulston, D *Tudor Music* (London, 1985)

18TH & 19TH CENTURIES

Bennett, J R S *The Life of William Sterndale Bennett* (CUP, 1907)

Burrows, Donald *Handel* (The Master Musicians, OUP, 1995)

Coleridge-Taylor, A *The Heritage of Samuel Coleridge-Taylor* (Dobson, 1979)

Dean, Winton *Handel's Dramatic Oratorios and Masques* (1959; Clarendon Paperbacks, 1990)

Dibble, Jeremy *C Hubert H Parry – his life and music* (Oxford, Clarendon Press, 1992)

Ehrlich, Cyril *The Music Profession in Britain since the Eighteenth Century, A Social History* (Oxford, Clarendon Press, 1985)

Fiske, Roger *English Theatre Music in the Eighteenth Century* (OUP, 1986)

Flower, Newman *Handel – His Personality and His Times* (Cassell, 1923; Panther 1972)

Foreman, Lewis *Music in England 1885–1920* (Thames Publishing, 1994)

Greene, H Plunket *Charles Villiers Stanford* (Arnold, 1935)

Hogwood, Christopher *Handel* (Thames and Hudson, 1984)

Howes, Frank *The English Musical Renaissance* (Secker & Warburg, 1966)

Jacobs, Arthur *Arthur Sullivan: A Victorian Musician* (OUP, 1984)

Johnstone, H Diack & Roger Fiske (eds) *The Blackwell History of Music in Britain: Volume 4 – The 18th Century* (Blackwell, 1990)

Kelly, Michael *Reminiscences of Michael Kelly* (edited by Roger Fiske) (OUP, 1975)

Langley, Hubert *Dr Arne* (Cambridge, 1938)

Mackenzie, Sir Alexander Campbell *A Musician's Narrative* (Cassell, 1927)

Parke, W T *Musical Memoirs* (London, 1830)

Pirie, Peter J *The English Musical Renaissance* (Gollancz, 1979)

Rainbow, Bernarr *The Choral Revival in the Anglican Church* (Barrie & Jenkins, 1973)

Routley, Erik *The Musical Wesleys* (Herbert Jenkins, 1968)

Scholes, Percy A *The Great Dr Burney* (2 volumes; London, 1948)

Scott, W S *Green Retreats – the story of Vauxhall Gardens* (London, 1955)

Smyth, Ethel *The Memoirs of Ethel Smyth* (edited and abridged by Ronald Crichton) (Viking, 1987)

Stradling, Robert & Meirion Hughes *The English Musical Renaissance 1860–1940* (Routledge, 1993)

Temperley, Nicholas (ed) *The Blackwell History of Music in Britain: Volume 5 – The Romantic Age 1800–1914* (Athlone Press, 1981)

Young, Kenneth *Music's Great Days in the Spas and Watering Places* (Macmillan, 1968)

Young, Percy *George Grove (1820–1900): A biography* (Macmillan, 1980)

20TH CENTURY

Anderson, Robert *Elgar* (The Master Musicians, Dent, 1993)

Bacharach, A L (ed) *British Music of our Time* (Pelican, 1946, 2nd edn 1951)

Banfield, Stephen (ed) *The Blackwell History of Music in Britain: Volume 6 – The 20th Century* (Blackwell, to be published September 1995)

Bantock, Myrrha *Granville Bantock – a personal portrait* (Dent, 1972)

Bax, Arnold *Farewell My Youth and other writings by Arnold Bax* (edited by Lewis Foreman) (Scolar Press, 1992)

Beecham, Sir Thomas *A Mingled Chime – Leaves from an autobiography* (Hutchinson, 1944; Grey Arrow, 1961)

Berners, Lord *First Childhood* (1934) and *Far from the Madding War* (a novel, 1941) (OUP, 1983)

Bird, John *Percy Grainger* (Elek, 1976; Faber, 1982)

Bliss, Arthur *As I Remember* (Thames Publishing, rev and enlarged 1989)

Boult, Adrian *My Own Trumpet* (Hamish Hamilton, 1973)

Brian, Havergal *Havergal Brian on Music – selected from his journalism* (edited by Malcolm MacDonald Volume 1: British Music) (Toccata Press, 1986)

Burton-Page, Piers *Philharmonic Concerto – the life and music of Sir Malcolm Arnold* (Methuen, 1994)

Carley, Lionel & Robert Threlfall *Delius – A Life in Pictures* (OUP, 1977)

Carpenter, Humphrey *Benjamin Britten – a biography* (Faber, 1992)

Cox, David *The Henry Wood Proms* (BBC, 1980)

Cox, David & John Bishop (eds) *Peter Warlock – a centenary celebration* (Thames Publishing, 1994)

De-La-Noy, Michael *Elgar the Man* (Allen Lane, 1983)

Elkin, Robert *Queen's Hall, 1893–1941* (Rider, 1944)

Fenby, Eric *Delius as I knew him* (1936; Faber, 1981)

Foreman, Lewis *Bax – A Composer and his Times* (Scolar Press, 1983, 1988)

Foreman Lewis (ed) *Edmund Rubbra – composer* (Rickmansworth, Triad Press, 1977)

Foreman, Lewis (ed) *From Parry to Britten – British Music in Letters 1900–45* (Batsford, 1987)

Frank, Alan *Modern British Composers* (Dobson, 1953)

Goossens, Eugene *Overture and Beginners* (London, 1951)

Griffiths, Paul *Peter Maxwell Davies* (Robson Books, 1982)

Hall, Michael *Harrison Birtwistle* (Robson Books, 1982)

Hamilton-Paterson, James *Gerontius* (a novel about Elgar's South American journey) (Macmillan, 1989)

Harries, M & S Harries *A Pilgrim Soul: The Life and Work of Elisabeth Lutyens* (Michael Joseph, 1989)

Herbert, David (ed) *The Operas of Benjamin Britten* (Hamish Hamilton, 1979)

Holbrooke, Joseph *Contemporary British Composers* (Cecil Palmer, 1925)

Holst, Gustav & Ralph Vaughan Williams *Heirs and Rebels: Letters written to each other* (OUP, 1959)

Holst, Imogen *Gustav Holst – A Biography* (1938, 1969, OUP paperback 1988)

Hurd, Michael *The Ordeal of Ivor Gurney* (OUP, 1978)

Hurd, Michael *Rutland Boughton and the Glastonbury Festivals* (Oxford, Clarendon Press, 1993)

Jacobs, Arthur *Henry J Wood – maker of the Proms* (Methuen, 1994)

Kemp, Ian *Tippett – the composer and his music* (OUP, 1984, 1987)

Kennedy, Michael *Britten* (The Master Musicians, Dent, 1981)

Kennedy, Michael *Portrait of Elgar* (Oxford, Clarendon Press, 3rd edn 1987)

Kennedy Michael *Portrait of Walton* (OUP, 1989)

Kennedy, Michael *The Works of Ralph Vaughan Williams* (OUP, 1964, 1965)

Kenyon, Nicholas *The BBC Symphony Orchestra – the first 50 years 1930–80* (BBC, 1981)

Lambert, Constant *Music Ho! a study of music in decline* (Faber, 1934; Hogarth Press, 1985)

Lutyens, Elisabeth *A Goldfish Bowl* (Cassell, 1972)

Macdonald, Malcolm *John Foulds* (Rickmansworth, Triad Press, 1975)

McVeagh, Diana & others *Twentieth Century English Masters* (articles from *The New Grove*) (Macmillan, 1986)

Matthews, David *Michael Tippett, An introductory study* (Faber, 1980)

Mellers, Wilfrid *Vaughan Williams and the Vision of Albion* (Barrie & Jenkins, 1989)

Moore, Jerrold Northrop *Edward Elgar – A Creative Life* (OUP, 1984)

Nettel, Reginald *Havergal Brian and his Music* (Dobson, 1976)

Palmer, Christopher *Delius, Portrait of a Cosmopolitan* (Duckworth, 1976)

Palmer, Christopher *George Dyson: A Centenary Appreciation* (Novello, 1984)

Palmer, Christopher *Herbert Howells: a centenary celebration* (Thames Publishing, 1992)

Panufnik, Andrzej *Composing Myself* (Methuen, 1987)

Ridout, Alan (ed) *The Music of Howard Ferguson* (Thames Publishing, 1989)

Rosen, Carole *The Goossens – a musical century* (Andre Deutsch, 1993)

Routh, Francis *Contemporary British Music 1945–70* (Macdonald, 1972)

Seabrook, Mike *Max – the life and music of Peter Maxwell Davies* (Gollancz, 1994)

Searle, Muriel V *John Ireland – The Man and his Music* (Midas Books, 1979)

Shead, Richard *Constant Lambert* (Simon Publications, 1973)

Short, Michael *Gustav Holst – The Man and his Music* (OUP, 1990)

Smith, Barry *Peter Warlock – the life of Philip Heseltine* (OUP, 1994)

Stevenson, Ronald (ed) *Alan Bush: an 80th birthday symposium* (Bravura Publications, 1981)

Tippett, Michael *Tippett on Music* (edited by Meirion Bowen) (OUP, 1995)

Tippett, Michael *Those Twentieth Century Blues – an autobiography* (Hutchinson, 1991)

Vaughan Williams, Ralph *National Music and other essays* (OUP, 2nd edn 1987)

Vaughan Williams, Ursula *RVW – A biography of Ralph Vaughan Williams* (OUP, 1964)

Walton, Susana *William Walton: Behind the Façade* (OUP, 1988)

White, Eric Walter *Benjamin Britten: His Life and Operas* (Faber, 2nd edn 1983)

PHOTOGRAPH AND PICTURE CREDITS